Creating
Room to Read

Creating
Room to Read

A Story of Hope
in the Battle for Global Literacy

JOHN WOOD

VIKING

VIKING
Published by the Penguin Group

Penguin Group (USA) Inc., 375 Hudson Street, New York, New York 10014, U.S.A. • Penguin Group (Canada), 90 Eglinton Avenue East, Suite 700, Toronto, Ontario, Canada M4P 2Y3 (a division of Pearson Penguin Canada Inc.) • Penguin Books Ltd, 80 Strand, London WC2R 0RL, England • Penguin Ireland, 25 St. Stephen's Green, Dublin 2, Ireland (a division of Penguin Books Ltd) • Penguin Group (Australia), 707 Collins Street, Melbourne, Victoria 3008, Australia (a division of Pearson Australia Group Pty Ltd) • Penguin Books India Pvt Ltd, 11 Community Centre, Panchsheel Park, New Delhi – 110 017, India • Penguin Group (NZ), 67 Apollo Drive, Rosedale, Auckland 0632, New Zealand (a division of Pearson New Zealand Ltd) • Penguin Books (South Africa), Rosebank Office Park, 181 Jan Smuts Avenue, Parktown North 2193, South Africa • Penguin China, B7 Jiaming Center, 27 East Third Ring Road North, Chaoyang District, Beijing 100020, China

Penguin Books Ltd, Registered Offices: 80 Strand, London WC2R 0RL, England

First published in 2013 by Viking Penguin, a member of Penguin Group (USA) Inc.

10 9 8 7 6 5 4 3 2

LIBRARY OF CONGRESS CATALOGING IN PUBLICATION DATA
Wood, John.
   Creating Room to Read : a story of hope in the battle for global literacy / John Wood.
      p.   cm.
   Includes index.
   ISBN 978-0-670-02598-5
   Export edition ISBN 978-0-670-01543-6
   1. Literacy programs—Africa. 2. Literacy programs—Asia. 3. Education—Africa. 4. Education—Asia. 5. Room to Read (Organization) I. Title.
   LC158.A2W66 2012
   374'.0124—dc23   2012019125

Printed in the United States of America
Designed by Carla Bolte

This book is dedicated to Amy,
with love and excitement for all of our future adventures together.

"Walk and move forward strongly. Your futures are in front of you."

—Phuong Giang, librarian,
Ngu Hiep #1 Primary School, Tien Giang Province, Vietnam

CONTENTS

INTRODUCTION Ten Years, Ten Thousand Libraries!   1

CHAPTER 1   Bold Goals Attract Bold People   10

CHAPTER 2   A Kilogram of Gold   17

CHAPTER 3   The Lottery of Life   25

CHAPTER 4   Blame It on Bahundanda   34

CHAPTER 5   Helping Others Help Themselves:
The Challenge-Grant Model   43

CHAPTER 6   GSD: Building a World-Class Team   54

CHAPTER 7   The Tsunami: One Year After   67

CHAPTER 8   "No Range Rovers": The War on Overhead   76

CHAPTER 9   Searching for Seuss   88

CHAPTER 10   Baby Fish Goes to School   99

CHAPTER 11   Sleepless in Siem Reap   109

CHAPTER 12   "I Was in Grade Two
When Our School Was Burned Down"   120

CHAPTER 13   "Sorry, but Your Money Has Disappeared"   129

CHAPTER 14   "We Picked Up the Phone to Call for Help"   141

CHAPTER 15   Nine Books Last Night   154

CHAPTER 16   On Her Narrow Shoulders
Rest a Family's Dreams   163

CHAPTER 17   Mr. X   174

CHAPTER 18   Now Departing for Cambodia: *Literacy One*   182

CHAPTER 19   Frantic Footsteps in the Night   195

CHAPTER 20   The World's Tallest Fund-raising Thermometer   203

CHAPTER 21   Whose Version of the Future Will Win?   217

CHAPTER 22   Boat to Read   228

CHAPTER 23   "If You Cannot Read, School Can Be a Torture"   240

CHAPTER 24   "Three Completely Pregnant Cows"   250

CHAPTER 25   Mr. Poet and Miss Library   260

Author's Note   273
Acknowledgments   275
Index   281
A Message from the Author:
How You Can Change the World   289

Creating
Room to Read

Ten Years, Ten Thousand Libraries!

In the shadow of Machapuchare, a twenty-three-thousand-foot Himalayan peak, the only sound I hear is laughter. Hundreds of students fill the school yard. Each wears a uniform of dark blue pants or skirt and a sky blue shirt, in contrast to their jet black hair and gleaming white teeth. They range from tots to teens and are nearly evenly split between boys and girls. What they all have in common is what they hold in their hands: books.

The Shree Janakalyan Secondary School has more than six hundred students stuffed into a single-story school building. But until today they faced a problem familiar to millions of students here in Nepal: They had no access to books. There were fewer than twenty to share among the entire student population—a situation that is, depressingly, all too common across the developing world. Countless times I've met parents eager to have their children be educated. But when the young students get to the local school, they find it desperately lacking in the most basic educational resources. A classroom without paper, pencils, pens, or books is not much of a classroom.

That situation had now changed abruptly at the Shree Janakalyan School, in Kavresthali, near the town of Pokhara, Nepal. A deluge of local people have gathered to help celebrate the opening of the school's new library. I am one small part of a very large crowd, one small light in a bright and populated constellation. In addition to the hundreds of students, there are at least that many parents, along with teachers, the school's headmaster, grandparents, government officials, and residents of the village. Grandmothers with pierced noses and faces lined with the crevasses formed by harsh sun and fierce Himalayan winds clutch newborns. Fathers hold aloft their three-year-old daughters, little girls eager to get a better look, anticipating the day they'll be able to explore the library's treasures. The students' energy level could power a village.

We're all assembled in front of a freestanding building newly bathed in an electric blue coat of paint. It's a small but cozy structure, about three hundred square feet. Across the door is a taut red ribbon, ready to be snipped by as many rusty scissors as the village can muster. Above the door and running nearly the length of the building is a banner celebrating the opportunities that literacy will bring to the village. It proudly announces an event that is not only game changing for the community but also a milestone in my life:

WELCOME TO THE OPENING OF ROOM TO READ'S
10,000TH LIBRARY

As I watch residents of the village continue to stream into the open courtyard in front of the library, I contemplate that number—ten thousand! I recall how different things were just a decade ago, when a tiny band of volunteers and I opened our first five libraries in rural Nepal. We had a tiny budget, no employees, and only a handful of advocates.

From a mere five to ten thousand, in a decade: This is the steepest growth curve I've ever been involved in, surpassing even my time in the technology industry. The number on that banner seems a bit surreal to me.

I feel a familiar hand on my shoulder. Turning around, I am greeted by my mother, Carolyn, a seventy-nine-year-old with a heart of gold, love of travel, and a crazed enthusiasm for the power of books. She is of hearty Norwegian stock and extremely healthy. Not many women of her age would insist upon flying halfway around the earth to the roof of the world to celebrate her seventy-ninth birthday. She attributes this love of nature, and of the cold, to having grown up in northern Minnesota.

Her eyes are as deep and blue as the many lakes of her native state: ten thousand lakes in Minnesota, ten thousand libraries around the developing world opened by her son and the organization he founded. I like the symmetry. She hugs me and holds me. Then she stammers through her tears: "I am so very, very proud of you."

"Me, too," interjects my eighty-four-year-old father, Woody, as he reaches out to shake my hand. Those two words are it for him. Like me, he is not one for overt displays of emotion; that short statement, piggy-backed on my mother's expression of pride, is about as good as it gets with him. Knowing this makes his statement all the sweeter to me.

Pulled between the extremes of my two parents, I gravitate toward my loquacious mother. Her words and embrace have caused my eyes to mist up. Then I hug my father and share a thought I've had for a long time but haven't spken: *None of this would have happened were it not for you two, who believed in my idea before the world did. You persuaded me to believe in this dream even during the tough times when it would have been easier to abandon it. We're only here today because of your faith in me.*

Most parents would not encourage their son to leave a lucrative corporate fast track at age thirty-five to devote himself to a highly improbable start-up charity venture. Parents are genetically programmed to do whatever it takes to help their children survive. Their dreams and aspirations for their offspring typically focus on a good job, the predictable place in society that comes with it, and financial security. Yet in 1999 when I told my parents that I planned to quit my executive position at Microsoft in order to focus "the rest of my adult life" on the quest for global literacy, they barely flinched.

I told them: "There aren't any charities building libraries across the developing world at a massive scale, so I'm going to try to start my own. I'll work for no salary for as long as I can, even if it means running down my savings. But don't worry; I'll never ask to move back in with you."

My mother laughed.

My decision could have fazed either, or both, of my parents. At the height of the Internet and technology booms, Woody and Carolyn went from telling people, "John is the director of business development for Microsoft's greater China region, has a full-time car and driver, and lives in a beautiful subsidized house," to telling them, "John delivers books on the backs of yaks to rural Himalayan villages." But their advice to me was as encouraging as it was succinct: "If that's what you want to do, then you should go do it—and do it well."

Woody told me: "I may be a little crazy, but you're not. You have your own wings, John, so fly."

As we open the ten thousandth Room to Read library, I ponder the fact that I lucked out in the parent lottery. Carolyn and Woody met in a bowling alley in Texas, where my dad was working for the Bureau of Public Roads. We were always middle class but lived in a home that was "rich in books."

These two believed in me, even when it looked like I was throwing away amazing opportunities to embrace a life full of risk and no financial upside. Their loyalty to me, and to my ambitious but risky dreams, is one of many reasons I pleaded with them to share this moment with me in Nepal on my mother's seventy-ninth birthday.

I knew they'd be proud of me at this pivotal point in the development of my now decade-old enterprise. Today, though, what's more important is to express how proud I am of *them.*

....

The courtyard at the Shree Janakalyan School is now teeming with hundreds of students bursting with excitement. They take turns peering in through the windows of their new library. Two dozen teachers are gathered. We hear the sound of snare drums as the band warms up, along with a wailing trumpet. Girls dressed in bright red saris, their eyes lined with charcoal, practice their ceremonial dance.

One of the teachers tells me that he and three others came from a village thirty miles away. "Are you here to help us to celebrate?" I ask.

"No, sir, we've come to petition you. We have over nine hundred students but no books. We would like a library in our school, too."

Hmm: Before we've even opened number ten thousand, we have a pipeline of projects to help get us started on the next ten thousand.

Standing next to these teachers is a smiling couple, both waiting patiently to hang a garland of marigolds around my neck. "It is an honor, sir, to have you here today. Please know that from the bottom of our hearts we parents so value this gift you have given to our children."

I want to explain that this community, with its outpouring of gratitude to us and love for its own children, is giving more to me than they realize. This is a grand bargain! Instead, I ask the father how he's gained such an impressive level of English proficiency.

"BBC Radio. I've listened to it since the age of nine! I still listen for an hour each evening. This is how I can not only improve my own mind but also encourage my children. It also helps the children who want to work in tourism; without English or other foreign languages, they can't have well-paid jobs like trekking guides or waiters."

I nod in the shared understanding that tourism is the biggest earner of foreign exchange in an otherwise dormant economy. Proudly he tells me and my parents of the roles community members have played in getting the library built. Three of the fathers helped to dig the foundation, while six mothers and fathers painted the exterior and interior walls. It feels quite awkward that they continue to thank me, given that they've done all the hard work.

This is part of Room to Read's "challenge grant" model. Rather than just sweeping in and handing local communities everything they need to get the school built or the library established, we ask them to meet us halfway. Our in-country teams start every introduction of Room to Read by saying in effect: *If you as a community are willing to put resources into the project, then we will do the same. But if you don't value the project enough to lobby the community to support it, and if the local people are not willing to pitch in with some of their resources, then this tells us that the motivation is not there to make it succeed.*

Today at Janakalyan School the offerings of gratitude are effusive. Our diligent translator lets us know that one mother "wishes to praise your team for allowing us to strive for greatness as we offer educational uplift to our children." I think of my own parents and their continual exhortations to study. This community reminds me that parents everywhere desire a better life for their children. It's a near constant: They understand the importance of education and crave it for their children, even as they are well aware of the sacrifice they will have to make.

With young children in classrooms instead of helping out on the family's small plot of farmland, parents here will face hundreds of additional hours of backbreaking labor. Still, they know that education is the best—or perhaps only—long-term ticket out of poverty for their kids. "Go, go," they tell their sons and daughters. "Without school, you'll remain a poor farmer, just like every other generation of our family."

Now it's time for the ceremony preceding the ribbon cutting. Few people enjoy speeches as much as the Nepalese. There seems to be no upper limit on the number of people taking the stage and commandeering the microphone. The crowd hears from the community's government leaders, the village elders, education ministry officials, the headmaster, teachers, parents, and anyone else who wants to take a turn. It doesn't seem to bother anyone that they all say basically the same thing. As the blazing sun traces a lazy arc across the sky, the speechifying enters a second and, I hope, final hour.

....

With ample time for my mind to drift back to 1998, I replay my fateful first visit to Nepal. During that maiden Himalayan trek, a chance introduction to a headmaster who showed me a library without books set me on this trajectory. The school he heads is actually not far, in Bahundanda, no more than seventy-five miles away as the crow flies—as long as the crow can fly above twenty-four-thousand-foot peaks. A mere mortal, walking along the mountains' numerous donkey paths, would need a week to make the walk.

These two villages are so close, yet so far. This is also an apt description for my life today as compared with a time when I had no resources, no employees, and no donor base—only the conviction that helping children across the developing world gain access to books was the only meaningful thing I could do with my limited time on earth.

Room to Read is one of the fastest-growing and most award-winning charities of the last decade. Its rapid evolution and steep trajectory have been beyond my wildest fantasy. Though we started by focusing on libraries, we experienced mission creep—the good kind—when we realized that libraries without readable books were not much help and that books sat idle on shelves, without engaged readers, despite the impressive new rooms housing them.

In addition to opening more than ten thousand libraries, we now support (as of May 2012) seventeen thousand young scholars in our Girls' Education program and have constructed and staffed (with help from our host-country governments) more than sixteen hundred school blocks. To fill the libraries, we've self-published more than seven hundred titles in local languages by training hundreds of local authors and artists to write and illustrate the first brightly colored children's books the local children have ever seen. After starting with building and stocking libraries, we evolved rapidly to also become a children's book publisher on a massive scale. In addition, we've now embraced training teachers on enhanced literacy skills and ensuring that girls are empowered through not just education but also the life skills they will need to negotiate key life decisions.

The need is global, growing more urgent by the day. Every day we lose is a day we can't get back. So we've also expanded far beyond Nepal and now bring books and libraries to Bangladesh, Cambodia, India, Laos, South Africa, Sri Lanka, Tanzania, Vietnam, and Zambia. The morning of the ceremony at the Shree Janakalyan School, I told the local team that Room to Read had become one of Nepal's most important exports. The model we'd established there was now having a huge impact on other parts of the developing world. Our role model, Andrew Carnegie, known as "the patron saint of libraries," helped open more than 2,500 in the United States, Canada, and Great Britain. Only a decade in, Room to Read has opened four times that number.

I look up to take in the mass of students sitting on the ground in front of the stage. The opening of the library will change their lives. In helping create opportunities like these for students in so many places, my own life has been radically altered. During my Microsoft years my focus was on revenue, sales growth, and market share—all things that were ultimately going to help make rich people richer.

My focus was also on ways to enrich myself: "What kind of raise will I get this year? How many stock options? Can I remain posted overseas so that the company will continue to pay my rent?"

Today I measure quite differently: How many additional books can we get into the hands of eager young readers each year? How many kids are visiting our libraries? How many books are being checked out each month? I think about the size of our team: The more employees we have, the more communities we can help to bring education to their young people. With more than six hundred people all over the world now on the payroll, and with over 80 percent of them being local nationals who are "close to the customer," Room to Read can accomplish quite a lot. The Nepalese team alone consists of sixty people. Thankfully, all of them are here today at the ribbon-cutting ceremony in Kavresthali, beaming with pride at how far they've come over the last ten years.

It's been a volatile and unpredictable ride with many highs and lows. At any number of points along the way, the idea of hitting the ten-thousand-library milestone seemed the ultimate impossible dream. More than once I debated running back, tail between my legs, to the relative stability, predictability, and fat paychecks of the tech sector.

Perseverance paid off: Thankfully, the mission and the work are no longer a lonely pursuit. Bill Clinton endorsed our work on multiple occasions by inviting me to speak at his annual Clinton Global Initiative and later to join its advisory board. CEOs of major companies have joined Room to Read's board. Volunteer fund-raising chapters have sprung up in fifty-six cities around the world. In our first ten years, more than seven thousand volunteers threw events that collectively raised over $35 million, fueling our rapid expansion.

One of the most exciting fund-raising campaigns happened totally out of the blue after Oprah Winfrey invited me on her show in 2007, when I published a book about the founding of Room to Read called *Leaving Microsoft to Change the World*—a novice author's dream come true.

Then lightning struck twice. Oprah got so excited about our work that she invited her millions of viewers to be part of "Oprah's Book Drive" to benefit Room to Read. Some of the very books we printed with the three million dollars she helped raise are housed here in Nepal. But to me the most important figure in all these millions is six million, the number of children who now have access to libraries Room to Read created. We've come so far, so fast.

It's difficult to process the difference between that first trip to Nepal and today's ceremony in Kavresthali. We've gone from being a disorganized, ragtag band of volunteers to being a global movement involving millions of people. I remind myself that today is a day of celebration. This is a moment to revel in all that we've accomplished.

....

As if on cue, the headmaster finishes his speech. Proudly he announces that it's time to cut the red ribbon stretched tightly across the door. We will officially open a magical and colorful place where students can develop a love of books and reading. The walls are painted in a riot of colors, and more than a thousand books are neatly nestled on the shelves, waiting to be picked up and loved.

The crowd charges toward the library as I look for my guests of honor. Grabbing my hand, my mother leads me as we walk together slowly. Each step is silent, but there are lots of *namastes* offered by the students: "The light in me bows down to the light in you."

On this beautiful Himalayan morning our bond and our happiness are as strong as they've ever been. My mother grips my hand tightly as my father walks a step behind. "Did you ever think you'd see this day?" she asks.

The only smile broader than those of the students is my own.

CHAPTER ONE

Bold Goals Attract Bold People

I am sitting at "the most famous desk in journalism," about to throw out an idea I've never dared express publicly. On the other side of the desk sits the one and only Charlie Rose, the best interviewer on television and a man who does not suffer fools gladly. He and his team do thorough research, resulting in questions that are pointed, concise, and challenging. This is the interview I've always wanted; yet here I sit with a look that can only be described as "deer caught in the headlights."

I'm scared as hell. On the way in, one of my board members texted me, "Don't screw this up!" We know that if I nail this interview, the results could be huge.

The intimidation factor is somewhat leavened by Charlie Rose's courtly southern manner. Opinionated yet charming, he could be the well-read uncle you always wanted but never had. Dressed in a charcoal suit with bold pinstripes, Rose sports a powder blue tie that forms a bit of sky on the cloudlike starched white shirt. Not a hair on his head is out of place, nor is a single word in the question he's just asked one I'd been anticipating.

The moment the call came that I was going to be on his show, and that he'd focus on my main messages in my book *Leaving Microsoft to Change the World,* I started pondering whether I'd dare to publicly declare a new goal I've been thinking about constantly.

"What do you really want?" he asks, leaning in the way he does, to suggest a measure of intimacy with his guest.

Gulp. Though I know what my answer will be, saying it in front of one of the world's most influential audiences is a bit terrifying. But somehow I don't miss a beat. I trust my gut and say without hesitation: "My goal is that *children everywhere* have access to literacy and books in their mother tongue from a young age."

There, I said it: the big goal. Every child. My heart is pounding. Charlie's gaze is fixed upon me intently, but in a very positive way. Both his silence and his eyes encourage me to expand upon my statement.

"I don't see any reason why we can't aim higher in an area of international development that is so critical to the escape from poverty, and to social stability. And I don't think we should stop until we reach that goal. Maybe it sounds hubristic, or egomaniacal, but I honestly see no reason why we can't get there."

"Every child," he repeats.

"Every one, without exception," I reiterate.

I've finally dared to articulate my next BHAG. The BHAG, or "big, hairy, audacious goal," is an acronym borrowed from *Good to Great,* one of my favorite books. *Every child:* Is it even remotely possible? After all, we live in a world in which 780 million people lack basic literacy. Won't the illiterate, like the poor, always be with us? And can anyone have that significant an impact with limited resources?

From the beginning, one of our "big picture" goals at Room to Read has been to put international education on the world's agenda. Now I have a unique platform, one that will help me explain why literacy is as vital as food, security, limiting population growth, and control of the environment.

Education, after all, is the one issue that affects every other one. I think of it in the same way as dropping a pebble into a pond and getting a ripple effect. Educated people make more money and are more likely to escape poverty. Educated parents raise healthier children. When a woman has finished school, she is treated better by her community and is more likely to vote. The list goes on, just as the ripples in a body of water emanate outward. If we can solve this issue, we will solve many others at the same time.

I've run the numbers, as have a number of journalists such as the *New York Times'* Nicholas Kristof, and am convinced that the world can make a major dent in the link between poverty and illiteracy if we just get serious about it. Let me give just three examples.

The United States spent nine hundred billion dollars fighting seemingly unwinnable wars in Afghanistan and Iraq over a decade. If just 10 percent of the ninety-billion-dollar annual cost of those wars had been dedicated instead to building schools, the change would have been radical. With nine billion dollars, fast-moving groups like Room to Read could work with local communities to construct 272,000 schools, resulting in more than a million new classrooms. At twenty-five children per classroom, we've just impacted twenty-five million students. I'm not making up these numbers: This isn't magic, just simple arithmetic.

A second example: The European Union spends thirty-nine billion euros per year on farming subsidies. Literally 40 percent of the annual EU budget goes to programs that distort markets and subsidize a coddled middle class, all while making it impossible for hardworking farmers from the African nations on Europe's doorstep to compete in EU markets. Redirecting just 10 percent of this money for a single year would allow one million school libraries to be created, or five hundred million children to gain access to books for the first time. It seems incredible that such a small redirection could have such a big international effect. But again, it's not voodoo or magic, but simple arithmetic

The third example focuses on girls, because two thirds of the illiterate people in the world are girls and women. Let's suppose that the ten countries with the highest gross national products decided to make a serious effort to educate girls across the developing world. Are you listening, America, China, Japan, Germany, Britain, France, Italy, Canada, Spain, and Russia? Imagine a day when the leaders of these countries, surrounded by young schoolgirls from around the world, sign a declaration that they will divert one tenth of 1 percent of their gross national product to providing education to girls in the poorest parts of the world, where on average only one of four girls makes it past seventh grade. One tenth of 1 percent of GNP—surely this amount is too small to move the needle, right?

Were the funds to be distributed through a network of efficient social entrepreneurs, the effect would be earth shaking: Eighty-three million girls would be able to go to school. Eighty. Three. Million.

This might just be the biggest no-brainer in the history of philanthropy.

Of course, it's not just a philanthropic issue. Getting this right would also have a huge impact on the global economy. Girls and boys who are educated today become tomorrow's middle class. If a person scrapes by on only one or two dollars per day (as two billion people, nearly a third of earth's population, do), he or she will never join the global economy. Higher-value products and services made in the developed economies will be completely irrelevant. Whether it's a computer or an iPad, an airline ticket or a hotel room, a savings account or a life insurance policy, it'll be useless to people living cruel, hand-to-mouth existences.

This might also be a much more logical way to defeat terrorism and the dark forces of nihilism that try to divide the world into "us" and "them." A young boy is quite unlikely to strap on a bomb and detonate it against a country that helped him to gain his education. I long for the day when people in the poorest parts of the world have proof that the developed world is serious about helping them educate their children.

Once a child is educated, he or she can start that crucial march from poverty to the middle class. It can happen in just one generation, all because of the power of the most wondrous device ever created—the human brain.

Within one generation a relatively small investment in basic human capital could more than pay for itself. A massively enhanced global middle class would accelerate worldwide economic growth. This would result in a higher tax base for governments and revenues that could be used to help grow budgets for education everywhere. It's such an obvious win-win situation, if only the world dared to be visionary and think long term.

Is this a pie-in-the-sky proposal? Is there proof that a big idea like this can actually work? I answer these questions with two examples: my father, Robert "Woody" Wood, and the tiger economies of Asia.

My father was one of millions of soldiers whose reward for serving in

World War II was a university scholarship underwritten by the U.S. government. The GI Bill was one of the biggest influences on the creation of a mass middle class in U.S. history. By educating such a large swath of its youth population, the American government helped to create a generation of engineers, scientists, doctors, teachers, and other white-collar professionals who helped to move the American economy to the highest levels the world had ever seen. Without the GI Bill, our family wouldn't have been middle class.

Woody worked hard for forty years. He helped design helicopters as well as the wingspan for Boeing's 707 jet. He was head of product safety for the largest fire engine company in the world. Eventually he became CFO of a large natural gas company. He earned money, faithfully paid taxes, and volunteered in his community. Over his life, the taxes he has paid to the U.S. government have been at least a hundred times what was invested in his education. And he's the first to tell people that he's just "a simple guy from a small town."

Had our family not been middle class, it isn't likely I would have been the beneficiary of a great education. Nor would I have been able to be part of the building of a great company that created tens of billions of dollars of shareholder value. Economic progress does not otherwise happen; world-class companies like Apple, Boeing, Google, Starbucks, and Twitter could not have been created by illiterate people with a third-grade education.

The United States is, of course, not the only nation to have used education as a driver of long-term economic growth. The last fifty years have seen the rise of several "Asian tigers," which offer a modern-day equivalent of postwar U.S. government intervention. The leap these societies have made—all on the back of universalizing access to education for their citizens—is awe inspiring.

It's hard to believe that just four decades ago, Asia's advanced economies were dirt poor, with the average family living in soul-crushing poverty. From Hong Kong to South Korea, from Singapore to Taiwan, the average family lived a subsistence existence. Malnutrition rates were high, and families lived in shacks in communities without sanitation or clean running water. Literacy rates were low, as were school completion rates for girls. Many of those girls began having babies by the age of fifteen. The cycle of poverty was perpetuated generation after generation.

And then the smartest and best-run governments in Asia decided to break out of the stasis that kept them among the world's poorest nations. Education was made one of the top funding priorities. Given a choice between that and massive defense spending, smart governments thought long term and chose to invest in human capital. Kids who were eight or ten or thirteen several decades ago are now some of the most productive citizens of today's economy. Hong Kong has a higher GNP per capita than New Zealand; South Korea and Taiwan are among the forty wealthiest countries. Singapore is now in the top five. Having realized that the country had no natural resources, the government of founding father Lee Kuan Yew directed massive investment in human capital. Today the self-proclaimed Lion City has a higher income per person than Japan, France, Germany, or the UK. It even tops oil-rich and scarcely populated Kuwait.

Let's examine that fact. A tiny nation-state with *no natural resources* and a large number of people living in a relatively small physical space has managed to outearn a country with some of the largest oil deposits ever found. *That* is the power of investing in and nurturing young brains.

Education alone may not be enough to guarantee economic success: Just look at Cuba. There are other success factors that matter, like good governance, rule of law, and access to trading routes and partners. But if you were challenged to assemble a prosperous society from scratch, education would be the first building block you'd want to develop. After all, can you name a single uneducated society that has ever risen from poverty to widespread prosperity?

I can't either.

Ensuring that "every child" can read is no doubt a big and audacious goal. But I sincerely believe it is achievable. In today's world we see a lot of great companies being built. Why not, in a similar manner, build a global movement around literacy and gender equality in education?

The time is now: In fact, it was yesterday. As I write, my goal is as audacious as it was ten years ago: to create independent readers and lifelong learners. Our motto at Room to Read remains "World Change Starts with Educated Children."

A decade in, Room to Read can show results in ten countries that prove the effectiveness of our approach and the no less compelling urgency of the need for ever bigger and better outcomes. In twenty years I'd like to have grown to reach so many more children that the ten-thousand-library milestone will look tiny by comparison. Could we open one hundred thousand libraries? Reach fifty million children?

Our long-term goal will always be to reverse the notion that any child can be told that he or she was "born in the wrong place, at the wrong time, to the wrong parents" and hence will not be educated.

That idea belongs on the scrap heap of human history.

CHAPTER TWO

A Kilogram of Gold

Half an hour before the sun rises, a young girl named Inkham, age eleven, wades along the shallow shore of the Mekong River bent over, staring into its halcyon waters. With no prior warning, her arm makes a lightning-fast strike, plunging into the river with empty hand and emerging clutching a silvery fish, which is then thrust into a small plastic bag tied to her loose white cloth belt. She does not take time to savor this victory, and less than a minute later she is holding a small crab—then another. She continues the hunt, fully engaged, not even noticing the small dugout canoes floating past or the sun rising over the horizon.

Within twenty minutes she has collected enough bounty to feed the family of five of which she is the youngest member. She knows her mother will be proud of her. They awoke, as they do every day, at 5:00 A.M. Together they stoked a small wood fire and put the rice on to boil. Her older brother packed up the thin blankets that had provided only marginal comfort against the night air. Part of the benefit of sleeping five to a bed, the only bed, is that proximity can be an antidote to a cold evening. Some of that chill still lingers in the predawn. But the family is up and about, sweeping with handmade straw brooms, collecting eggs from their three squawking chickens, and then bribing those angry birds with a few handfuls of corn kernels.

Inkham strides quickly and with a fierce determination away from the river and toward the family's straw hut. If she is fast, there will be time to study her homework prior to breakfast. If she can keep a *really* accelerated pace, there might even be an opportunity to read a few of the treasured Lao-language storybooks she has checked out of the school's small library. Greedy with intellectual anticipation, she makes double time along the dirt path. Inkham's face is lit with fierce concentration. Her goals are simple: first, ten minutes to review her Lao-language homework. *I will be the best student in the entire nation at the Lao language.* Then ten minutes to read aloud two storybooks to her mother. *She will cook, and I will share with her some good stories. And then we get to eat my favorite food—deep-fried crab.*

....

Not many people would associate the joy and optimism felt by Inkham with her home country of Laos. As she happily skips home, she passes people walking along the side of the dusty road pushing small carts and riding rusty antique bicycles. These adults have not had many lucky breaks in their lives. Laos is landlocked and sits in the heart of one of the poorest regions on earth. It has long been isolated from the rest of the world. Knowledge of English and other foreign languages is low, which means that most Lao people cannot communicate with 99 percent of the world. The country has few natural resources that could help it earn precious foreign currency. Even in the tourism department it can't compete against neighboring attractions like the beaches of Thailand, the temples of Cambodia, and the famous noodle soups of Vietnam.

As if that weren't enough, the country also suffers from damage done by the United States during the 1960s and 1970s. There are four words that, strung together, form the reason that the United States heavily bombed Laos on a daily basis for nearly eight years: Ho Chi Minh Trail. Because the United States controlled large parts of central Vietnam, the North Vietnamese weren't able to move soldiers or supplies from the north to the south without significant risk, at least not through their own country. Instead they took ingenious advantage of geography. Central Vietnam is the narrowest part of the country. If you drew a straight line from Hanoi to Saigon, it would pass through large parts of Laos.

So pass through the Vietnamese army did. The Ho Chi Minh Trail was an informal series of roads and jungle tracks that never appeared on a map. Some sections of the trail shifted over time. The United States eventually started to bomb the trail but, realizing that soldiers and armaments were still getting from north to south, it increased the geographic scope of its bombing. Since it's nearly impossible to accurately target a site for which there is no fixed set of coordinates, indiscriminate bombing became a key part of the escalation plan. The people of Laos, most of whom were rural, agrarian, peace-loving Buddhists, watched helplessly as buildings were destroyed, forests burned, and family members killed.

By the time it was over, a new record had been set: The United States had dropped more ordnance on Laos during the Vietnam War than had been dropped on all of Europe, by all parties, during World War II. This was all done despite the fact that the United States never made a formal declaration of war against the country it was punishing.

From 1964 to 1973, more than 270 million cluster bombs were dropped on Laos. By the time the war was over, the government of Laos decided that it wanted no part of this madness and sealed itself off from the outside world. Perhaps isolation would offer something more closely resembling peace.

Granted, the rebuilding would be difficult. The majority of the bombs dropped had not detonated, meaning there were tens of thousands of what were euphemistically called UXO, or unexploded ordnance. In addition, thousands of Lao's best and brightest had fled the country, seeking to avoid the postwar political struggle for power and the coming closure. Isolation is never a brilliant economic strategy, and as the country stagnated, the people of Laos found themselves in a familiar catch-22: They were too poor to afford education, but until they had education, they would remain poor.

The nation's fate could have been Inkham's. But thankfully we live in a world where fate does not always come wrapped in dark clothing. What if fate can actually be a positive thing? Rather than watching negative outcomes from the sidelines, can the world we live in change the word's meaning and tone? Inkham's auntie believes this is both desirable and entirely possible.

....

Auntie Vankham looks in frequently to make sure that Inkham and her two brothers are doing well. Over the small wood fire, the family's only source of heat for comfort and cooking, Inkham's mother stirs the pot of rice. Observing the full bag of her daughter's river treasures, Inkham's mother smiles but says nothing. Instead she points to the books overflowing from Inkham's backpack, then signals toward her husband, indicating that they should form a small circle. Inkham's father smiles but is silent as he stands close to his only daughter. After scanning the books before her, Inkham picks her favorite, one that she's checked out of her school's small library on numerous occasions. She beams as she opens to the first page of *The Happy Little Monkey.* She reads aloud in Lao: "The happy little monkey wakes up in the morning. He brushes his teeth."

With a look of intense concentration, she focuses on sounding out each phrase. "The happy little monkey eats his breakfast. He puts his books in his backpack to go to school."

With each page Inkham's parents beam with pride. Inkham continues, telling her hushed and attentive family that the happy little monkey is kind to his parents. He is a good student. He reads books before going to bed and then says his prayers every night; the End.

Though this is perhaps the fiftieth time Inkham has read the book, she still enjoys the look of victory as she quietly closes the book and places it gently, like a treasured object, on the shelf. Her auntie claps and praises Inkham for her reading skills. The youngster smiles modestly and then looks over to her parents.

Their faces tell her what their voices never will. They have taken in every word with stoic concentration; their eyes shine with happiness. They can, however, say nothing. Both were born, and remain, mute.

....

Gainful employment opportunities in rural Laos are few and far between. For those who cannot speak, the odds are even grimmer. Inkham's family lives on the small amount of vegetables they can grow on a tiny plot of land, the rice for which they can barter, and the fish and crabs the young girl catches each morning in the river.

With no cash income, the family could not afford the "luxuries" of a school uniform, a book bag, school supplies, or the small fees required to help subsidize the teachers' salaries and textbooks. Inkham was likely to become yet another statistic, a small rounding error in an indifferent world that sees—or rather chooses not to see—that two hundred million young girls and women wake up every day and don't go to school.

One of Inkham's best friends is a "social mobilizer" named Nipaphone. She is employed by the Laotian office of Room to Read. Her role is akin to that of a social worker—she looks out for several hundred girls like Inkham who are in our Girls' Education program, monitors their progress, encourages them to study hard, and steps in to help out when there are problems or obstacles. She is also perpetually on the lookout for ways Room to Read can reach more girls. Nipaphone heard from a local headmaster that Inkham had to drop out of school (we immediately checked to make sure this was not a school Room to Read had built) and went to investigate. After asking around the small village, Nipaphone was able to find the family and introduced herself. Neighbors helped to quickly locate Uncle Maita and Auntie Vankham to help the communication flow. As Nipaphone explained her goal of finding bright young girls for whom finances were the only barrier to education, the adults got excited about the opportunity to get their precocious Inkham back into the classroom.

"How grand it would only be," her auntie practically sang aloud, "for Inkham to be the first in our family to finish school!"

The girl herself was skeptical. Later she explained to our Laos team: "I must confess that when I first heard about Room to Read coming to our village, I did not pay much attention, because I was convinced I would never qualify for the program. I have parents who cannot speak and who have very little education. We have no books in our home. We are poor. Why would I be deserving of an academic scholarship?"

Her status did not matter: All that did was the kinetic energy of her auntie and uncle, who regaled Nipaphone with stories about how Inkham awakens by 5:00 A.M. to help her mother with the household chores, followed by her daily expedition to the river. At which point Inkham interjected: "I love to catch crabs. They are my favorite food. I bring them home and my mother turns them into deep-fried crabs. When I used to go to school, she made sure that every day we had breakfast early, and were ready for school by 7:30 A.M. I love deep-fried crabs so much that sometimes I push my luck and see if we can have it for all three meals!"

Nipaphone then inquired about Inkham's love of reading. Had she previously brought books home to read after school?

"Yes. Despite this challenge my family is able to communicate well, for my brothers and I have learned to 'read' our parents' expressions and hand movements. Even though they cannot speak, I know my parents are proud of me.

"They are also happy to have me read storybooks to them. Often while reading a book to them, I look at their faces and long for a magic wand to grant me a wish that would give my parents the ability to speak. Then we could talk about these stories and discuss them over our dinner. I wish I could hear their thoughts about the characters and the lessons. But maybe it doesn't matter, because I still love them. I am proud that they are my parents."

A week later, the family received the news. Inkham recalls: "Much to my surprise, I was picked! I remember one of my teachers telling me afterward that I should always expect good things and to be optimistic all the time. Now my favorite quote is 'Expect the unexpected!' "

Her uncle and auntie's intervention helped convince the Room to Read Laos team that Inkham was likely to succeed because she had four adults and two older brothers looking out for her. With her work ethic, her personality, her smarts, and this support structure, how could Room to Read not invest in Inkham?

Auntie Vankham was equally thrilled. "When I first heard that Inkham was selected by Room to Read, I could not sleep that night. It felt as if I had won a kilogram of gold!"

There are 35.27 ounces in a kilogram. As I write this in early 2012, the spot price of gold is $1,608 per ounce. A kilogram of gold is therefore worth $56,714.

....

Room to Read established a library in Inkham's school so that students would take books home. As always, we started with a challenge to the local community to pitch in. Early in the development of Room to Read, my founding partner, Erin Ganju, and I heard from our country directors that the best way to assist local communities was to help them help themselves, not to provide direct "charity." Whether with "sweat equity" or small contributions that added up, the people in Inkham's village staked a claim in providing books and education for their kids. If they'd lacked this motivation, the project might not have sustained itself over the long haul.

Just building a school or library won't suffice. Our goal at Room to Read is also to monitor programs carefully and to follow through with the necessary resources for students' ongoing success.

Nipaphone (the social mobilizer) and her team also provide Inkham (and others like her) with everything she needs for school. They pay the monthly school fees and have bought their young prodigy two school uniforms and two pairs of shoes. They make sure she has textbooks to read, notebooks to write in, and pencils and pens with which to fill them. She gets a small home library of books to encourage literacy and the habit of reading. Nipaphone regularly checks in on her academic progress. Finally, Inkham regularly attends "life skills camps" run by Room to Read, at which she learns the skills she will need to make key life decisions as an independent and educated woman. These include financial management, self-confidence, communication skills, knowledge about her own health and body, and an understanding of the advantages of delaying marriage and having children until after she's finished secondary school.

This integrated approach to girls' education is one developed by Room to Read after extensive feedback from the field. Sunisha Ahuja, head of Room to Read India, reflects: "I think that our success has much to do with a holistic approach to the problems we encounter in each country in which we work. You can't just build schools and fill libraries with books: You also have to examine the skills of the children reading those books and the lives they lead. Girls still face substantial barriers to education due to economic and social pressures, especially in the rural areas."

Inkham now attends school every day.

"I study hard at school, especially in Lao-language class, my favorite subject. I want to have the highest grade on every test and be the best student of Lao—first at the level of the district, then the province, and then the entire country. I love reading books, which helps me improve my knowledge and vocabulary. I visit the school library regularly and check out books to read at home."

These are big goals, but apparently not grand enough.

"I am also dreaming of graduating from high school with a Red Certificate, which means I have to score no less than ninety percent for all eight subjects. This will result in getting a scholarship and automatic enrollment in university either in Luang Prabang or Vientiane, so I can pursue my preferred choice of study, health science." She pauses as her brown eyes look up to the sky. A wide smile crosses her face. "I know I can do it."

Whenever I hear reports of Inkham's progress and her self-confidence, I marvel at the changes we've seen in just three years. Back in 2008, she was convinced that because her family was poor, her parents mute and uneducated, and her home lacking in books, she would not qualify or be chosen for a scholarship. Today she expects to be number one not only in her class but in the entire nation.

To effect this radical change must be a very expensive proposition, yes?

The all-in cost of providing Inkham with everything that she needs to succeed academically, to be the first in her family to finish secondary school, and to have the life skills she will need to be an independent and educated young woman is $250 per year. Yet to Inkham and her family, this is valued as highly as a kilogram of gold (more than $50,000).

When I nervously proposed my "every child" goal to Charlie Rose, these numbers played a big role. Though the cost of our intervention is low, the value of education is insanely high. As long as we continue to raise funds to support girls like Inkham—whether it's $250 at a time or $25,000 at a time—social mobilizers like Nipaphone can continue to recruit new girls to join our program. Today we employ more than one hundred of these talented mobilizers in countries across the developing world.

If they can support a million more Inkhams out there, then the future will be a much brighter place.

CHAPTER THREE

The Lottery of Life

From my elementary school library to the small but well-stocked community library in my hometown to the book stacks at the Norlin Library on the University of Colorado campus, the insides of libraries have always provided me a warm feeling of heaven on earth. If I have been blessed with this good fortune, shouldn't I strive to provide that same blessing to every child who has not yet experienced it?

It was not always this way. As a young MBA graduate, I focused on how much money I was making, what kind of car I drove, and how large a team I had reporting to me. As I look in the rearview mirror, that part of my past seems to belong to a different person. My highest priority today (indeed, it might be accurate to call it an obsession) is for children everywhere to have access to those magic portals to the wider world called libraries. I won't be satisfied until hundreds of millions more children have the same access I enjoyed while growing up, which I took for granted then.

At age forty-seven I am prosperous and healthy. I can reasonably expect (I'm painfully aware that I'm tempting fate by writing these words) to live for another forty years. What a deal! I've already had a really full life: read thousands of books, filled five passports, run a dozen marathons, and met all kinds of interesting people. I can envision working full time at my passion and traveling the world for two more decades, then maybe working ten more years at half-time pace, and then enjoying another ten or so "sunset" years in my rocking chair reading great books.

Thanks to the lottery of life, I was born in the right place at the right time. Life expectancy in the wealthiest parts of the world—Australia, Iceland, Israel, Japan, Hong Kong, Singapore, Sweden, the United States—can be up to four decades longer than in the poorest parts of the world. You can double your time on earth if you're born in Switzerland rather than Swaziland, in Andorra rather than Angola, in Liechtenstein rather than Liberia.

Let's say instead that I live in Mozambique.

I'm dead.

Zimbabwe?

Ditto.

Malawi?

Same.

The Central African Republic?

D-E-A-D.

Pushing up daisies.

Six feet under.

This is not just a medical or "lifestyle" issue. Education affects every other issue, even life span. Research and data analysis show that the more education a person has, the more income he or she is likely to earn. A person who is above the median can afford shelter, clothing, better food, and a wider variety of it.

An educated woman is twice as likely to vaccinate her children. Those with cash on hand don't have to decide *which* child to take to the doctor if he or she is sick or whether they should skip the medicines recommended due to their lack of affordability. Parents watch their children die at age five, while teenagers bury parents who have passed on at age forty-seven or fifty-three—all because they lost the lottery of life.

I was one of the lucky ones.

Our family still had its ups and downs. Though my father graduated from the University of Denver in civil engineering and worked in aviation, he was laid off from his chosen field in the recession of the Nixon years. We moved from Connecticut, where I was born, to Pennsylvania when Dad went to work for a company that produced shelters used in war zones by the U.S. Air Force. Later he worked for a company that manufactured engines for fire trucks.

My father never tired of reminding my older brother and sister, Bruce and Lisa, and me that we were only one generation removed from poverty. "I could not afford college, so without that scholarship we would not today be a comfortable middle-class family. As a result, you kids have access to good public schools with caring teachers, to libraries, to books. We are by no means rich, but nor are we poor." Our job, he and my mother constantly reminded us, was to read constantly, to study hard. "Once you have an education, no one can ever take that away from you."

They believed this so strongly that they were willing to make sacrifices—one of which showed up on my eighth birthday.

....

In January 1972 I couldn't sleep. It was the night before my birthday, and for weeks I had listened to my parents hint that this year there might be a present that was extra special.

"You're only going to get one present this year, but trust us—it will be something you love."

It was a long day. I couldn't focus. Playing with my friends after school was merely a way to fill time before dinner and the birthday cake. *When, when, when, when could I open my big present?* Looking back, I can imagine Bruce and Lisa chortling silently as they watched my level of anticipation build.

The cake my mother had made—in the shape of a bucktoothed rabbit with floppy ears, gumdrop eyeballs and whiskers made of black licorice—had been sliced up and consumed. The big moment was upon us. I had to close my eyes and promise not to open them until I was told to do so. Finally, three . . . two. . . . one . . . open! And what did I see but the most beautiful thing I'd ever cast my eyes upon in my young life—a brand-new bike! It was bright green, with a long banana seat that was all the rage in bicycle design. Our grainy home movies show a hyperexcited boy jumping for joy and waving his arms over his head, then running outside to ride over icy roads as winter snow drifted down.

Economically times were very tough, and to this day it seems a minor miracle that my parents were able to scrape the money together to buy my new treasure. Our family had converted part of our backyard to a vegetable garden as one way to save money, and at night before we were allowed to play we'd instead gather for a working session of taking corn off the cob to freeze it, or cleaning and canning the green beans we'd grown. How my parents had found the funding to buy a new bike is still a mystery.

My memory of the day's soundtrack replays my father's words: "Now you can go to the library on your own, whenever you want." Though not a big reader himself, my father was nevertheless a fan of libraries.

Growing up in Denver, he remembers being too busy playing outside to sit still and read: "I was a typical boy, one of seven children. My father was a meat cutter and my mother a homemaker. Our family is of German, British, and Irish descent—mostly German. On the British side, I have ancestors who arrived in America in the seventeenth century and fought in the Revolutionary War. I was the first in the family to graduate from college."

Even if Woody wasn't a big reader as a child, he knows the value of education firsthand.

Though my father didn't often share much of his family history when I was growing up, he did tell me one story with some frequency. When he found me sitting quietly with a book, my eyes aglow, he'd often say: "I didn't grow up in a family with books. My parents were not well educated. But my dad could tell you how much you owed for a pound of meat without reading the scale."

My paternal grandfather only went to school through the fourth grade, my grandmother through the eighth grade. "I cannot remember my parents ever reading—to themselves or to me or any of my six brothers and sisters," Woody would tell me. "But your mother did. You know how Mommy Booka (the nickname of my maternal grandmother) is always reading to you, and how your mother loves to curl up at night with a good book while I watch TV? That's the difference between her side of the family and mine."

Great Books Versus the Boob Tube

"I wish I was a reader, but the reality is that this never happened. I think that love of reading either hits you when you're young, or it forever passes you by. You should follow her example. It's the better one."

I took his words seriously. Despite what I recall of his childhood admonitions, Woody does read today, mostly adventure stories set in the Southwest, featuring the Navajo tribe, Kit Carson, and others. "I don't read highfalutin literature like you and your mother," he often jokes.

My mother, Carolyn, was, and still is, a voracious reader, a member of an active book club. Her mother was a teacher in a one-room schoolhouse in Minnesota. "Reading was always instilled in me," she recalls. "I was an only child and often complained that the other kids in our neighborhood had brothers and sisters to play with. My mother would consistently counter this by saying, 'If you have a good book in your hands, you will never be lonely.'"

My sister was seven years old when I was born, and my brother five. Because of that age gap, my mother often said that I was like an only child. But there was a benefit to this, as she had a lot of time with me when the other two were in school. She tells me: "You would sit and listen. At night we'd crawl in bed and read a book—then another. Then a third. By then you'd fall asleep, and I'd try to take the book out of your hands without waking you up."

Dr. Seuss books were my favorites: *Yertle the Turtle, There's a Wocket in My Pocket.* What young boy doesn't love *Hop on Pop* or learn his colors and numbers with the aid of *One Fish Two Fish Red Fish Blue Fish*?

Throughout my childhood my mother and I read constantly, at times together, curled up on the sofa. She'd engulf me in her arms and read me an adventure. At other times, we'd read independently in adjacent chairs—alone but together, united in our love of quiet reading time.

Looking back, it seems that all the members of my family were jointly plotting to encourage my habit of reading. My maternal grandmother, the teacher, always inquired about what I was reading. At a time when I was going through a period of intense fascination with comic books, she did not discourage me.

"No matter what you are reading, it should not matter. Don't let anyone tell you what to read or what not to read. The important thing is to simply be in the habit."

I'll never forget one of the final times I saw her alive. Although healthy as a horse, she died suddenly at age seventy-five, when I was only eleven years old. She may have known that her time on this earth was limited; she'd insisted that my mother and I visit her in Duluth, Minnesota, during my summer school holiday. She sent us two bus passes, a perk from her deceased husband's three decades of driving for Greyhound, to make the thirty-three-hour trip from Pennsylvania. We couldn't afford to fly, so even a long bus journey seemed like the adventure of a lifetime.

Our two weeks with my beloved grandmother in Duluth went by all too quickly, even the time I scared myself by accepting her mischievous dare to dip my entire body and head underwater in the frigid waters of Lake Superior. On our final day, she mentioned to me that we had a long bus ride ahead and that I'd need entertainment.

"How many comic books can you buy for a dollar?" she inquired. My face lit up as I told her that was enough for ten copies of Archie, Richie Rich, Scooby-Doo, and the Flintstones.

"Well, then," she said as she reached into her small pocketbook and handed me three crisp bills, "I guess this will be enough for you to buy thirty."

This pattern would permeate my childhood. Once a stack or collection of books was finished, I'd begin the hunt for more. My father once told me that some of his saddest moments as a dad were the days I'd come home from school with my monthly book order form from the Scholastic Book Club. As a voracious reader, I took the attitude of "rather than either/or, let's pick both."

I would tick off book after book: "Mom, I want this book about the bear that joins the circus. And this one, about a dachshund named Pretzel who can tie himself up into knots to entertain the children in his neighborhood."

Then my parents would begin to whittle down the list.

"I feel bad about this," my father would say to me in a rare display of emotion. "I don't want to tell you no when it involves something as important as books. But maybe it would be best right now to order four books instead of twenty."

Thriftiness was part of our family ethos as much as reading. At one time or another, both of my parents were employed as bookkeepers. When they lent money to me and my siblings, they charged interest.

As for my thirst for books, there was a cost-effective solution to the problem of my desire for more, more, more: The shiny green bike would be a part of it.

....

Spalding Memorial Library was built in Athens, Pennsylvania, in 1897. Jesse Spalding, a wealthy industrialist, funded the library to honor the memory of his son Robert, who had died shortly after his twenty-third birthday. The red brick building was two stories tall and looked solid enough to last for at least a hundred years. Built on a narrow strip of land between the Chemung and Susquehanna rivers, the building was set back from the main street by forty feet of lawn and a small, well-tended garden. Four Ionic columns supported a handsome portico. You needed only to climb six stairs to walk through the handsome oak doors and into another world.

It was a glorious journey I was to make hundreds of times during my childhood. It's fair to say that the small town of Athens was not a hotbed of intellectual thought or discourse. It was very much a blue-collar town that didn't seek or accept much contact with the wider world. And yet within the walls of the Spalding Memorial Library, that world awaited anyone with the curiosity to explore it.

Library day was the biggest day in my week. In the kitchen my mother would spread my favorite chunky peanut butter on two slices of freshly browned toast, the "fuel" Mom insisted I would need to pedal the six miles round trip. She knew me well enough to understand that I'd rather read than eat. My backpack was full of books devoured over the last week: *I Love Dogs,* an encyclopedia for young readers, the *Guinness Book of World Records,* a collection of Encyclopedia Brown detective stories. I was in a hurry to exchange this treasure trove for the next.

"No time to eat," I explained urgently. But my mother knew that once I walked through those doors, I'd be lost for hours. Since she insisted, I ate, slipping clandestine bits to Pretzel, our strategically placed and perpetually mooching beagle. Pretzel was, of course, named after the character I'd first encountered in one of my treasured storybooks. Unlike the svelte dachshund of literary fame, my Pretzel was semiobese; but I loved her anyway. She scarfed down food the way I devoured books. Working together, we finished off the meal within minutes. The Green Machine was soon pointed south, making good time in the direction of the library.

Once inside, I was immediately transported to a world where camel caravans trekked across the Sahara and dogsled teams raced in the Alaskan tundra. There were biographies of historical giants like Abraham Lincoln and Susan B. Anthony, written in a style designed to appeal to the young reader; books chock full of baseball statistics, as well as bios of my favorite players. There were fantasy stories about boys who got to spend a day being a policeman and then the next day a fireman. And what about full-color photos of the wonders of the solar system, including the multiple moons of Jupiter and the rings of Saturn, or guides to diabolical practical jokes you could play on friends?

There was only one problem: The number of books I wanted to read exceeded the check-out limit. Spalding Memorial Library only allowed eight books to be taken home at a time.

Thankfully, I had a special understanding with Mrs. Tidlow, the kindly librarian, who was like the friendly aunt that every child wishes he or she had—always willing to talk, to suggest books that might be of interest, and to say proactively how proud she was that I read so voraciously.

Since I considered her to be an ally rather than a repressive authority figure, one day I took a risk: "Mrs. Tidlow, why is there a limit like this? It's such a low number. I can read more books than that in a week. So why limit me to such a small amount?"

Perhaps figuring that this wasn't a bad problem for a library to have, she agreed to a side deal. But she admonished that this was strictly between us. Since she'd noticed that I'd checked out nearly all of the Encyclopedia Brown mystery novels, she resorted to that lingua franca.

"We'll have a top-secret agreement. We must never tell on each other, no matter who asks. You can take twelve books home. But if you snitch and tell anyone, then the deal is off."

"You can trust me," I assured her as I conjured a secret handshake that could be part of the ritual.

Each week we exchanged a conspiratorial smile as my emptied backpack was once again filled with books that would ignite my brain and inspire my imagination. Within the warm and child-friendly space that Mrs. Spalding had created, a lifelong reader was born. It's impossible for me to imagine a childhood that wasn't filled with books.

And yet one day that exact situation would confront me on a Himalayan trek that set my life on a completely different course.

CHAPTER FOUR

Blame It on Bahundanda

The village of Bahundanda lies in the shadow of the massive Anna-purna range of the Himalayas. The terrain is so rugged, the cliff faces so steep, the vertical plunges so vertigo inducing, that building paved roads is a near impossibility. A complete circumnavigation of the range requires one to walk for eight to ten hours a day for eighteen straight days on dirt paths shared with the local equivalents of eighteen-wheelers: donkeys and yaks. During that time the trekker will not see a car, a television, a functioning telephone, or a newspaper.

This remoteness appealed to me when I first heard about the famous Around Annapurna trek. At the time, I was seven years into a fast-paced and stressful career with Microsoft and in need of a holiday. I flew from Sydney to Singapore, then onward to Kathmandu. A sense of jubilation hit me upon seeing the prayer flags, Buddhist temples, *tuk-tuks,* and chaotic streets of Nepal's capital. But I was not here for an urban experience. Upon landing, I was thrilled to think that the trail-head for the Annapurna circuit was less than one hundred miles away.

The nine hours it took to travel those final hundred miles on an over-crowded and rickety bus was the same amount required to fly the 3,200 miles from Sydney to Singapore. And yet what a blissful trip it was! Kitted out in my shiny new trekking gear, I was euphoric at the thought of the adventure ahead: 190 miles of dirt trails shared with donkeys, goats, yaks, and local people walking between mountain villages. What struck me most during the long hours on the bus was the friendliness of my fellow passengers. Every time my eyes met those of a stranger, a welcoming smile would grace his or her countenance: "Hello? Where are you from? Are you here to trek?"

After I told one man in his early twenties that I wanted to learn some Nepali words, he wasted no time in initiating my education.

"Water is *pani*," he explained. If I wanted cold water for drinking, I should ask for *chiso pani*. If I needed a small tin of hot water for bathing, the words were *tato pani*.

An old woman next to him joined in, teaching me the words for "up-hill," "downhill," and "river." Soon half the bus was formed into a semi-circle, shouting new words and grinning with encouragement. Deep belly laughs accompanied my stumbles over certain phrases. They had probably never before heard someone request a "hot beer." General good-will and merriment filled the bus as it climbed uphill toward the literal end of the road.

On the first day of trekking I took it easy. By 4:00 P.M. I was sitting on the stone patio of a local *bhatti* (a combination tea house and bare-bones lodge). The breeze off the Marsyangdi River was refreshing after hours in the hot sun. Ready to celebrate the first day of a well-earned holiday, I flagged down the only "employee" minding the shop at the *bhatti*, the owner's eight-year-old son, and asked for a beer.

Seconds later, when he delivered a bottle of Tuborg, I had an immediate opportunity to practice the rudimentary Nepali I'd learned during the long bus ride.

"Thank you. But it's *tato* [too hot]. Do you have *chiso* beer?"

"No *chiso*. Only *tato*."

A quick scan revealed that refrigeration had not made it to this part of the mountains. Just then, the young boy's face lit up.

"*Tin minut, dinush,* okay?"

I agreed to wait the requested three minutes as my young waiter took off at a fast gallop downhill toward the river. Within seconds he had the bottle submerged in the glacial-melt waters. He waved, gave a thumbs-up, and smiled at his customer-satisfaction skills.

I laughed and returned his thumbs-up. Noticing that an older Nepali man at the next table had joined in the laughter, I asked him if all Nepali children were this clever.

"Here we have to improvise, as we have very little," he replied. "This is something you will see a lot of on your journey. Are you trekking the circuit to the pass?"

I replied that I was, and that it was my first trip to Nepal. With that, Mr. Pasupathi Neupane and I started a conversation that was to last for the next decade.

....

Bahundanda: That's where Pasupathi suggested we trek together. For two hours the previous evening, he'd filled me in on his life story. He served as the district resource officer for the Education Department of the province of Lamjung, where I was currently trekking. There were seventeen schools in the district, and his role was to visit each one and hear about its needs: more teachers, textbooks, storybooks, crayons, chalk. The list went on and on.

His explanation was at once simple and revealing: "I am a district resource officer. But I have no resources."

Given that he was on his way to visit the small school at Bahundanda, he invited me to join him. I accepted immediately. At eight the next morning we met for tea. Pasupathi greeted me: "Today is the day you see Bahundanda. I can assure you, we do not need your map. I have walked this trail dozens of times."

Within half an hour we were ready to begin the day's journey. My backpack was overstuffed. Every square inch was filled, and it weighed in at forty-five pounds. Pasupathi had a small briefcase and was wearing the same clothes as the day before—an early indication of the differences in our respective resources. Despite being two decades older, he set off at a brisk pace; I struggled to keep up.

As we walked, he explained that Nepal is one of the world's poorest countries. These mountains might be picturesque, but they created all kinds of hardships. It was nearly impossible to grow sufficient crops at higher altitudes and difficult to trade with neighbors when the geography prevented the building of roads. Furthermore, the self-absorbed monarchy running the country did not seem to care about the needs of the people. The list went on and on.

"You will see it at the school," he told me. Then he repeated a comment he'd made the night before: "You will see that in Nepal, we are too poor to afford education. But until we have education, we will always be poor."

The statement that had hit me with incredible force the night before was no less resonant this morning. Could this catch-22 be a huge factor in why the most resource-deprived parts of the world didn't see much improvement over time? It seemed so simple; but was it *too* simple?

....

"I don't understand. How can this be reality?"

My question was directed to Mr. Rajeev, the kindly headmaster of Bahundanda's school, who'd shown us all around the eight classrooms. Everything we saw confirmed the enormity of Pasupathi's challenge, and the nation's. The school was decrepit and decaying, with fifty students crammed into a tiny room. The dirt floors were bad enough, but with the recent rain, they were more mud than dirt. The school did not have desks, so the students sat on long benches and balanced their notebooks on bony knees. The sheet-metal roof baked in the sun and cooked the room at one hundred degrees, a problem exacerbated by the lack of windows and adequate ventilation. Each room we toured was a sad mirror image of every other, with the only variable being the ages of the children trying to learn in such an inadequate environment.

The pièce de résistance was the school's library. When Mr. Rajeev suggested we end the tour there, followed by tea, I got very excited, given my background as a lifelong library nerd. But my idealized vision could not have been more inaccurate. Other than a sign above the door reading LI-BRARY, there was nothing even remotely librarylike about this space: no desks, no chairs, no lights to read by, no shelves, and most important, no books. It was a big empty space where theoretically a library could have existed; could have, but clearly did not.

Rajeev rushed to enlighten me: "We have only a few books. We keep them over there," he explained, pointing to a small cabinet nearly hidden in the darkest corner of the room. The size of the cabinet—close to that of a hotel minifridge—was made only more depressing by the rusty padlock on its doors. "The books, they are so precious and so few. We must protect them."

Maybe they'd crammed several hundred storybooks and early-childhood readers into the cabinet, I thought. Then the moment arrived that would change my life forever, when the meager contents of the bookcase were revealed.

"A few trekkers who've come through our village have left books for us," Rajeev explained as he handed me a copy of Umberto Eco's *Foucault's Pendulum*. It was written in Italian, no less, just in case the book was not impenetrable enough in English.

The headmaster and several teachers nodded along with me in sympathy, then helpfully handed me a dog-eared copy of the Lonely Planet guide to Mongolia. I sighed again and then accepted not one but two books by everyone's favorite children's author, Danielle Steel. The bodice-ripping covers of *Wanderlust* and *Five Days in Paris* were enough: I asked if we could call it quits on the library tour and have that tea they'd offered earlier.

Six teachers joined Rajeev, Pasupathi, and me for tea in the headmaster's spartan office. The world map on his wall was filled with geographies that no longer existed: unified Yugoslavia, East Germany, and the Soviet Union. Headmaster Rajeev and Pasupathi translated for me as the teachers told me of their situation in rapid-fire Nepali. What I heard from each of them was a similar variation on Pasupathi's earlier theme, as they spoke of their frustration. They wanted the children to learn, but . . . "Our village is poor. Most parents are farmers. We have no extra money; our resources are near zero. Many months, we teachers have to work for half salary, even though we only make fifteen hundred rupees [about twenty U.S. dollars] a month."

Then the headmaster said nine simple words that would cause me sleepless nights, and eventually cost me a very large sum of money, and upend my life and world.

"Perhaps, sir, you will someday come back with books."

....

When my father talks about all the jobs on his résumé, he says, "This is how I supported my family. But the most rewarding part of my life has been as a volunteer."

The first people I called with a pitch to join my crazy scheme were my parents, who heard from me shortly after my successful circumnavigation of the Annapurna circuit. Even during the toughest parts of the trek, including the climb to nearly eighteen thousand feet, my mind had returned continually to Bahundanda and the electrifying idea of filling their library.

Carolyn and Woody have always been community-minded people. Carolyn was a Cub Scout and Brownie leader and volunteered for almost twenty years at Robert Packer Hospital in Pennsylvania, taking patients to their tests. She and Woody were both active in the Lions Club, gathering donated eyeglasses for children.

One of the most powerful bonding experiences I recall from my childhood is filling sandbags with Woody to hold back the floodwaters then engulfing our little town in Pennsylvania as a result of Hurricane Agnes. This storm killed 129 people and caused three billion dollars in damage, at the time setting a record for the most destructive hurricane to ever hit the United States. Even the news reports of its raw fury were not enough to keep the Wood family bundled up in our basement, warm and dry. We were all out on the front lines, filling sandbags. At the tender age of eight, I did not understand why we were doing this: After all, we lived on the highest hill in town. Our house was safe.

"This is not about us as a family," my father explained as he wiped the rain from his three-day growth. "This is about us as members of a community who look out for each other."

Alas, those sandbags were not enough, and our downtown streets were soon flooded to a depth of twelve feet. Even then, my father found a way to help. He put our small water-ski boat into immediate action. I rode in the back of the boat as my father navigated the streets, rescuing both people and their possessions from their homes and handing out Carolyn's sandwiches to the firefighters.

They had taught me well. And now I was asking them to help with my own charitable project. I'd promised Headmaster Rajeev that I would return with books in hand—hopefully hundreds or perhaps even a thousand of them. I was living overseas, but most of my friends were in the United States. So my e-mail marketing campaign asked people to send the books to my parents' home in Colorado. Soon their garage was overflowing. As my father unpacked boxes and sifted for quality, my mother hit yard sales and discount stores that offered used children's books "ten for a dollar." My eight-year-old niece even did a book drive in her school, with the winning homeroom being rewarded with a pizza party. The Wood family was back in philanthropic action!

....

Six months after my first visit to Bahundanda in 1998, we had thousands of books and were eager to get them into the hands of the students. My father had lobbied to join me, and in April 1999 I greatly annoyed my boss by once again slipping away for a visit to Nepal. Now here we were just hours away from the return to Bahundanda. On the hotel patio Abin, the young boy whose cold-beer solution had originally broken the ice and started my conversation with Pasupathi, was still serving as the lodge's waiter. He was now nine years old.

"Do you still go to school?" I asked.

"Yes, yes, every day," Abin assured me as he thrust his thin arm out and pointed uphill in the direction of his school.

Pasupathi was with us, drinking cups of *duit chia* (milk tea) as we warded off the morning chill rising from the rushing Marsyangdi River. He reported that the people of Bahundanda had spent weeks planning a welcoming ceremony for us. "It's going to be a big day," we were assured. "Hundreds of students will be lined up, and they have composed a special song for you about the importance of reading."

Though excited, I was also a bit skeptical. A big day? All we were doing was showing up with some donated English-language children's books. I could picture Headmaster Rajeev's look of elation—but the entire community?

Woody, Pasupathi, and I walked along the thin trail paralleling the river. The roaring Marsyangdi River was full of glacier melt. Two days ago, this water had been frozen. This morning, it cascaded downhill. A breeze cut across its waters, and the chill hit me. As I zipped up my fleece, my father turned to me and said: "I hope you don't mind, but I took five of the books out of one of the boxes."

Without waiting for an answer, he explained: "I asked Abin, the young boy serving us, if he has books in his school, or in his home. He said they have very few. Obviously he is very bright. So I gave him some books."

"When did this subterfuge take place?" I laughed.

"Last night. Abin was so excited that his face just lit up. This morning he told me his name and shook my hand and said that he'd been reading until late at night. Then I noticed that all morning, Abin would walk out to check on us or to refill our tea and then run back to the kitchen. He was in the corner reading. His mother was cooking and said that she couldn't thank us enough."

In a parallel to my own childhood, my father had met a smart boy and immediately wanted to inspire him. I was close to Abin's age when my parents bought me the bike that enabled my weekly trips to the Spalding Memorial Library.

Pasupathi interrupted my musings, pointing out that we were about to "enjoy" the very steep climb up to the school and that I might want to fill my water bottle before we climbed out of the river valley.

On top of the hill, a huge crowd of students and parents were lined up in a receiving line. We bowed and exchanged literally hundreds of *namastes*. Children hung marigold garlands around our necks, while the youngest presented us with flower petals they'd picked in the forest during their morning walk to school.

And when the big moment came, and it was time for us to unpack the books, the children went crazy. Having never before seen brightly colored children's books, their eyes lit up. As Woody, Pasupathi, and I handed out books, the scene became a bit of a mosh pit. For the next hour, we watched as children scattered around the school yard enjoyed their new treasures. Some read alone, while others sat in small groups, helping one another to sound out the words.

One of the teachers, whom I'd met the year before, held my hand. Looking into my eyes with both intensity and love, he said, "You have given us so much. We have so little that we can give to you in return."

I could not find the words to describe to him what I'd be taking away that afternoon as we left our friends in Bahundanda.

Woody and I talked for hours afterward. Over a beer on the stone patio of our *bhatti*, the Trekker's Lodge, again served by young Abin, we relived the day. Woody asked, "Okay, what's next? I'm signed on for another book drive."

My mind was racing; it was obvious that I had a unique opportunity here. This emotional day had made me acutely aware that my "lottery winnings" from Microsoft stock might have a higher calling. An abrupt U-turn lay ahead.

Just as the journey of a thousand miles begins with a single step, the path to the ten thousandth library had begun with Bahundanda. It was the first drop of paint on what was destined to be a very beautiful canvas.

CHAPTER FIVE

Helping Others Help Themselves:
The Challenge-Grant Model

By 2005, our fifth full year of operations, Room to Read was opening libraries at a faster rate than Starbucks opened coffee shops in its fifth year. My little dream was scaling rapidly. In addition to opening school libraries, we were also building schools and running a program to provide long-term support for girls to continue their education through the end of secondary school.

"One of the reasons we've succeeded," says my cofounder and trusted colleague, Erin Ganju, "is that we have a really simple mission, one that touches people emotionally: It's very hard to argue with educating children."

As Room to Read grew to its current size, I was often asked, "How did it happen? It's easy to quit your job; any fool can do that. But how is it that you could go from one library in 1999 to ten thousand by 2010?"

One of the key elements in our success has been our insistence that local communities get involved in our projects: We are instigators, not administrators. We scale up by being nimble, lean in our operations, and determined to get the best results for our donors. The challenge-grant model is one of the cornerstones in the school-construction process. We go into communities already identified by members of the local Room to

Read team as ready and motivated. Our local teams focus on customizing our programs so that they fit the local context and are culturally appropriate. They also work closely with the provincial and national ministries of education. For example, we don't agree to build a school unless the ministries are able to assure us, and the village, that they'll be able to provide teachers. Typically, Room to Read will fund the building of a school or library for three to five years. Then it is expected that the local government will take over. We're also pragmatic in that we don't always insist on starting from scratch but instead will often build on what's already there. A school may be overcrowded, or may run only grades one through three, so in those cases we will build on incrementally to what already exists. Or we may find a school that lacks a library, and for a small investment we can greatly improve the quality of the learning by adding one on.

....

The sun climbs, rising over the tops of a row of palm trees. Nourished by the near-perpetual Sri Lankan sun, the line of trees forms the back perimeter of a small play area attached to Rathmalgahaela Primary School. The flat, dry earth, burned to a cocoa color, becomes more vibrant as vendors lay blankets across the ground. There is a flurry of activity as several dozen local people set out their wares. Every month this small but bustling farmers' market draws hundreds of local customers. The farm-fresh offerings are vast: eggs, coconuts, mangoes, and rice all compete for the consumer's attention. Stretched out on a bright blue cloth are the yellowest bananas I've ever seen, while one blanket over is stacked a pyramid of pineapples, which sell for twenty rupees each, or about twenty U.S. cents.

My business goes to the coconut vendor. With a grateful smile for her first sale of the day, the dark-haired merchant pulls out a machete. It's not meant to frighten me but instead to hack off the top of my purchase. Once the dismembered bit of hard "exoskeleton" has been thrown to the ground, she uses the tip of the machete to gently poke a hole through the soft membrane. Inserting a green plastic straw, she hands me a thirst-quenching beverage straight from the tree. Her teeth are the color of the milky bits of the coconut. As I give the drink an instant thumbs-up, she smiles, happy that her first customer of the day is satisfied with the product.

There is only one thing unusual about our transaction: The coconut seller is only seven years old. The boy selling bananas next to her seems to be no older than nine. On the next cloth over, the girl selling a kilogram of rice appears to be in first or second grade. In fact, looking around, I note that this farmers' market is apparently run by children.

....

Two thousand miles north of Sri Lanka, it's a beautiful day in the Nepal Himalayas. The sun traces a lazy arc across a cerulean sky, illuminating the glaciated peaks that hover over the village like a larger-than-life mirage. Along the worn dirt paths of the village of Dumre, there is heavy foot traffic this afternoon.

Tiluk Pradhan is one of many dozens of farmers walking downhill. His family's small plots of land sit above the village center, neatly arranged in terraces that stretch several hundred vertical feet up the verdant hillside. Tiluk, his ten-year-old daughter, Mithi, and his seven-year-old son, Anup, make their way carefully over small boulders and tiny streams that are part of the village's irrigation system. The descent is particularly precarious for Tiluk, as he carries a heavy burden on his back. Hunched over beneath his load—a one-hundred-pound bag of sorghum—he makes his way slowly down the trail. Skipping ahead, his children encourage him.

"*Chito, chito,*" they yell, encouraging him to move faster. "We will be late for the festival."

Unburdened by sorghum and excited by what lies ahead at the Tihar (Nepali New Year) gathering, they have the speed of cheetahs, while their father resembles a plodding donkey. Seeing the radiant smiles of his children, he moves a bit faster, breathing a sigh of relief when they reach level ground. The family joins a caravan of other locals making their way to the town center. A remarkable number of the adults are also carrying large bags of grain. Some adults have split the burden, with both the husband and the wife bearing loads, while others have enlisted donkeys.

Even these overloaded beasts of burden seem caught up in the spirit of the day, moving at a faster pace than their usual reluctant plod.

Brightly colored prayer flags strung between trees are flapping gently in the afternoon breeze. Several hundred people use these trees as a refuge from the harsh afternoon sun. The women are dressed in their best saris, forming a tableau of reds, greens, and purples. Many are adorned in what looks like all the jewelry they own, including nose rings, necklaces, and sparkly silver bracelets. Some have a red dot between their eyes, indicating that they have been to temple that morning. The men are mostly in slacks and short-sleeve shirts, and almost all wear cloth *topis,* the national hat of Nepal. Generations are gathered, from grandparents to toddlers.

The cacophony of the crowd is soon silenced as a village elder offers a prayer for the continued well-being of the village and its people and for another bountiful harvest. He then invites a farmer to join him on the elevated stage. A small man about fifty years of age, with glasses, slowly makes his way up the four steps. Placing his large canvas bag on the ground, he puts his hands together, bows, and offers a *namaste* to the hundreds of village residents. He opens the top of the bag and uses all of his strength to hoist it above his head. Then he pours his crop onto a tarp stretched for twenty meters on the ground beneath the stage. When the falling golden grain turns from a trickle into a torrent, the crowd responds with loud applause.

A second farmer is waiting to repeat the process. Indeed, there is now a long queue, in which Tiluk is in the number-eight position. Clutching his hand, Mithi pleads with her father: "Can Anup and I join you on the platform and help to pour out our grain?"

Her father agrees. Excited that he has granted her wish, she then plays big sister and teaches Anup how to perform the perfect *namaste.* She instructs, and they practice together. "Palms together at the head level. Bow from the waist, and say, '*Namaste.*'"

Meanwhile, several more bags of grain have been poured onto the pile, which is beginning to broaden and rise higher. The queue of farmers has grown even longer, with more than one hundred ready to join in. Soon it is Tiluk's turn. He follows behind Mithi and Anup as they bounce up the stairs. Together they add one hundred pounds of sorghum to the growing stockpile below and then walk offstage with their empty canvas bag. Anup cannot resist one more *namaste,* slightly delaying their departure. Near the stage they find a place to sit, knowing that the ceremony has just begun.

....

I thought of those farmers years later, during a visit to a farming village in the landlocked nation of Zambia. Joined by a group on our summer "Teen Trek," fifteen of us toured a library that the local Room to Read team has established in a rural school. Agnes, the librarian, proudly walks our small group of investors past the well-stocked shelves. Posters on the walls encourage children to read regularly and to check out books. The library's list of rules includes the familiar (keep your voice low; be sure to bring back the books you have checked out so that other students may enjoy them), along with a few that seem surreal to us (no smoking; you may not be in the library if you are drunk). Judging by the cherubic faces of the fifth and sixth graders reveling in their library period, I am guessing that the latter rules must apply to the adults in the village. Or at least I hope so.

Agnes tells me that she opens the library each morning at 7:00 A.M., one hour before the start of school. It stays open until 5:00 P.M. five days a week. More than one thousand students have access. She tries to encourage all of them to read at least one book per week.

"Isn't it difficult to have that many students in here? And to be in here fifty hours a week, in addition to your administrative duties—isn't that a challenge for you?" I ask.

She smiles broadly, her eyes alight. "Yes, it can be challenging. But when you love something"—(here she pauses)—"when you love something, you do it with all of your heart, all of your passion, and all of your energy. If my students learn to read, they will be set up for life. And I will be a very happy woman."

A member of our investor group praises her dedication to the school's students.

But Agnes is not yet done with the tour. "The pigs," she says. "You have not seen the pigs. We must take you out behind the library to see the piggery."

Our group is perplexed. What role, we wonder, does a litter of pigs play in a properly functioning library?

....

The children selling produce in Sri Lanka, the farmers pouring grain into a community stockpile in Nepal, and Agnes the librarian with a small on-premise "piggery" in Zambia have one thing in common. All are taking part in Room to Read's challenge-grant model, by which each of our projects—a new school, a freestanding library building, or a classroom library—is established with a coinvestment business model. Rather than us giving them everything they need to get the school built or the library established, we offer to meet them halfway.

As Dinesh Shrestha, who started Room to Read in Nepal, likes to say, "We can't want this more than you want it. We can't help you unless you want to help yourselves."

Dinesh originally proposed the challenge-grant model to me during the first full year of Room to Read's operations in 2000. After starting with libraries, we'd quickly progressed to building schools to house them. For over a year I had fantasized about one day surprising my parents by opening a school in their honor. Corresponding via e-mail, Dinesh told me of a small farming village he'd visited that needed a new building. The school was teaching only grades one through five. The nearest secondary school was a hilly two-hour walk. Many families could not afford to lose their children's labor for the entirety of a school day plus a four-hour commute, so for most children education ended after grade five. But with a new building, and with the promise of teachers being trained and paid for by the local Ministry of Education, they'd be able to make grade ten the new norm.

I loved the idea and asked Dinesh the total project price. When I heard how low it was, I immediately responded, telling him I'd wire the money the next day. His response speaks volumes about who Dinesh is:

Dear John,
Please wire only half the money that is needed for this project. I will try to convince the community to find the resources for the other half. They are very motivated in the village of Ngadi, and I think they can all be convinced to donate labor to the project. Also, the Village Development Committee is

willing to collect small donations from all the families in the area—it may
be as low as 500 rupees per family, but it will add up. If we end up needing
more money, I will inform you immediately. But I don't think we will.

Thus the challenge-grant model was born. Like many of the best innovations at Room to Read over our first decade, the idea did not come from me or from anyone sitting at the central headquarters but from the local team in the field. Over the years it has succeeded wildly.

Now operating across ten countries, our teams have found that there are three main advantages to the challenge-grant model:

1. It allows us to work only with motivated communities. We can quickly sift through which proposed projects are worth doing and which should be avoided. It is the local people, after all, who will be running the library or school after it is built. So if the up-front motivation is not there, then there is a low probability that the project will be sustained in the long run. The developing world already has enough projects that, for all their good intentions, did not meet their lofty goals. Often this is because the local community was not involved in their design and implementation.

2. It allows us to make our money go further. If the true cost of a library construction project is forty thousand dollars, and the local community finds the resources to cover half, then this means that Room to Read can catalyze the development of twice as many libraries. As an early "proof point" on this theory, I was so excited by how Ngadi responded to Dinesh's challenge that I offered to fund a second school if he could find an equally motivated community. He could, so I did. And rather than having one school built in their honor, Woody and Carolyn now have two. (And yes, my mother did cry when she visited the school and saw her name on the dedication plaque, on which their "loving son John" thanked Woody and Carolyn for investing so heavily in my education.)

3. It greatly motivates Room to Read's investors. People like knowing that they are providing "a hand up, not a handout" to communities in need. Many people are understandably skeptical about how "aid" can foster a never-ending cycle of dependency. If you donate food aid to a com-

munity, for example, how can you guarantee that a month later it won't need another donation, and perhaps another after that?

In today's world, there are paths to dependence and paths to independence. We are big fans of the latter. But it's not just us. Many of the community residents tell us how much they appreciate being treated with dignity and being asked to help. Nobody welcomes the condescension that comes with being treated as if they were helpless, or in the words of a mother in India: "You do not treat us as passive spectators. We are active and proud participants who go to sleep at night knowing we've been part of creating a better future for our children."

Our team believes that by requiring the community residents to pitch in, we are saluting their inherent dignity.

....

In the community of Dumre, Nepal, word had gone out back in 2002 that a new school was on the planning boards. To make good on their pledge to Room to Read, the village elders were hoping to collect cash contributions from local families. But after one month, their success had been extremely limited. At a school construction committee meeting, a village elder pointed out that most of the families had no cash income and lived mostly by barter. How could cash be collected in a cashless economy? I knew two answers—pigs and produce. Here came a third.

A member of the construction committee spoke up: How about getting each farm family to donate grain? The rains and the sun had been good that year, and healthy crops of sorghum, millet, and corn had been harvested. Why not, he suggested, ask each local family to donate some of that grain to a "community stockpile"? Since most families came into town for the Tihar festival, they might respond to a request to bring a hundred pounds each as a small contribution to the school construction fund. If two hundred families each donated one hundred pounds, they'd have ten tons of grain. After this was trucked to the nearest city market to be sold, the resulting cash could then be contributed to the construction fund.

Though each family would do something relatively small, the collective impact would be hugely significant, especially since Room to Read's

Nepal team had already agreed to match all funds raised by this community effort on a two-to-one basis.

The pigs in rural Zambia were also a response to our challenge-grant model. Our team had worked with the local community to build the library that was now open fifty hours per week under Agnes's leadership. The parents of the students who would benefit had already helped by digging the foundation and building bookshelves. But the school needed additional help, as many children from the surrounding villages had been orphaned due to the HIV/AIDS epidemic and could not afford the school fees, the uniform, or school supplies.

Room to Read was asked to help, but our team pointed out that we were not a billion-dollar foundation but rather a cash-strapped NGO that had to earn every dollar we deployed. Our budgets were tight, and we were already stretching just to keep our commitment to open 150 libraries in Zambia during 2010. While we wanted to help those orphans, we just could not say yes. They had experienced enough disappointment and hardship in life without our adding to it further by making a commitment we couldn't afford to keep.

Fortunately, the residents of the small, dusty hamlet came up with a workable solution. A member of the school's management committee pointed out that the school abutted a local farm that had unused buildings; perhaps they could be put to good use? The committee would ask some of the community residents to donate pigs. If the school had a few male pigs along with some sows, a predictable annual litter of piglets would be born. The majority could be sold off and the proceeds used to fund scholarships for needy orphans. A few could remain to increase the size of the drove. As more pigs mated, more piglets would be born, and more scholarships could be funded in this innovative way.

Many of the teachers were inspired by the idea and contributed part of their small monthly salaries to help get this piggery party started.

"How many scholarships are now being supported?" I asked Agnes.

"Thirty," she reported proudly.

My grin matched hers. I always love seeing entrepreneurial energy. When people hear of a great idea, very often they want to invest in it. I was not able to resist this temptation. On the spot I offered to give the school enough funding to buy two new pigs, one male and one female, to help them scale up their innovative solution.

Back in Sri Lanka, the small farmers' market was one more example of the success of the challenge-grant model. The school's innovative head-mistress had proposed a bold vision that the parents supported. Each family was asked to contribute a small amount of produce to the monthly farmers' market. The students would lay out blankets and colorful cloths on which to display their wares and contribute all funds generated from sales to the school's general maintenance fund. A few bananas here, some coconuts there, and it would all eventually add up to . . . what?

In this case it would result in the purchase of ten gallons of paint, the headmistress explained. Working with Room to Read, she had con-structed a large freestanding library building for the school's 350 chil-dren. As part of the challenge grant, the community had agreed to donate paint, paintbrushes, and labor. They'd give enough to cover all four inte-rior walls and then move on to the exterior ones.

As of that day, the community had painted all of the interior walls and three of the four exterior ones. After fifteen months of continued effort, they were so close. Our team wondered if today's market would put them over the top. "How much have you raised?" the headmistress was asked.

"We will not know until three days' time," she responded. "Monday is when the fifth-grade math students count the money. It would be faster for the adults to do the calculations, but when the students are fully in charge, it keeps them motivated. They can then also learn math, and they're realizing a lot about running a business—that if you sell products that people want, you make some good money. So I think my students benefit from this market in many ways that are not obvious."

Did she think they'd be close to success on the final exterior wall?

"Oh yes," she said, smiling. "It is virtually certain."

Inspired by this creative example, our team could only ask one more question: "Is there anything else your school needs, with which we could help you?"

By then we'd seen enough to know what a good investment we'd made in this hard-pressed but determined and fully engaged community.

As with the piggery in Zambia, it seemed obvious that continuing to co-invest alongside the motivated community of parents and teachers would pay significant dividends. Over the years, we've seen similar sacrifices and coinvestments being made by over ten thousand communities.

Our team at Room to Read works hard, smiling, and secure in the knowledge that we're helping others to help themselves.

CHAPTER SIX

GSD: Building a World-Class Team

Over the years, Room to Read has continued to grow at a frenetic pace as we hit new milestones continually. Looking back from the vantage point of the ten thousandth library opening in Kavresthali and wondering how it had happened, I recalled the words of an Urdu poet:

I embarked alone towards the goal, and towards my dream.
People joined along the way, and it became a caravan.

We've been fortunate to have thousands of people join our caravan: By journeying together, we've managed to reach this destination.

And fortunately, most of them have been what I call GSD people. I lifted one of Room to Read's early directives from my old boss Steve Ballmer: "Get shit done!" Steve was the biggest influence in my eight-year career with Microsoft. I watched him very closely to learn what made this hyperactive perfectionist tick. And it was very quickly clear to me: In every internal meeting he focused not on what was going right but on what was going wrong.

I still cherish his directive to get the job done no matter what the circumstances. Whining does not cut it, either in fighting for greater market share in Asia for a high-tech giant or in looking for ways to adapt to challenging circumstances in developing nations in a quest to build new schools and libraries.

Steve was able to get so much accomplished only because he had a great team around him. Starting a nonprofit organization has, as they say in the world of diving, "a high degree of difficulty." The founders have to simultaneously hire the core team, design and implement programs, and build a funding base. All of this requires an insane amount of time, energy, and commitment. Our early team had all of that. We simply worked our butts off, with one person often doing the job of three or four.

Take my cofounder, Erin Ganju, as one example. I had been impressed with her background from the day I met her: two degrees from Johns Hopkins, three years as an analyst with Goldman Sachs, then three years running business divisions for Unilever in Vietnam. But what was more impressive was her ability to GSD. In a given day, she would interact with our country offices in Nepal and Vietnam, write grant proposals, have breakfast and lunch meetings with potential investors, review country requests for new school and library projects—and the list went on. We worked long days with little support staff. There were times we would go hours without exchanging a word, as both of us liked to "crank quietly."

Though we'd hired more than a hundred employees by the fifth year of Room to Read, our staff and some members of our board of directors kept telling us that we needed to hire faster. I often rationalized that this was easy for others to say, as they were not "sweating the payroll" as I was, constantly circling the globe in hopes of bringing in more donations. Fortunately a visit with one of my early mentors helped to persuade me to move even faster to build a global team.

In 2004 I paid a visit to one of my former Microsoft managers, Bruce Jacobsen. A brilliant guy who had studied philosophy at Yale, he was one of the rare breed at Microsoft who could reportedly go head to head in arguments with Bill Gates and not back down. When I visited Bruce in 2004, he was hard at work on his second post-Microsoft start-up. The first, Starwave, an online sports site that was acquired by Disney and then became part of the foundation for ESPN.com. His new baby, Kinetic Books, was producing online lessons with Advanced Placement (AP)–level tutorials in chemistry, physics, math, and other weighty subjects.

We got reacquainted over a cup of coffee at the nearby Pike Place Market in Seattle, after which he offered to give me a tour of the office. As we walked through, he talked about the view overlooking Elliott Bay and the distant Olympic Mountains and how he hoped this would inspire creativity in his workforce.

But what I noticed most was all the empty space. At least a third of the office was full of desks without people. Another third had no desks at all.

"This seems like expensive real estate," the cost-conscious accountant in me opined. When he didn't disagree, I continued. "It's a lot of space to pay for and not use."

Bruce explained the method to his seeming madness.

"Yes, lots of empty space. But I figure this company—like both Microsoft and Starwave—is going to get really big, in which case we will need all of this real estate and more. Or we won't get big, in which case I'll have to shut the company down and just make payout terms on the lease. If it's not going to be big, then it's not worth spending my time and effort on."

Flying back to San Francisco, I ruminated on Bruce's words. Like him, I wanted to either *go big* or *go home*. What was the point of devoting my life to Room to Read if we did not aim ridiculously high in terms of the number of young children we could help to gain access to the improved life trajectory that literacy and education provide? I quietly vowed to work on increasing the size of our own office and filling it with great people.

Although money was very scarce in the early days of Room to Read, I knew that hiring too slowly was probably a bigger danger than hiring too quickly. We would not be able to establish many libraries or build schools without large in-country teams who could work with the local communities.

As Erin articulates it: "Local leaders know how to navigate complex political issues and how to hire and build on community support. This is much better than having foreigners try and figure out local issues whose complexities they can never really understand. It's all about decentralization: empowering people at the level that is closest to your beneficiary, or your customer."

Just as we needed more staff for program implementation, we'd never be able to raise sufficient funds if I was the sole "rainmaker." If the enlarged local teams were visiting hundreds of additional communities and green-lighting new projects, we'd need to triple the amount of funding we were bringing in, then double it, then double it again.

Erin and I quickly went into GSD mode. She put out feelers for a larger office, and jointly we wrote up job descriptions for positions on the education programs team, in fund-raising, and in finance. I sent out word via countless phone calls and e-mails to let our network know that we were looking for great people. With little money in the bank, we were both nervous about increasing the monthly cash flow we'd be expending on payroll, benefits, and real estate, especially in our expensive headquarters city of San Francisco.

As we posted the new positions online and entered into lease negotiations, we devised an elegant new theory. If we had more people working for Room to Read, we could get more schools and libraries built and put more girls on scholarship. If we were getting really impressive results, we could go out to potential donors and make the argument that we were getting a lot done (again, GSD). Inspired by our progress, they would buy in and write large checks. But we needed a bigger fund-raising team to help us make these pitches.

But *when* (not *if*) we were successful, the increased funding flow would mean that we could get even bigger results with our programs. In turn this would help us get new investors and ask our existing ones to write even larger checks and introduce us to their networks. If our theory held, we'd have on our hands what technologists call a positive feedback loop. But if Room to Read wasn't able to make the leap from scribbles on the office whiteboard to reality, we'd have what's called a flameout.

Recognizing that we'd never know if we didn't get started immediately, we moved into action mode and were soon interviewing a steady stream of job candidates. The decisions on these early hires would prove to be some of the most important we'd make. The success or failure of our whiteboard theory was hugely dependent on whether we succeeded at getting the right people on the bus.

We were very clear on three key attributes we sought.

The first was passion. We knew the job ahead would be tough, requiring long hours, constant travel in the cheapest seats on the plane, and limited holidays. We were a start-up environment where if you wanted to get something done, you pretty much had to do it yourself. When people presented Erin and me with their brainstorms, we often joked: "Great idea. When can you implement?"

We needed to test for whether the person we were interviewing would possess the stick-to-itiveness to make things happen. Where the candidate had gone to school, or what prior jobs he or she had held, was no guarantee. We probed in every way possible to learn how passionate the candidate was, not only about education but also about building a large and world-class organization from scratch on a limited resource base.

Three of our earliest hires were off the charts on the passion meter. I'll never forget interviewing both Ami Ehrlich and Stacey Warner, who were brought on to work on our school library program and geographic expansion strategy, respectively. Both had been teachers in Namibia, a poor country in southwest Africa that had only recently been freed from colonization. Each had spent two years teaching English in rural villages, one with WorldTeach and the other with the Peace Corps. They had lived with local families, sharing meals, sleeping on the ground, and battling numerous illnesses over the years.

And yet both described not the hardships but how much they had felt privileged to be helping children in rural Namibia to be among the first in their families to learn to read and to speak and write in both their mother tongue and English.

At one point in her interview, I asked Stacey about some of the famous places making Namibia a newly popular adventure travel destination. "What was Etosha National Park like?" I asked.

She had no idea.

"How about the famous, eerie Skeleton Coast?"

She had never been.

"What about Fish River Canyon?" I asked, throwing out the name of a famous six-day hike that was Africa's equivalent of the Grand Canyon. There was no way she could have spent a year in Namibia and not gone there.

Again, she could not tell me. "I was there as a teacher, not as a tourist," she said with a gentle laugh that was more ironic than didactic. "My job was to teach. Even though there were a lot of hardships in the village, especially since I had virtually zero privacy as the sole American—I could not bring myself to leave it."

Within a few days, we made offers to both Ami and Stacey.

And then there was Emily. Having grown up in comfortable Sonoma County, California, she had become fascinated at a young age by the struggle of the African National Congress and its allies to free South Africa from its oppressive history of apartheid and racial discrimination. She enrolled, sight unseen, in the political science department of the University of Cape Town to pursue her master's degree.

During our interview I asked her what had been the most enlightening parts of her graduate study.

"That's an easy question," she replied as her eyes lit up with a fire I'd come to know well over the years. "In 1994, South Africa was finally going to have elections that would hopefully bring Nelson Mandela into power as the country's first black president. I could already envision the day when the world's most famous political prisoner would become the world's newest head of state. But voter registration amongst the black population was low, as to many of them the right to vote was not yet something they fully understood. Even if they did, the system for registering to vote was not yet clear or logical. So I spent the majority of my free time, even cutting classes to do so, going from home to home—or in most cases shack to shack—to educate and register voters and encourage them to come to the polls. I was knocking on doors morning, noon, and night."

I asked her if that was not a bit dangerous—the Cape Flats was known as one of the most violent parts of an often-violent country.

Her answer was what we'd eventually refer to as "classic Em."

"Yes, full-on dangerous!" She smiled as though danger were a good thing, an old friend whose presence she welcomed. "But this work had to be done, or democracy might have been stillborn. And I felt that the danger I was putting myself in was so minor compared with what Mandela and the other freedom fighters had experienced. They lived under constant threat of political assassination. The question for me was simple: Would I be a bystander as a new democracy was born, or would I be a participant?"

Needless to say, we hired Em on the spot. Eight years into her tenure at Room to Read, Emily Leys is now global director of our Girls' Education program.

The second key attribute we were seeking in new hires was corporate experience. Most of our board of directors and the majority of our early funders, along with Erin, Dinesh in Nepal, and me, came from a business background. Our bias was to make sure many of the early hires shared a business-oriented view of the world. We felt strongly that it helped distinguish Room to Read from other nonprofits. Yes, we wanted to "do good" and "make a difference in the world." But with a nearly unlimited demand for Room to Read's "products and services" (300 million kids out of school, more than 780 million illiterate people), we needed to build a team that could create, grow, and run a massive organization with the rigor, accountability, and best practices that characterize the most successful for-profit companies. Like any well-run business, but unlike a lot of charities, we'd watch our expenses like hawks. And we'd constantly set bold goals, and then when they were hit, we'd raise the bar again and again.

From our research we knew that 90 percent of nonprofits in the United States have a budget of less than three hundred thousand dollars per year. Many times this was due to the fact that the founding team didn't think like a business. We wanted to be a hundred times that size, at least thirty million dollars per year. So we'd need people who had experience in growing and leading fast-moving companies.

Erin often tells university and business-school students in now-popular classes in "social entrepreneurship": "A lot of people have this idea that the fund-raising side of the organization is somehow bad—that it's the evil business you have to do in order to do all the good stuff. The story of Room to Read is that we've truly tried to own the fact that raising money, raising awareness, building the momentum around the mission is as important as the mission itself. You can't deliver great services without a sustainable funding base."

My theory is similar. One of my ten laws of fund-raising is simple and succinct: No Money = No Mission.

One of our first full-time fund-raising hires was Bella, an acquaintance I'd met through a local marathon group. I jumped when she said that after seven years working for investment firms, she felt that she was only making rich people richer and sought more meaning from her work. But most nonprofits scared her, as she felt like they were run very chaotically. She did not want to devote her life and "the fourteen-hour days I like to work" to an organization that was not well run.

Another early hire was Jayson Morris. Upon sitting down to our first interview, my initial comment was that his background looked quite interesting. He was number three in his class at Georgetown and had three years under his belt working as an analyst for Credit Suisse in both New York and Melbourne. This was followed by three years of backpacking through thirty countries in Africa, Asia, and Latin America.

How, I asked, did this make him qualified to work for our start-up?

"Well, I've seen thousands of children whose lives will never get better if they don't have education. That was the number one takeaway from my years backpacking through many of the countries where Room to Read either currently works or will work one day. But lots of people have empathy: What I bring to the table is my unique skill set with spreadsheets, financial analysis, forecasts, and budgeting. If this organization is going to get big, you will need those skills. You probably need them now. When a corporation that funds Room to Read gets a report I've written, it will look every bit as good as a Wall Street research report—except that you will have paid a lot less to get that report produced than a bank would have, as I know how low salaries are here at Room to Read." He laughed.

Jayson and Bella were soon working at Room to Read, sharing space in a bullpen so small that the desks were touching.

The third major attribute we interviewed for was in my opinion the greatest litmus test: the strength of the candidate's work ethic. It would be impossible for us to make Room to Read a major player unless every person on our team was willing to work insanely hard during the early years. The amount we could spend on payroll was limited, so each new employee would have to do the job of two or three people. I needed to be convinced that each candidate knew that this was not a Monday-through-Friday, nine-to-five kind of charity (in fact, I so dislike the connotations of the word "charity" that I refer to Room to Read as a company).

Potential hires needed to convince me that when they faced a brick wall, they would run over, around, or through it and that they would then celebrate the achievement by burning the midnight oil.

Dinesh Shrestha was my role model. During the first few years of our work in Nepal, he acted as the country director but worked for no salary. He had a "day job" working for the United Nations' World Health Organization and considered Room to Read to be his second job. It received his full attention on nights, on weekends, and probably during some e-mails tapped furtively from his comfortable UN office.

On weekends he would drive six hours one way and then walk for three hours on mountain paths, just to visit our first schools and libraries. He would leave Kathmandu at sunrise and return home seventeen hours later, close to midnight. He used his own car and never even asked for reimbursement for petrol. When I tried to get him to join Room to Read full time, his answer spoke volumes about his commitment: "John, you are not taking a salary. As long as you are doing so, I will do the same. I can work forty hours a week for the UN and forty for Room to Read, and it will be my pleasure, because I know Nepal will only develop with education. My father taught me that. Our family had a little extra money when I grew up, so my parents funded our village's first library. So this is my way of honoring them."

Stephanie Scott is a final example of a classic interview where I saw a work ethic so strong that as soon as her interview was over we started the reference checks. Stephanie had been a teacher in inner-city Newark and during her summer break volunteered at a school in Nepal, staying on for two months because the school needed help.

I asked about her role at the school: Was she primarily teaching English?

"Of course I did that. The children so loved showing off their new vocabulary. They'd yell new words at the top of their lungs, and even at night I could hear new English words being shouted from nearby homes.

But I did more than that. The school was in a really bad state of disrepair. They needed a new roof, as the current one leaked, and the walls had a lot of holes, as they had been constructed from mud more than twenty years ago."

"So you rolled up your sleeves and became Bob the Builder?"

"Exactly! I got the kids to help out, too, so that they learned that it was their responsibility to help maintain the school."

"What did you use to patch up the holes?"

"We collected cow dung and mixed it with dirt and then just scooped it up and filled the holes."

"Cow dung?"

"Yes," she said with a big grin on her face. "Cow dung was not only free; it was also really effective."

I was in awe that an Ivy League graduate who grew up on the Upper West Side of New York City would be willing to go to these lengths to get the job done. Before telling her that we'd be making her an offer, I explained our concept of GSD and suggested that she might be taking GSD to the next level.

. . . .

With these key hires made, we could begin to really put our machine into motion. Our model was simple and easy to comprehend while also having the potential to be world changing:

- Ami, Emily, and Stacey would lead the programs team, which designed the education programs we provided to communities.
- Bella, Jayson, and Stephanie, as part of the fund-raising team, would bring in the dollars, pounds, euros, and yen we needed to scale these programs in our existing countries and launch them in new ones.
- The in-country teams, with strong entrepreneurial local talent, would set bold targets, write their business plans, and set in-country budgets. They'd then engage the local communities to implement hundreds (and eventually thousands) of projects: school construction, the opening of libraries, long-term scholarships for girls, etc. By 2004, we had hired our country directors for Nepal, Vietnam, Cambodia, and India.

Each team would play a unique and well-defined role, with the success of one team reinforcing that of the others. The more well designed our programs were, the more likely it was that the fund-raising team could find the donors to provide the cash needed to implement them. As the money came in, Dinesh, Sunisha, and the in-country teams could work with more communities. And the bigger those results, the more likely it was that the world would take notice of Room to Read, meaning that we'd be able to attract more great new hires, launch additional fund-raising chapters, garner more media attention and public-speaking opportunities, and bring in still more donations.

The machine was built. Now we simply had to unleash it on the world.

....

I'll never forget a dinner conversation with a trusted mentor shortly after *Leaving Microsoft to Change the World* was published. From the first days it had gone on sale, the book had brought Room to Read an unprecedented number of donations. During 2005 our team had brought in a record $4.7 million of contributions. With the success of my book and the events attached to it, we had nearly doubled that total during 2006 to $9.3 million in cash inflow.

My "inner finance nerd" loved to spend time calculating how much good we could do for the world with an extra $4.6 million. Jotting in the white space of an in-flight magazine, I would do longhand math and realize that this capital would be enough to fund an additional 18,400 spots in our Girls' Education program. Or it could be used to open 1,150 libraries serving 460,000 children. With donations trending skyward, I found it impossible to say no to all the offers I had for public-speaking opportunities, media interviews, and fund-raising events.

I had dinner with Muneer Satter, a senior partner at Goldman Sachs who somehow also found time to serve on our board. As I gave him the book tour highlights, he saw the writing on the wall and made a bold prediction. "Nine million dollars is a great result. I can't think of an organization that's come this close to an eight-figure budget this quickly in its life cycle. But get ready. You will be a twenty-five-million-dollar organization before you know it," he stated with absolute clarity and confidence.

I was skeptical. We'd already grown way beyond my wildest dreams, and many people were telling me we'd soon hit a ceiling. They spoke of a "law of large numbers," which dictated that once you hit a certain size, your growth rates would inevitably slow.

Muneer scoffed at the notion. "What ivory-tower academic is telling you—the perpetual motion machine—to slow down? I know you well enough to know that you're not buying into that idea. I'll bet the people telling you that have never seen you onstage in front of a room full of people. You remind us that without education we would not be in the position we're in today. You challenge us to put some of that good fortune to work by providing a similar opportunity to children in resource-starved parts of the world. Every time I turn around, I'm bumping into a colleague telling me they've funded a school through Room to Read. They share the news with incredible pride and enthusiasm. They are hooked—for life! You took a lot of their money, and they love you for it.

"So don't listen to the so-called experts who want to talk you into slowing down. You know in your heart of hearts that you don't believe it. Instead, accelerate into the curves. You'll be at twenty-five million dollars per year before you know it. But you'd better be ready for it. You're already behind on your hiring, and you'll triple in size over the next five years."

Responding to the challenge, we hired new employees as quickly as possible. Thankfully, Erin was holding down the fort back in San Francisco, scrambling to keep up. She could not count on much help from me, the road warrior. She had already doubled the physical footprint of our office in San Francisco's historic Presidio. Every day she looked at empty desks she saw them not as vacant but as a challenge.

In addition, she was leading our expansion onto the African continent, with South Africa as the first country and Zambia next in the queue. This did not worry me much, as she was an old pro at this by now, having launched Vietnam, Cambodia, India, Sri Lanka, and Laos: five countries in five years. This played on the strengths she had had in her prior career in international business expansion at Unilever.

She faced additional pressures, not the least of which was to effectively and efficiently deploy the cash we had coming in. Our strong preference was not to have large sums of money gathering dust in our bank account. We wanted that money to immediately be used to buy the cement to build schools, to fund teacher-training programs, to print more books, to underwrite more scholarships.

We had doubled the size of our staff in just twelve months. We'd agreed that we'd refuse to compromise on the quality of the people we brought into the family. Some we hired, as I have said, on the spot; on many occasions our team would go through twenty or thirty interviews before finding the right candidate.

Calling in from the road and hearing what Erin was going through, I often felt as though I had the easier of our two positions. But the pace at which Room to Read was growing, and the quality of the people willing to join us, infused our operation with an infectious energy and made me feel that I was doing what every founder should—building a team of superstars so that the organization never has to depend on any one individual. With a solid foundation, we could grow to the sky.

CHAPTER SEVEN

The Tsunami: One Year After

Nowhere had the ethos to "get stuff done" been more effectively displayed by a Room to Read team than in Sri Lanka in the wake of the disastrous tsunami that swept across the Indian Ocean at Christmas 2004. More than two hundred thousand people were killed and thousands of communities destroyed. Our strategic plan included the launch of Room to Read Sri Lanka in 2007. Upon witnessing the televised scenes of flattened coastal villages and hearing a report that more than two hundred schools had been destroyed, we made an immediate decision to bring the launch forward to . . . tomorrow . . . no, today!

Though launching operations in such a devastated country was far from an easy decision, the results illustrate the critical role Room to Read played in the rebuilding of the ravaged island nation. By the one-year anniversary of the tsunami, Room to Read had helped to build or rebuild thirty-nine schools (the number would eventually rise to more than two hundred in Sri Lanka alone).

....

Amid a towering canopy of trees offering welcome shade from the omnipresent Sri Lankan sun, the residents of a small village form a receiving line one hundred yards long. As I step out of the minibus, the first person I see is a dark-haired man who reaches out to grasp my hand in both of his. A thick mustache is set against his caramel-colored face. His ivory teeth magnify an already radiant smile. As he shakes my hand vigorously, I try to steal a glance at the name tag pinned to his crisp white shirt so that I can greet him by name. "Father of Ganesh," it reads. Little Ganesh is clutching the man's other hand. As he hides behind his father's leg, the four-year-old looks up, wide-eyed and silent. His father is effusive: "You have helped my son, and I will always be thankful."

The next person in the receiving line, "Mother of Sathi," enfolds her daughter in loving arms. As we exchange a smile, I notice that at least a hundred "mothers of" and "fathers of" line the path leading to the school, exchanging greetings and handshakes with our visiting party.

Two Room to Read staff members encourage me to quicken the pace: "The opening ceremony needs to start on time."

I laugh and remind them that while the people of Sri Lanka have many wonderful qualities, punctuality is usually not one of them. I want to greet each parent personally, to congratulate them for having contributed to this new school's construction. This day is theirs, and it seems a shame to rush it.

The school is symbolic of how a community can come together to rebuild in the wake of tremendous devastation. In the tsunami of 2004, tens of thousands of people were wiped off the face of the earth. Whole communities were swallowed by the suddenly monstrous ocean. The people we are meeting today once lived on the coast and worked as fishermen. Those who survived, terrified of the sea that previously provided only sustenance, have moved five miles inland. They are starting a new village, from scratch, with the few possessions that remain.

We are proud that the community is finding a way to move forward despite the despair. Cutting a red ribbon seems sterile and clinical compared with shaking each hand, including the floppy and tiny ones offered by the children in imitation of their parents.

....

The ceremony at Shilpa Preschool was one of two our group was attending on this sunny morning. We were in the Weligama Division along the southwestern coast of the island nation. During our 160-kilometer drive south from the capital, Colombo, we hugged the coastline as we witnessed the greatest destruction any of us had ever seen. Buildings had been flattened, train tracks ripped up. A fifteen-car train had been tossed into the ocean like a leaf blown by a fall breeze. In many villages, the most prominent feature was the graveyard, overflowing with fresh tombstones. Crosses, incense, and offerings of flowers stood sentry atop minuscule mounds of fresh earth.

The Weligama area is famous for its two large forts along the coast, built by the Dutch in the seventeenth and eighteenth centuries, and a forty-foot-high statue of Buddha. The Aukana Buddha statue is carved out of a single rock and is the tallest Buddha statue in the world. (The Bamiyan statues in Afghanistan were taller. They were dynamited and destroyed by the Taliban in 2001 after being declared idols that were forbidden under Sharia law. This great moment in religious tolerance was brought to us by Mullah Mohammad Omar.) The local economy is one of basic subsistence, with tea, rubber, coconuts, and fishing as the major industries.

Fishing is a profession with many occupational hazards, most rarely encountered on land. But as they slept, many thousands of fishermen and their families had been in the path, the dark shadow, of one of the largest walls of water of the past century. Rising to a height of up to a hundred feet, it was fierce enough to kill more than 230,000 people in fourteen countries. Those who had survived now lived with the trauma of lost family, and also a newfound fear of the sea. Tsunami survivors were moving inland. New villages were being established five to twenty kilometers from the coast, while previously existing inland villages dealt with a migratory influx.

Our first stop had been Lassana Village Nursery School, which had been built in a newly established village populated mostly by coastal refugees. An American donor, working through a Sri Lankan NGO, had paid for twenty-five homes to be built, and that number was expected to increase. The men would continue to fish but would commute each morning before sunrise by bicycle to the coast. The preschool would serve thirty-two children to start, and that number would likely increase as the village grew and families began to repopulate.

The school that would be attended by Ganesh and Sathi was Shilpa

Preschool. Run by a Montessori-trained Sri Lankan woman named Chintha Samanmali, the school had existed prior to the tsunami but had been in a cramped building that was so overcrowded that it had been turning students away. As more families had moved inland, this problem had been exacerbated. Chintha's husband, Shantha, had traveled to Colombo to seek Room to Read's support in building a new 850-square-foot building large enough for seventy-five students.

Shantha had been so excited by the idea of rebuilding a combination preschool and village library that he had offered to volunteer for Room to Read on a full-time basis. He had told our team that he didn't need money and that for him it was enough to gain access to resources to help the village's children begin their journey back to a normal life. All he wanted from us was the money for construction materials and books.

Grateful to Room to Read for our financial help, the couple had vowed to keep costs as low as possible by having every hour of labor needed be donated by the community. Each morning the couple and their four children had come to the building site to organize the day's labor.

This was yet another example of the power of the challenge-grant model. Even in the wake of devastation, Sri Lankans were eager to pitch in. The youngest volunteer at the Shilpa Preschool was Chintha and Shantha's son Kavith. Just four, he would make multiple trips from the brick pile to the building site. Brick by brick, he would do his handoff to the busy masons putting up the walls. Our team e-mailed us the story, saying that Kavith was "just like his father, there are no complaints, [he is] just doing what he thinks he should be doing."

Kavith also boasted to his friends that he was the "owner" of the new preschool. When told by our team that the school would actually belong to the entire community, he seemed a bit disappointed. Asked if he would like something else as a substitute, he inquired whether he could have a new Room to Read schoolbag like the ones all the students would get the day of the school opening ceremony.

Chintha's parents, who were retired and living near the school site, also pitched in. They donated the land for the building site and for an adjacent playground where the children would enjoy two sets of swings, a slide, and a climbing pyramid. As in many Room to Read projects, they also gave their "sweat equity." They decided that the best way to keep the volunteer workers fully focused was to avoid having them leave the building site for lunch and a siesta that might possibly follow. So each day Chintha's parents would cook a hearty lunch for the team of laborers. Steaming pots would be delivered to the building site, and ten to fifteen people would dig in to heaping plates of rice and curry.

Chintha had sent a message to us in San Francisco via our local team. She asked that we thank our donors for making her dream come true. Without our help, she said, the children would not already be in such a beautiful building that was conducive to learning. When the school was almost finished, she said, she "went every day to the site to touch the freshly painted walls. I was filled with happiness."

Three generations of a single dynamic family had come together, each doing what it could do to help its nation to rebuild.

If ever there had been an opening ceremony that I wanted to attend, this was it! I had vowed to visit the village one day in order to meet this extraordinary family and to shake little Kavith's hand. That day had arrived.

Our receiving line continued to move at a snail's pace, but that was fine by me. I was enjoying the eye contact, the smiles, and the handshake with each parent. As I made my way up the line, I thought of all those whom I was representing, who had made this and many other happy moments possible. Vowing to capture as much detail as possible to share with our incredible global network, I noted the bright yellow walls and the children's art that had so filled the interior that it spilled over to the outer walls, which were thirteen feet high. The height, combined with the open-air windows, allowed the school to be flooded with light and fresh air and a feeling of openness. The scent of the surrounding forest wafted in. Verdant plants lined the sides of the building, and the flag of Sri Lanka flapped proudly in the breeze.

....

My first visit to Sri Lanka was starting off well. I'd been anticipating it for a long time, as over the previous year the country had played a big role in my life. Our original long-term plan called for Room to Read to launch operations in Sri Lanka in 2007. But as news of the tsunami's devastation reached us, we moved that date forward. We didn't know how we would do it, as we didn't have a team in place there yet. But we couldn't let that slow us down. We knew in our hearts that we wanted to be part of the rebuilding process. I was interviewed twice on CNN about our plans, and the phones were soon ringing off the hook with offers of volunteer help and financial contributions.

Leaders are often forced to make quick decisions despite limited information and confusing and often contradictory signals. Ideally the leader's brain trust is quickly convened, risks are assessed, and a vigorous debate helps to ensure that the final decision is not made in a vacuum. But even after several hours with a group of trusted and hypersmart people, the leader retreats into an internal monologue, an echo chamber of reasons for and reasons against, of opportunities and risks and risk-mitigation strategies. The brain races, synapses fire, neural networks light up with kinetic energy. And after all that, the center of action moves to a new location: the gut.

The gut does not debate, it does not weigh pros and cons, it does not do SWOT analyses. Like Eeyore in the Winnie-the-Pooh stories, it just is. (A SWOT analysis, a popular business strategy and planning tool, looks at an organization's strengths, weaknesses, opportunities, and threats.) Basketball has the twenty-four-second shot clock and looks slothful in comparison. Whenever I believe our team, or I, have spent enough (perhaps too much?) time in debate mode, my favorite "forcing factor" is invoked: "Okay, suppose God came down to earth right now and said you had five seconds to decide, and that your answer has to be as simple and straightforward as possible, with no clauses, contingencies, ifs, ands, or buts. Your answer is . . . ? The clock is ticking. Five . . . four . . . three . . ."

Of course I had to follow my own advice and give a clear recommendation to the board and to our management team. In early January 2005, I told Erin that I was ready to recommend to the board that we go in, but only if she agreed. We were equal partners and had always vowed that we'd never decide anything major unless we were in sync. As I had expected, she said her gut was in the same place.

Her face, however, showed her stress. She clearly knew all too well that the challenging work of implementation would fall to her in her already overburdened role as chief operating officer. But this was not about us; it was all about those who needed us. We had a policy of "no looking back." Once a decision was made, all members of our team were expected to stop talking about obstacles and instead focus intensely on solutions. "Don't tell us all the reasons this might not work. Tell us all the ways it *could* work."

The next day we recommended to the board that we launch operations in Sri Lanka with an immediate focus on rebuilding schools. We'd also initiate and accelerate a fund-raising campaign with a goal of $2.5 million for Sri Lanka. Our plan was unanimously approved by the board after a long discussion of the three key factors that made this a logical choice:

1. Psychologists believe that when a child experiences trauma, the best thing one can do is to help him or her return to normalcy. School and the home are the places where children spend the most time. Tens of thousands of homes had been destroyed, and the Sri Lankan government estimated that more than two hundred schools had also been flattened and washed out to sea. Immediate rebuilding was therefore, in my mind, the best way for us to help the children, especially the many thousands who had been orphaned. After they'd experienced the hell on earth of losing their friends, neighbors, and families to the largest natural disaster in the world, the least we could do was welcome them back to a clean and airy school full of supportive adult teachers.

2. Expansion of Room to Read's programs into Sri Lanka was already part of our long-term strategic plan. After a thorough analysis of the needs across Asia and the potential fit between various countries and Room to Read, we had identified our priority countries and launch dates: Laos, 2005; Bangladesh, 2006; and Sri Lanka, 2007. Erin and I therefore felt comfortable that opening operations in Sri Lanka was not a total shot in the dark. In essence, we were recommending an acceleration of our planned launch by twenty-four to thirty-six months.

3. Last, but certainly not least, I was driven by the desire to take immediate action to help solve what looked to be large and intractable problems. My view of the charity world is that compared with business, there

is too much talk, way too many meetings and expert panels and blue-ribbon commissions, and not enough action. Or as an Australian friend of mine once opined: "Sometimes you just have to have a go and get on with it, mate!"

Our hastily assembled Sri Lanka team was proud to host our visit and show us some of the new schools. Because we were the new kid on the block in Sri Lanka, we'd built many of our first schools with existing charities, as they had more employees and long-standing relationships in many of the communities. We often try to work with others so as not to reinvent the wheel. By combining forces, like-minded organizations can leverage one another's unique strengths and assets. The media were filled with stories, many of them justified, of aid dollars not getting to the places where they were needed. In contrast, by the one-year anniversary of the tsunami, our team had helped to open thirty-nine new schools. The goal was to then more than double this number during our second year.

From a standing start, the team had moved with all deliberate speed. The example set for the NGO community was significant, as was the fact that donors could see immediate results and be encouraged to reinvest the next year and the one after that. But of greatest importance was that thousands of little Ganeshes and Sathis had a place to go each morning and an earlier-than-expected opportunity to begin to return to a normal life.

....

The last stragglers now walked in haste toward the preschool's entrance. It was impossible to keep their energy bottled up, and the students had burst into song and dance. Aligned in five rows of ten each, they were moving to a fast-paced, upbeat Sinhalese tune. Dressed in red shorts, short-sleeved pink shirts, and tiny red ties that looked borrowed from a 1980s new wave band, each youngster pointed at the floor, then the audience, and finally the ceiling. They were roughly in sync, with only one confused kid facing backward and using his dancing hand to hold up his shorts. Inspired by the syncopated Sinhalese beat, our group joined the dancers on the floor.

....

As I pointed to the floor, audience, ceiling, I wondered if this was the first time the local people had been subjected to the white-man overbite. My hips moved mechanically, more Al Gore than Ricky Martin. Ten feet away, I saw my friend Sonya, one of the leaders of the Hong Kong fund-raising chapter who'd raised hundreds of thousands of dollars for Sri Lanka, holding hands and trying to dance with a five-year-old. Confused, he kept facing the wrong way. But soon he understood her pantomimed instructions. She led and he followed. Their faces lit with effusive smiles, they were every bit as beautiful as Fred and Ginger.

I lost my self-conscious paranoia and danced like a dork. Sonya's energy was infectious—not to mention that of fifty gleeful children filling the light-drenched room. My brain raced to process the enormity of this day. The adults standing on the sidelines had experienced two decades of civil war. They had lost parents and siblings and friends in a hellish display of nature's power. The children dancing had lost aunties and uncles. They had awoken to discover that some of their little playmates who yesterday had been holding a cricket bat were now . . . gone forever.

Yet today it was as if the entire village were breathing a significant sigh of relief. Pain still lingered. Life was not perfect. But our group's visit had been an excuse for the community, for the first time in thirteen months, to celebrate. Today a down payment was being made on the return to a stable and peaceful life. If that is not a reason to shake your groove thing, I don't know what is.

CHAPTER EIGHT

"No Range Rovers": The War on Overhead

One of the major challenges in starting Room to Read was that I had no previous experience in running a charity. The whole sector was a brand-new world whose norms and rules were unknown: I rationalized that this could be either a weakness or a strength. If I had what Buddhists refer to as "beginner's mind," I could always claim naïveté if I felt like doing things differently. Though I realized that not every established procedure deserved to be discarded, I also felt strongly that the nonprofit world was ossified in many ways and ready for a reboot.

During the early years, our team declared four key areas where we would do things differently.

First, we'd never call Room to Read a *charity*. We banished that word from our vocabulary from day one. The typical definition of a charity, which I found in www.dictionary.com, rubbed me the wrong way: "Something given to a person or persons in need; alms." Maybe it was the verb "give" that turned us off. History is full of giving that led to overdependence. You could give someone food, but then wouldn't that person need for you to return with more food the next day or the next week? The only thing we wanted our young organization to *give* was an opportunity. We would say to children and to their families: "If you are willing to work hard and make sacrifices and think long term, then Room to

Read is the best organization for you. If you're looking for a handout, then you should look elsewhere." This was especially true given that the communities we worked with, such as the one rebuilding Shilpa Preschool in Sri Lanka, would be coinvesting. So step one was easy—we referred to ourselves as an *organization* and as a *movement* but never as a *charity*.

A second point of differentiation was that we'd never ask people for a *donation*. We instead referred to it as an *investment*. Anyone who *invests* in the capitalistic sense of the word expects to see a long-term return. We rationalized that there are no greater returns than those yielded by education. It might seem like a minor difference, but to me one of these sentences has a much more pleasant tone: "Can you give Room to Read a donation?" "Can you make an investment in Room to Read and the children we serve?"

Our third key point of differentiation was the fact that Room to Read was "run like a business." An important part of our pitch was that Erin and I had spent years in the business world. We knew how to build teams, set bold goals, track performance closely, and keep our costs low in order to run an efficient operation. This would help us to attract only star performers, as during the interview process we made it very clear that this was not yesterday's slow-moving charity but instead a new breed where strong performance by every member of the team was the only acceptable outcome. It's amazing how many interviewees you can lose when you specify these expectations up front. We knew this would also appeal to the hard-core capitalists whom we'd be asking for investments.

The fourth and final way we'd try to do things differently was in running the most efficient operation possible. During the early days of Room to Read, we conducted informal research by asking people what motivated them to invest in certain causes and what turned them off. My friend Chris opined: "If I believe in a mission, I will invest, but only if I know the funding is going to its intended purpose. If you're one of those groups that is spending forty or fifty cents of my dollar on overhead, then you're not getting a check from me."

That immediately seemed like an obvious competitive advantage. Potential investors would have an additional incentive to invest if we could assure them that the majority of their funding would go directly to the education programs that served the children, not to fund-raising or administrative expenses.

This made inherent sense. Any organization needs money to keep the wheels turning, of course, but the point is to use your funds in the most efficient way possible. I recalled my own decision to cut off a charity I'd supported for years after receiving a monthly direct-mail solicitation—half the time with a fake red EMERGENCY APPEAL stamped across the front. I would promptly walk the mailing to the recycling bin. *How much of my investment,* I wondered, *are they spending just to ask me for more money?*

We were determined to find innovative ways to minimize costs. With that came a battle we'd fight every day for years to come: the war on overhead.

....

The first act in our declared war was to initiate a "no Land Rover" policy. This inspiration didn't originate with me. Like many great ideas, it was borrowed, this time as a result of a chance encounter at a dusty crossroads in Tanzania in 1999 after I'd come off a successful summit of Kilimanjaro. I was excited to be back in "civilization," even if the tiny town of Arusha was the big city on offer. Checking in to one of the few hotels in town, I looked into a mirror for the first time in seven days. Not pretty.

Within an hour I'd left six days of dirt in the shower, seven days of razor stubble in the sink, and a lot of freshly laundered clothing draped everywhere. Making a mental note to myself to slip the maid a few dollars upon my departure, I headed into town in search of a cold beer to celebrate standing—at 19,789 feet elevation—on the roof of Africa.

There was only one other bloke in the pub, a bearded guy in his midthirties in jeans and a dark T-shirt set against deeply tanned arms. Like me, his head had been down for thirty minutes as he wrote in his notebook. Though I usually respect other people's space, after too many solo hours on the mountain I felt like a monk who had just ended a seven-day silent retreat. I asked if I could join him.

Simon was a British journalist, apparently every bit as chatty and eager for companionship as I was.

"Bloody hell, I've been covering the Rwanda genocide trials, and I can't think of anything more depressing. I spend my entire day listening to testimony, or at least I would if the chief justice did not keep declaring these abruptly announced long-weekend holidays. Yesterday, for seemingly no reason, a five-day holiday was announced. So now I've got nearly a week to kill."

I admitted that like many UN employees, I was a do-gooder. What had he learned from the UN? I asked. "Any advice to share?"

"Just avoid buying a bunch of Land Rovers; that's my advice."

"I wasn't really planning to. Tell me, why is that the first thing that comes to mind?"

When Simon poured his bottle of Mosi lager, the condensation on the glass formed a mirror image of the perspiration on his forehead.

"The UN came in here a few years ago to set up the International Criminal Tribunal for Rwanda. Nothing happened for a long time. Journalists who were here to cover it were bored to tears. Then one day a rush of activity sent a bunch of us to grab our notebooks and head over to find out what was going on."

"Was it the arrival of prisoners—the start of the trials?"

"No, it was heavy equipment, tractors and graders that had come to pave the bloody parking lot."

"Parking lot?"

"Yeah, an order went out to pave it, because they were about to accept delivery of a bunch of Land Rovers. The entire fleet arrived a few days later. I was really annoyed."

"I know *exactly* what you mean! In Cambodia a few years back I went to dinner on Friday night at a place very popular with the expat aid workers. As far as I could tell, all of these organizations were doing work that was desperately needed. But I was taken aback by the insane lineup of Land Rovers, Range Rovers, and Jeeps outside the club. Every one of them had the logo of some charity or aid agency painted on it. Why would they want to advertise that they were wasting people's money?"

Simon chuckled and drained his beer.

"You know, when I travel in Cambodia, I pay a local kid a dollar to put me on the back of his motorbike and drive me to the Foreign Correspondents' Club. He was one of a dozen boys hanging outside my little guesthouse, desperate for business. His family depends on that income. I originally used the local motorbikes," I admitted, "because I'm a cheapskate. But later I realized that there was an even better reason—to help create employment in a country where people are trying to rebuild their lives."

Simon brought us back to Tanzania. "The irony, of course, is that most every road in this country is packed earth, interspersed with a heavy dose of potholes. Why is it that a vehicle designed to be driven on dirt needs to be parked on asphalt?"

He was just beginning to work up steam. "What bothered me more is that within a week there were twenty bloody Land Rovers in the parking lot, all with the UN's logo painted on the side. Some bureaucrat in Geneva had punched up a purchase order using the latest in procurement software, because that, of course, is what's written into his job description as a procurement officer.

"Now here we are, several thousand miles away. What's your guess on how much twenty Land Rovers cost?"

"Let's go with fifty thousand dollars each and call it a million."

"Probably more! That's at least a million dollars that can't be put into building or running hospitals or clean-water projects or that can't go to a guy like you who wants to build schools."

"Have you written about this?"

"I tried, but my editor killed it. Said it would make me too many enemies within the system, and then I'd not be able to get their cooperation on my stories."

It was in Simon's honor that I declared Room to Read's no–Land Rover policy.

. . . .

The no–Land Rover policy proved to be not just effective at keeping our overhead low. It was also a story that we could share with others—an iconic image we hoped they'd remember long after they'd left the event. In each of my slide shows I talked about applying the lessons of the business world to the social sector. "If a business lets its costs get out of control," I'd remind people, "it gets undercut by its more efficient competitor and eventually goes bankrupt. But in the charity world, organizations can run so inefficiently that they spend fifty or even sixty cents on the dollar on their overhead, and yet they stay in business year after year.

"Our approach is to try to find every way possible to keep our overhead low. In a way, overhead is like cholesterol. There is good overhead, and there is bad overhead. Paying for an audit is good overhead, as you want to make sure investors' money is not disappearing. But in reality a purchase is good overhead if it's something you need. A great accounting system, or giving a corporate investor a report on how your team spent its funds, or a world-class CFO doing tight expense control—those are all good investments.

"But then there is bad overhead—like sending endless fund-raising letters to donors. How many times have you sent one hundred dollars to an organization and then wondered whether it was their goal to spend all of it sending you monthly solicitations asking for more money? Or buying first-class overseas flights?

"But our favorite example of bad overhead, I'd say, is this . . ."

Waiting a moment for the drama to build, I'd then click forward to a brand-new, shiny white Land Rover. Invariably people in the audience would chuckle. I'd click again, and a big red *X* would blot out the vehicle.

Surfing the momentum, I'd continue: "Seventy-five thousand dollars spent on a Land Rover means you can't put three hundred girls on scholarship for a year. That is over sixty thousand days a young girl does not go to school. Seventy-five thousand dollars means you can't print seventy-five thousand copies of a local-language children's book. It means you can't set up fifteen bilingual libraries in rural parts of Asia serving seven thousand children. And that's if you just buy one of them! But Land Rovers are like potato chips—nobody stops at one!"

The anecdote had its intended effect. We had created an iconic image, one that was "notable and quotable." Our type A audience would immediately go into problem-solving mode, their brains buzzing with other ideas that we could utilize to make sure more money got "to the kids." They were now foot soldiers in our battle against inefficiency.

....

One of the best methods of keeping our overhead low came as a spontaneous idea at one of our board meetings. As we enjoyed ten minutes of social chat before diving into a heavy agenda, one of our board members and my trusted mentor, Muneer Satter, told us about his insanely packed travel schedule.

"In the last week I've been in Brazil, Japan, and now here in San Francisco. I fly between Chicago and New York so frequently that it's gotten to the point where on Monday morning, right before the door for the 6:00 A.M. flight to LaGuardia is about to close, the American clerk smiles at me as I rush towards the gate and says, 'Good morning, Mr. Satter.' I was depressed that they now knew me by name.

"And then the other day my statement arrived and I discovered that I have three million frequent-flier miles. That's a sign I've been on the road too much." He sighed.

"Did you just say the number I think you said?" I inquired, trying to be discreet.

Discretion is apparently not a tool in this actor's kit bag. He smiled, shaking his head at my audacity.

"Yes, three million—I already know what you're thinking, Mr. Low Overhead Cheapskate."

"Cheapskate?"

"Yes. Hilary told me that every time you guys travel together, you walk around the hotel lobby stockpiling pens, like a squirrel storing nuts in preparation for winter." (Hilary Valentine was at the time the board cochair with Muneer.)

All three of us looked down. Sure enough, my pen gave me away—RITZ-CARLTON TOKYO. I'd been caught red-handed.

Sensing a chink in my low-overhead armor, Hilary pointed out that this was not exactly a "cheap and cheerful" hotel.

"It is for me," I responded. "Super cheap—as in free!—and megacheerful, the best home away from home a guy could ask for if he has an action-packed week in Japan. Our Tokyo chapter leaders presented a personalized and signed copy of my book to the property manager, who promptly offered to put me up for free on all future trips. He told me when we first met: 'I can't afford to fund a school, but this is something within my zone of influence.' He's also introduced us to other hotel managers, and our chapter leaders have gone in to make the pitch. I have unlimited free rooms in London, Hong Kong, Mumbai, Singapore, and Sydney. So now . . . *ahem* . . . all I need are a few free plane tickets to connect the dots."

Muneer chuckled and reached for his BlackBerry. "There you go again—Mr. Never Afraid to Ask for the Order. I'm mailing my assistant right now to tell her that you have carte blanche to use my miles for your travel."

Just as interest compounds over time, so do good ideas. I added Muneer's example to my standard slide show, right after the Land Rover story. Audiences got to hear not only what we didn't do but also the creative actions we were taking. Within a few months, four other bankers had each offered me enough frequent-flier miles to fund more overseas trips. (If you've got 'em, I'm on e-mail 24-7: wood@roomtoread.org.) A donor who sat on the board of a major airline gave us some of his "friends and family" tickets for use by our staff. Ketchum, a global communications firm, brought us on as its client on a pro bono basis. Muneer then donated a galaxy of Starwood points to provide free hotel stays in various cities. We'd gone open source: soliciting the best low-overhead ideas from the widest variety of people.

. . . .

When it came to saving money on overhead, our network of fund-raising chapters was the secret weapon of the organization. When *Leaving Microsoft to Change the World* launched in the middle of 2006, we had nine fund-raising chapters. Today we have fifty-six. They range from smaller communities like Aspen and Greenwich to big cities like London, New York, Hong Kong, Singapore, Tokyo, and Zurich.

The various volunteer fund-raising chapters contribute a third of Room to Read's annual budget. (The remainder comes from grants from individuals, corporations and foundations.) The leaders in these communities know who's who locally: who makes the big bucks, who has business and alumni networks, and who might have recently traveled in the developing world and had their heart touched.

Originally dozens, then hundreds, and then thousands of people got involved by throwing events in their towns and cities. Because they were volunteers, we didn't have to support additional payroll. They worked out of their homes or the offices of their employers. Again our costs were minimized.

Most important, we asked each person to make sure his or her event was "cheap and cheerful." This could lead to challenges. Many of the volunteers were not used to our model. They respected us for trying to run an efficient operation, even if it could lead to certain challenges. I recall a conversation Erin and I had with a new chapter leader in Atlanta who was planning her first event.

"What's my event budget?"

"Start with zero, and let us know if for some reason you need more than that. But we hope you don't."

"Seriously?"

"Yes, sorry."

Pushed to think beyond the "hotel ballroom with rubber chicken" model of fund-raising, our virtual team members got really creative. They'd pitch their boss to allow the use of her fancy new home as the event venue. Room to Read parties were hosted at furniture stores, bookstores, wine shops, and high-school gyms. Vineyards and wine writers would be asked to supply libations, and we ended up with a Moby Dick–sized aggregation of donated sushi from local restaurants.

It became standard operating procedure for the chapter leaders, during their welcome speeches, to announce that the cost of the evening's event was zero, so every dollar donated would go directly to Room to Read. Hearty cheers would follow. A few stories would be told about the creative approach taken, which helped give the event a unique personality. People imagined the busy young software engineer or banker beating the street on weekends to solicit the very wine they were drinking out of plastic cups, as well as the spicy tuna rolls on their paper plates.

The examples continued. In the same way that Wikipedia so brilliantly harnessed the power of the crowd, we found a way to let everyone do his or her own small part to add up to a significant outcome.

In 2006 I was invited to speak at the Forbes European CEO Conference in Copenhagen. I was honored to be on a panel focused on corporate social responsibility with Michael Philipp. The CEO for the EMEA (Europe, Middle East, and Africa) region for Credit Suisse, Michael was a bearded, extroverted, gregarious, and friendly guy with whom I instantly hit it off. We grabbed a table together at the lunch session following our panel. He immediately proceeded to close a deal I had not realized we were in the midst of negotiating.

"What do you need from me? What can I do to help—besides giving you money?" He laughed while waving his BlackBerry in the air, as though by punching a few keys he could make lightning appear from the sky or make any dream come true.

"Thanks for asking. We just sent Bella, from our San Francisco office, over to London to get a European fund-raising operation off the ground."

"And she needs connections?" he interrupted. "Send her my way. I've worked in the finance industry my whole life and know a lot of people from my days at Goldman Sachs and Deutsche Bank. We'll get her set up with some new donors."

"Excellent! Much appreciated. But what I was actually thinking is that right now she's working out of her cramped apartment. And it's on the outskirts of London, for cost reasons. I'd love to see her in a real office in a central location, so that she is closer to potential investors. It would be a lot more productive, but of course real estate in London is really expensive."

"No problem. What do you need, one desk or two? We will get her set up. When you come over, we can get you a loaned conference room so that you can have meetings."

Michael was true to his word. Within a few weeks Bella had a place to sit in Canary Wharf, surrounded by potential donors. Within six months, as we began to take the steps to open an Asian fund-raising office in Hong Kong, Michael lobbed an e-mail to his counterpart in the Asia HQ, Paul Calello. Paul quickly agreed to provide a desk. That office eventually expanded to five people, and ultimately the bank also catalyzed the launch of our offices in Sydney and Tokyo, again with donated space.

Other companies joined in. The *Financial Times* gave us office space for seven employees in midtown Manhattan. Reliance Life did the same in Mumbai. Lafarge, the biggest cement company in Zambia, gave us an "all you can eat" deal—it'd donate and transport to the building site every pound of cement we could use in building libraries. Recognizing that we had a strong bias against buying expensive vehicles, its executives also pointed out to us that it's impossible to get very far on rough Zambian roads without them. Their solution: They donated two of their used trucks to us. We painted a Room to Read logo on the side, along with the words DONATED BY LAFARGE. Again and again, the theme was "free stuff, no invoice." I could get used to this.

Through thousands of small acts, and some quite large, we had enlisted a great many foot soldiers in the war on overhead. Warren Buffett writes frequently and compellingly about the power of compounding to build up a large fortune. We found a parallel system—the power of hundreds of great ideas compounding in a way that kept overhead expenses well below 20 percent of total donations.

Why be so fanatical about this? Don't I have better things to do with my time, some people ask, before begging for frequent-flier miles, hotel rooms, and office space? My reply is that every dollar we save really counts, because it aggregates over time. Room to Read is now close to being a fifty-million-dollar-per-year organization. If we can save just two percentage points of overhead, that is an additional one million dollars per year we can use to fund our education programs. That is enough to support four thousand girls in our Girls' Education program or to print five million children's books or establish a thousand libraries. That's five hundred thousand additional children who gain access to their first library. If we save 4 percent rather than 2 percent, that number is a million.

Given what's at stake, I would say I have a million reasons, or maybe more, to continue to be a proud cheapskate. Our team continues to watch the ratio of donations to expenditures like a hawk. We deploy more than 82 percent of donated funds to our programs rather than to overhead. Charity Navigator, the most popular rating service for charitable efficiency, has given Room to Read its top "four-star" rating each and every time it's evaluated our financials, or six years in a row. Only 3 percent of charities can make this proud claim.

The hotels, however, are safe. As a gag gift at Christmas 2010, Hilary's mother, Rachel, surprised me with a large box filled to the brim with one thousand pens, all proudly bearing the Room to Read logo.

Last time I checked, however, Muneer's frequent flier account was close to zero.

CHAPTER NINE

Searching for Seuss

One goal at Room to Read was always to run a very data-driven organization. Overhead was only one of the important metrics we tracked. We also carefully measured community contributions to each project under the challenge-grant model and commissioned frequent surveys—often using independent evaluators—of customer satisfaction. That is, did teachers, parents, and students value the projects we'd created together? Where did they see strengths, and where were there opportunities for improvement? The analysis of the data always revealed interesting truths, as there is nothing quite like holding up a mirror in order to see your organization as the customer sees it. And there are days when that feedback can knock you on your butt.

Our Nepalese country director, Dinesh, was phoning from Kathmandu. It was a big week: We'd just received a report with the first formal evaluation of the effectiveness of our programs. His call to us in the home office marked a crucial moment in our young organization's history.

Once, during the mid-1980s thaw in U.S.-Soviet relations, Ronald Reagan was asked about his budding relationship with Mikhail Gorbachev. He responded with one of the most famous quotes of his presidency: "Trust, but verify."

From the start of Room to Read, we developed a similar philosophy: We knew that it would not be enough to donate books to a school and then hope that an effective and well-utilized library would spontaneously result. We'd need to go back to schools to see what was working, what was failing, and what improvements were needed.

We were fortunate to receive guidance from many experts who told me candidly that what I had done in the early days was not really going to solve the core problems. The model of the foreign visitor taking yaks and donkeys into remote mountain villages to drop off books—with no formal plans for training the librarians or monitoring utilization of the library—would not create long-term systemic change. It wouldn't even come close.

My small team and I were told that the developing world already had enough one-off projects in which well-intentioned foreigners performed what is referred to as an "aid drop," when they brought used computers, food, or medicine to a village. Or perhaps thirty years of back issues of *National Geographic,* an ancient set of World Book encyclopedias, or used textbooks that taught world history from the American perspective. These drops made people feel good but ultimately failed. They were like sugar highs: The photo opportunity felt great, but without local staff, plus training, plus follow-up, good intentions wouldn't be good enough.

It wasn't easy to hear my early projects referred to in such derisive terms. This, after all, was my dream. I'd sacrificed a great deal, only to hear: "naive, well meaning, but destined to fail" or "been there, done that."

I rationalized, at least to myself, that Andrew Carnegie had donated the buildings for his libraries and relied on local communities to do the rest. He hadn't even donated books. Things may not have been perfect at first, but eventually the communities sorted themselves out. One hundred years on, Carnegie's project was viewed as one of the greatest philanthropic investments in human history. And hadn't we out-Carnegied Carnegie by providing books and also bringing down the cost per community to such a low point that massive scale was now possible?

Yet we were also thankful to those experts who were willing to advise us. We were a start-up, and they were the authorities in the field. The experts we liked best were the ones who not only criticized but would also take the time to brainstorm on solutions. Both these informal advisers and the members of our board encouraged Erin and me to invest in an early evaluation of the first libraries we'd established in Nepal and Vietnam. They suggested we ensure impartial feedback by hiring outside evaluators who had no stake in the outcome, people who would dare to "speak truth to power."

We would not rely solely on the outside evaluators. We also built into our employees' training the critical importance of monitoring their own work and closely tracking results. We wanted to build it into our young company's DNA to always be out in the rural communities to "talk to the customer." They'd ask questions of the students, the teachers, and the parents to find out whether our library program was delivering on its potential.

We were excited to learn the initial results of our first monitoring exercise. But we might have been less so had we known that the data would show that we weren't doing nearly as well as we'd thought. Disappointment in our early performance lay ahead.

....

One day as Erin and I looked at some depressing statistics issued by our evaluators, we paused to pick up the ringing telephone. At that point, our burgeoning organization had one shared phone line at the grandiosely named world headquarters. No matter who you were, you played receptionist.

Erin greeted our cofounder in Nepal. "*Namaste,* Dinesh. We were just getting started in talking through the implications of the monitory report. John was just going through his top-line observations."

I jumped right in, focusing not on what was perfect but on the biggest weaknesses. "What stood out for me was that over half the students surveyed are telling us that we're failing them by not giving them the 'products' they want. Over half! That's a pretty harsh indictment on our work."

Students using our libraries in Nepal had been asked what factors would influence them to use library resources on a more regular basis: longer hours? staying open on weekends, or at night? The number one answer had not been any of these. Instead, 52 percent of the students surveyed said that they would use the library more often if there were more books available in the Nepali language.

"Okay, so that number is alarmingly high. But I'm surprised it's not higher. Of course the students want books in their mother tongue," I opined.

Erin agreed. "That's how children learn to read—by starting with the language they hear spoken in their home environment."

Dinesh explained the issue from the Nepal team's perspective. Every year the team built money into its budgets to purchase Nepali-language children's books. But there simply weren't many available. Year after year, that line item of the budget went unspent.

He explained: "In Nepal, seventy percent of adults are illiterate. They didn't grow up reading, so their mind-set is not focused on buying books for their children. But even those few with the desire to do so are usually too poor to afford them anyway. If you live on a dollar a day, then a three-dollar children's book is a luxury item."

Most of the books available in the local market then were in English, imported from either India or overseas and targeted at private-school students. They were also not around in large quantities. The local-language books that were available were for upper grades such as eight to ten or even higher. There were virtually no books for primary-school students written in the students' languages.

"Publishers don't have any economic incentive to produce children's books," Dinesh continued. "The people of Nepal aren't illiterate because they're dumb or lazy. They were simply born in the wrong place—in a country with very little children's literature. If a kid's lucky, like me, he might be part of a family that could afford to send him to an English-language boarding school. But that's maybe ten percent of the population."

Erin agreed with Dinesh and backed this up with a second data point. She explained that this was also a common problem in Cambodia and Vietnam. It turned out that in those Southeast Asian nations, our local-language book budgets, which enabled us to fill shelves in a limited number of libraries, were also underspent. The Khmer language is one of the world's oldest written scripts, dating to the tenth century, yet a thousand years later the number of children's books in Khmer was infinitesimal. The situation in India was a little different when Room to Read started there in 2003–2004, because there was already a well-developed children's book publishing industry in the country. But though there were many books in local languages, few were aimed at the crucial early grades.

I responded by challenging both Dinesh and Erin: "Look, we've all read *Good to Great*. And you remember that section where Jim Collins talks about data collection, right?"

Having zealously studied the bible of creating and leading a world-class organization, Erin paraphrased the relevant passage: You collect the data, and then you stare the cold hard facts in the face, without emotion and without denial. You do the pattern-matching and admit whatever it is the data are trying to tell you.

"Right," I said. "And this one pesky little data point—fifty-two percent—is trying to alert us to the inconvenient fact that over half our customers are not satisfied. They would use our product—the library—more often if we set it up better. What are the numbers for Vietnam or Cambodia? Are they similar?"

We leafed through the thick report and realized that yes, they were. It was not just the kids in Nepal who were telling us we were letting them down. So I made a dare to our brave and beloved cofounder: "Dinesh, since you're the country director with the most experience, let's nominate you to break this logjam. Can we do a pilot program this year to publish ten children's titles using local authors and local artists?"

"Where will we get the funding?"

"Well, to start, we'll tap into those underspent line items in your budget. I hope you haven't spent that money on your favorite *momos*." I laughed, referring to the buffalo- and chicken-filled dumplings popular in Nepal.

"We can also talk to Skoll," I suggested, referring to a foundation recently established by Jeff Skoll, who had been the first full-time employee and first president of eBay. "Erin, what do you think?"

"That's a natural. They're not afraid to take a few risks on a new idea, unlike some of the foundations we know," she said as we both simultane-

ously rolled our eyes at the memory of some of the old-fashioned foundations that had treated us like poison ivy at a summer picnic just because
we were young and trying to do new things that had never been done
before.

Mentally Erin and I were moving forward. I could read her mind, and
she mine. I knew that she was beginning to visualize the grant proposal
she'd start writing that very night. She knew I was already visualizing a
walk to the bank with that hypothetical check. This is a weakness of
mine: Once a decision is made, I consider it a done deal. If it's decided,
ipso facto it's ancient history.

Dinesh burst our bubble: "There's only one problem now that you two
have so quickly found the funding." He laughed with characteristic understatement. "I don't know how to do this."

"Dinesh *bai* ["younger brother" in Nepali], we don't either," I said with
the best brotherly voice I could muster. "But I'll tell you what one of my
mentors always told me: 'You are smart; you will figure it out.' I'm well
aware that this is a compliment, while also being a challenge."

I tried to imagine his face at the end of the long phone line as I continued: "We can't give you the road map, because one doesn't exist. What
we can offer you is Rob Campbell, a really smart guy from Seattle who's
moving to Nepal. His wife is going to be teaching at the American school
for the next two years, and he's looking for a full-time volunteer project.
He can be your right-hand man on this. And once you succeed, we'll take
the program into Cambodia and Vietnam. Assume the funding is going
to happen. I will sell, sell, sell the proposal to Christy Chin and Sally Os-
berg at Skoll. I think they will get behind this, but if not, I promise to
find a plan B, or a plan C or D if necessary. This is important, and we
have to get it right. When I get to Nepal in a few months, we can talk
more over a plate of yak *momos,* my treat. For now, my only advice is to
get started."

....

I left the office at 10:00 P.M. that night, the frigid fog rolling in from San
Francisco Bay engulfing me. I beat a fast path to the warmth of my car.
While the foghorns guarding the Golden Gate Bridge groaned their
mournful warnings, I replayed key elements of the meeting.

I felt bad that I had immediately homed right in on the most negative part of the evaluators' report. After all, there had been many positives as they reviewed the early progress of our library program, such as the community coinvestment. But I had immediately gone straight for the jugular and picked the most negative-seeming data point. I was aping my former Microsoft boss, Steve Ballmer, who'd been the biggest influence in my eight-year career at the company. In every internal meeting he focused not on what was going right but on what was going wrong. If six subsidiaries in the room were in a regional meeting, and five were exceeding their plan, he would relentlessly hammer on the subsidiary whose revenues were below target. "Why, why, why? What were we doing wrong? How can we improve?"

The country directors who had worked so hard to make their numbers looked confused. Steve was not talking to them at all. They awaited his comments on yet another year of strong performance and are probably still waiting.

"We'll get to you later," Ballmer would thunder, his arms waving crazily in the air as he zeroed in on the poorest-performing country director in the room.

Steve was the same when meeting with customers. His first questions to them were always focused on "Where are we weak? How are we screwing up? What is it that you need that we should be providing but aren't?"

Ballmer wanted to talk only about the stuff that wasn't going well. His theory seemed to be that this was a waste of time and that all of his focus should be on the areas where there was more room for improvement. Some might say that this is management by intimidation. But having Steve breathing down my neck also made me the best leader I could be, knowing I'd be held accountable for every single number. What gets measured gets done!

As I reviewed the negatives in our evaluation, I acknowledged to myself that I'd known this day would come, the point at which all the tough decisions we'd avoided would manifest themselves. The chickens had come home to roost.

It's not easy to listen solely to negative feedback, especially when it concerns something as emotional as the dreams in which you have invested your life. Thankfully, I had mentors who told me that a real leader will have the guts to set his or her ego aside and seek to improve by embracing any and all opinions. A B-plus leader will listen carefully and respectfully to constructive feedback if it's offered but not stress out if it's not. An A-plus leader will proactively seek it out.

During Room to Read's early years, one of our board members persuaded Erin and me to learn about how others saw us as leaders by submitting to a 360-degree-feedback study. It was yet another way in which we tried to bring best practices in business to the nonprofit sector. The goal was to learn how we were perceived—strengths but especially weaknesses—by our employees, board members, chapter leaders, and funders. It did not matter where they were on the org chart; we would still ask. Each recipient was promised anonymity in exchange for complete and total candor.

Of the twelve pages of data and quotes, I will never forget one simple passage:

"John's start-up story is cool. But he now needs to get over his fixation with low overhead and begin to make the serious adult investments that will help to make Room to Read a true force in the world."

"Serious adult investments"? That hurt. But as the data about the students' desire for mother-tongue literature showed, we had been relying far too heavily on donated English-language books. We'd had great success convincing publishers like Scholastic, Macmillan, McGraw-Hill, and Penguin and its corporate parent, Pearson, to donate new children's books in huge quantities—often twenty thousand or more books at a time. And this was a good thing, as Room to Read was working only in countries that teach English as a second language.

But it was obviously not good enough: We needed books in the children's mother tongue. It was time to change course and expand the mission. We simply had to become a children's book publisher, even if that would require money, energy, and brainpower we didn't have at that point.

I also wondered whether or not I'd been too tough on Dinesh in throwing this problem to him and telling him it was his to figure out. As I replayed the call, I was mortified to recall that I had tossed the ball to him, said good luck, made a lame joke about talking over steamed *momos,* and then hung up. Here he was out in the middle of an isolated and distant country, with a skeletal staff, and I was challenging him to break a logjam on a long-standing problem.

This is another one of my weaknesses as a leader. Once someone has made it through the gauntlet of our hiring process, I have a lot of faith in him or her. Immediately I push new hires relentlessly. If we've just had a record quarter of fund-raising, I ask how we can set the next three quarters up to be barrier shattering, too. If we establish a new library every four hours, I ask what it would take to get to the point of opening one every two hours. Though I love having more than seventeen thousand girls in our long-term education program as of 2012, I'm pushing hard for the day when the number is twenty-five thousand, and then one hundred thousand.

As a result, some people may not always enjoy working for me. There are days when I am deeply unpopular: "John pushes too hard." "Why isn't he ever satisfied?" "For him, too much is never enough."

I know this; and yet it doesn't slow me down. I've learned that I can at least partially alleviate the downside by stopping to praise coworkers frequently. Pause. Praise. Celebrate each milestone and victory. But then I go back to pushing. I have such a passion for our education programs that I want them to reach more kids in more places more quickly. If that means that not everyone loves me, then that's a price I'm willing to pay.

Pulling into the garage, I grabbed a few logs for the fireplace. It would be another late night of e-mail. I rationalized that I was not pushing anyone harder than I was pushing myself. Nobody traveled more than I did. Nobody spent more time and effort asking for money. It wasn't as though I were making demands from the beach or the golf course.

I owed Dinesh an explanation. My next e-mail would be to him. I had to explain that my comments had been predicated on a belief in his abilities. I knew he'd figure it out. In my gut, I trusted his intelligence. I knew he'd come up with a solution.

....

Comfortably ensconced in front of a roaring fire as heavy winds and fog blew past my living room window, I had a sudden brainstorm. Maybe *I* could write a children's book that would be published in Nepal. I had long joked that the best way to tell the story of Room to Read's humble beginnings would be to publish a book that I'd mentally titled *Zak the Yak with Books on His Back*. Zak would be a smiling and talking yak. He'd be big, cumbersome, and clumsy looking, as yaks can be. But the only thing bigger than his physique would be his heart. He'd not let the fact that he was so different stop him from doing good for the world. Zak would deliver books to children everywhere. If your village lacked books, you could expect a visit from Zak. He would be a literary Santa Claus! Maybe he'd even be a latter-day Tintin, I mused, traveling to dozens of countries besides Nepal, all with the intention of being a force for positive change. Maybe, I brainstormed, it was time for me to step in and help to solve the problem.

Or maybe not. As I pondered the idea, I realized that though it sounded fun, it was also antithetical to our young organization's core values. We'd always been committed to finding local solutions to local problems. We did not send well-meaning foreigners to Nepal to "build a school for the local people," as this risked turning community members into passive aid recipients. Likewise, I noodled, the solution to the lack of local-language children's books in places like Nepal and Cambodia should come from Nepalese and Cambodian authors, artists, and editors.

Zak the Yak would have to wait for a later date. But I already had my opening lines that would make Nepal come alive for young readers:

> *In the land of Nepal,*
> *the hills are so high,*
> *that the snow-covered peaks*
> *almost block out the sky.*

....

Dinesh later recalled from his perspective the challenge we'd laid out and the progress he made: "When we decided to support publications, it was a nightmare for me, because I was not from that background. It had not yet been Room to Read's role to publish books for our libraries. Initially the idea was to work with existing publishers: to support them and produce additional titles in a pictorial format in the Nepali language. I went to the publishers and explained: 'Okay, since these books are not available here, why don't you publish some, since you are the commercial publishers? We'll buy the books that you produce.'

"They were hesitant: 'Well, you might be buying only five hundred or a thousand copies. And what about other titles: Where do we go and sell? There's no market. Parents here would rather buy food or cigarettes or drinks. They will not buy books for their children. And the books that you're asking us to produce are costly, because they are pictorial. We cannot partner with you.'

"I got so frustrated. I wanted to help, but they were not ready to take my challenge. Luckily I found an organization called the Nepalese Society for Children's Literature. I was introduced by my colleagues. But these guys in the society were all in their sixties or seventies! I wasn't sure how they could understand the sentiments of young children.

"They did help. Working with them, I came to know a lot of authors. I showed them books in English as samples. 'Okay,' I said, 'you have to provide me with the story, one sentence in one page. Not more than one sentence. You have to give a very short story that will be fun reading. I will work with the illustrator.'"

Nepal went first, and within a few years a similar challenge would be taken up in other Room to Read countries. We could not find high-quality and colorful children's books in languages like Lao, Khmer, Rajasthani, or Vietnamese. Around the developing world, we were searching for Dr. Seuss.

CHAPTER TEN

Baby Fish Goes to School

Several months later I returned to one of the many cities that now felt like a comfortable second home, Kathmandu. Driving straight from the airport to the office to meet the team, I observed the usual chaos in the streets. Overloaded diesel-belching buses swerved to avoid *tuk-tuks,* the motorized rickshaws that zip along Nepal's streets. As the *tuk-tuks* careered out of the way of cows munching on plastic garbage bags, traffic lights were either broken or ignored. Large trucks bore the ubiquitous HORN PLEASE sign on their backs, as if daring the city's residents to add to the cacophony.

All was peaceful and orderly inside the Room to Read office. Dinesh and Rob Campbell (the volunteer from Seattle) had made great progress on finding authors and artists who had ideas for children's books. One artist was writing a book about a family of mice who lived in an old abandoned shoe and were constantly avoiding attacks from the neighborhood cat. Another was working on a book about wildlife, using a *topi*-wearing (traditional Nepalese cloth cap) monkey as the guide.

Dinesh brought out from a manila folder a manuscript of which he was particularly proud. *Chameli ko Basna* told the cautionary tale of a girl named Chameli from a rich family. One day she borrows a piece of gold jewelry without her mother's permission and wears it to school, basking in the admiration of the students, all of whom come from poorer families. Rather than scolding Chameli, her indulgent mother instead gives in to her daughter's incessant demands for her own jewelry collection.

Every day Chameli shows up at school wearing something new. The jewelry collection continues to grow. When she gets to school, she insists that the other students gather around to admire her: and while they're there, why not also draw pictures of her? Obsessed with her beauty, Chameli is soon spending more time staring in the mirror than studying. She misses school to go to the goldsmith to window-shop or to have repairs made to her necklaces and bracelets. Her grades put her in danger of failing.

"You used to be one of the best students, but now you have the lowest grades," the headmaster tells her.

Chameli has no one with whom to commiserate, since by now she's alienated all the other students. She asks the headmaster for one last chance. He explains to her that true beauty comes from within and that studies are more important than material objects. Chameli asks her mother to return the jewelry and comes to school the next day unadorned, ready to study and to win back her friends.

Next Dinesh showed me a series of books being planned around a new character named Tommy Tempo. *Tempo* was the Nepali word for *tuk-tuk*, and Tommy would be an anthropomorphic, hell-raising version constantly escaping from its hapless owner, Ramji, and creating chaos on the streets of Kathmandu. He would drive through puddles to splash pedestrians, steal policemen's hats, and perform high-speed 360-degree loops at traffic roundabouts while blowing his horn.

I thought of that morning's commute from the airport and wondered what *more* traffic chaos in Kathmandu would look like.

All joking aside, I was impressed. Just four months after the phone call telling us we had to respond more effectively to our local customers, the team had four quality books that would soon be ready to print. I told Dinesh and Rob how thrilled I was with the progress they'd made.

My belief that smart people will usually find ways to get things done had been vindicated. Many leaders feel guilty if they throw a challenge onto someone else's plate. They may have the *coworker impulse*, which is to solve the problem for them. But most times the answer cannot be found right there on the spot, as it takes some time and mental energy to brainstorm, talk to others, and find a creative solution. I knew that Dinesh, along with Rob, would succeed, even if none of us could yet visualize what the path would look like.

In the case of Nepali-language publishing, it turns out that the solution was sitting there just waiting to be discovered. Once word got out that Room to Read was willing to pay local authors and artists, we had sixty-seven manuscript submissions within one month. The Skoll funding had come through, thanks to Erin's always-convincing grant request and my in-person lobbying of the foundation's leaders. We had enough to fund and produce the first ten titles. All would be done by local authors and artists, which we viewed as being critical not only to the relevance of the content, but also to the scalability and sustainability of the program. Dinesh and team would be able to choose the best ideas and still have a healthy backlog. And with budget to print ten thousand copies of each book, we'd soon have one hundred thousand answers for those children who had challenged us to provide more books in the Nepali language.

....

Well-run organizations are structured in a way that allows great ideas to spread like wildfire. Every year, we bring our country directors and program directors together in one place for a week in which they learn from one another.

In 2004, Dinesh was one of the stars of the show. As he later recalled: "We published fourteen books during the first two years: I was so, so happy! In Nepal we single-handedly created a market for children's picture books. All those commercial publishers who didn't agree with me are now producing similar books. We made a real contribution."

As Dinesh proudly showed the new hot-off-the-press Nepali-language titles, our teams from other countries began to visualize how this program could be brought to their children. In a very short time, there were requests to approve budgets for publishing in a dozen additional languages.

Within three years, our teams in Cambodia, Laos, India, Nepal, Sri

Lanka, and Vietnam were producing more than a hundred new and original titles each year, using local authors and artists. Starting in the landlocked Himalayan kingdom of Nepal, we had not just found Dr. Seuss; we'd recruited dozens of *Doctors* Seuss.

We also continued to talk to the students, parents, and teachers to hear their feedback. Sometimes the results could surprise and even delight us.

One evening I was at home catching up on e-mail. India, fifteen time zones ahead, had just opened for business. With a steaming cup of milk tea at her side, Jaishree, one of the program managers for our library program, was sending me an anecdote from her travels.

Dear John,

I've just returned from a field visit to a district called Betul in the state of Madhya Pradesh yesterday. It is so, so heartening to see the poorest of poor kids from the tribal areas come to the library every day and read the books with sparkle in their eyes. They are vying for attention to read and to share with me the story.

And . . . believe me, no exaggeration . . . the teacher is complaining that "Now that we have encouraged them to have free access to books, they hide the books inside the text book when I'm teaching them math. How will I finish my curriculum if they do not pay attention?"

It reminded me of our good old school days. Quite an achievement, I thought, one that speaks volumes about how excited these children are about reading. This is not to say that all is as rosy. Challenges are many, and it's a long road ahead. Still I just felt like sharing my excitement!

> *Thanks,*
>
> *Jaishree*

Smiling, I replied immediately to Jaishree: "Stories like this one give me the energy to work harder than ever. And congratulations! This is the classic *good problem to have!*"

. . . .

We continued to invest resources in gaining feedback on our programs. Some of the students told us that they didn't want only to read children's books; they also wanted to write them. Other students showed their artwork to our local team members and asked if they, too, could be published artists. Seeing the zeal of the students, the local teams were soon running young writers' and young artists' competitions, with the winning entries being published.

As the winning stories filtered back to us in San Francisco, we were constantly inspired by the creativity of the students. One of my own favorites was a title from Sri Lanka, *Baby Fish Goes to School.* The book was written in both official languages of Sri Lanka—Sinhalese and Tamil. What follows is my best paraphrase:

Baby Fish is swimming by the side of its pond when it sees a young rabbit hopping by with a big smile on its face.

"Hi, Mr. Rabbit, why are you so happy?"

"I've just come from school. It's a really happy place. We sing songs, dance, play games, read books, take naps, and eat rice and curry. I love school!"

Baby Fish decides that this sounds like a great place. That evening, she swims close to her mother and declares her intention to go to school the next morning.

"You can't," the mother explains. Baby Fish frowns, her eyes drooping.

"Why not? I really want to go."

"The school is on land. And you're a fish. Sorry. Life is not fair, but it is what it is."

Baby Fish is sad. She can't sleep. Life seems bleak.

The next day Baby Fish swims to the side of the pond and explains her predicament to the rabbit. Rabbit explains that he has talked to some of the other animals to ask for their help. Pig has opined that there is "no reason to help the fish—fish are different from us. They don't belong in school."

The rabbit has nobody to help him. The other animals did not care. Baby Fish would not be going to school anytime soon.

Let's pause here to reveal that this story is written by a fifteen-year-old Sri Lankan girl named Pradeepa. The illustrator is a seventeen-year-old girl, Chandanayah, from the same village. As young girls living in a rural community in Sri Lanka, they certainly know something about exclusion. If you're born poor, female, and rural, life is pretty much stacked against you. Add to that religious and ethnic discrimination, and it's obvious that these girls have heard a lot of rationalizations for why life is not fair. But they were inspired by our local team to not let these barriers get in the way. Both girls excelled at school and were excited to now be published. Thankfully, our flop-eared friend is the GSD (get shit done!) kind of rabbit. After assuming a pondside pose seemingly inspired by Rodin's *The Thinker,* Rabbit has a eureka moment. He hops away, returning a short time later with a fishbowl he has purchased. With a fast and deliberate motion, he scoops up Baby Fish and carries her triumphantly to school. Once there, Baby Fish is plunked down next to the blackboard. Seeing the happiness of their new classmate, the animals give a hearty cheer.

Which is exactly how I reacted when this book first fell into my hands. I loved the lessons: exclusion converted to inclusion. A problem turned into a solution; a GSD attitude as a key attribute of character development. Most important, this was a tale of young people refusing to accept the excuses and inaction of earlier generations.

At the 2007 Clinton Global Initiative in New York, I was invited to participate as a speaker on an education panel. I was nervous as could be, sitting next to Andre Agassi and facing a room packed with dignitaries. Those with whom I was sharing the stage were more well known and had much longer track records. I felt like an impostor.

To make the work of Room to Read come alive, I told the Baby Fish story. As I summarized the story line, the audience was silent. Not a single person was checking their BlackBerry. At the story's conclusion, there was spontaneous applause. In the front row sat Toni Morrison, one of the guests of honor. Her eyes were silvery with tears. Two Sri Lankan girls had struck a universal chord. Their storytelling prowess had made a Nobel laureate in literature cry.

What I loved most about the Baby Fish story was that it proves the adage that talent is evenly distributed. You never know how many talented people are out there until you invite and inspire them to be creative. It wasn't an adult who'd come up with the compelling metaphor (a fish out of school) and the obvious and cost-effective solution (the fishbowl). Had our team not run the young storytellers' competition, the world might not have heard the story that adults had missed but that the teenage girls understood intuitively.

....

As in all of our programs at Room to Read, we focused intently on scale. By the end of 2006, the teams had produced 144 original children's book titles in seven languages: Hindi, Khmer, Lao, Nepalese, Singhalese, Tamil, and Vietnamese. Eighty-two more in 2007 brought the total to 226. And 2008 was a milestone—the first time we published 100 titles in a year. The total would grow to more than 500 titles by the end of 2010, and more than 900 by the end of 2012. The local teams had published in more than twenty languages! We'd grown to become one of the broadest-reaching children's book publishers in the developing world. In every presentation I give, I show dozens of these titles and joke with the audience that "Room to Read is the biggest publisher you're never heard of"—because, of course, we're doing it in what I have come to refer to as "the forgotten languages." And we are publishing millions upon millions of these books.

From Baby Fish to Chameli the jewelry lover, from Tommy Tempo to the wildlife of Nepal, the characters of our rapidly growing publishing arm were greeting hundreds of thousands of eager young readers—all because students in Nepal, the opinionated 52 percent, had dared to tell us how we could do better. Little did we know that a much bigger day lay ahead as we were challenged to stop thinking in such small quantities and focus on producing books in the *millions.* Now we have a full-time global program officer for our book-publishing program, Willi Pascual.

"When Room to Read first started, and soon realized that the children were not reading the books they donated, they knew they had to provide books in local languages. But the problem was that they didn't have these books for kids at all in most of the places where we work. The few that were there didn't necessarily promote the habit of reading. They were text heavy and didn't focus on storybooks.

"Before you can get a child to have the habit of reading, he or she has to learn how to read. So we needed books for early-grade readers. We actually commissioned the author of *Baby Fish* to come up with a second edition more geared to younger readers, with fewer words and more illustrations. Our authors and illustrators get a one-time payment, understanding that it's nonprofit. Our primary goal is not to sell the books. We donate them to Room to Read libraries. We also work with our library program and our literacy-instruction program to make sure teachers and librarians know how to use these books. Many are designing activities around the stories.

"In addition, we publish nonfiction books that are related to the curriculum. If you start producing books related to the subjects children are learning in the classroom, then the government or the schools are more willing to have those books used. For example, in Cambodia this meant topics around hygiene and the family or the community. When we talk with government officials in Vietnam, for example, they want more of these 'big books,' the oversized ones ideal for shared reading. Children can read together, guide each other, or be guided by the teacher. The illustrations are huge, almost poster-sized.

"We always try to observe local traditions. For instance, one of the plans in Africa is to have some of our work inspired by oral narratives or folklore. We're hoping to have some books produced and inspired from stories that are documented in the communities where we work. This is especially important in South Africa, where for much of their history books were available only in the Afrikaans or English languages. Now locals can write stories in their own languages, of which there are eleven in South Africa."

Our South African country director Chris Mothupi's life experience inspired a story titled *The Honest Caddie.* The protagonist is a thirteen-year-old black South African boy named Stephen. His family is poor, and to help them keep food on the table he works hard at the local golf course. Most of the people for whom he caddies are, inevitably in a place like postapartheid South Africa, white. Stephen catches a bus from school to a crossroads town, then a second bus to get to the club. Or at least close to it, as we all know that the notion of a bus entering the hallowed ground of a country club is . . . well, it's ridiculous enough for us to know that Stephen will get dropped off by the bus at the discreet distance from which every "service employee" walks.

None of this seems to bother Stephen. He carries clubs for the ladies' league and gets paid by the club. Given his charm, he often takes home a small tip. And then one day everything changes.

Stephen is in a thicket of trees. The man for whom he is caddying today has hit yet another shot into the native flora. As the man waits only semipatiently for his "boy" to correct his error, Stephen stumbles upon a small billfold. It's red and looks like something that would be carried by a lady. Opening it, he sees one, two, three, four, five, six, seven, eight, nine thousand one-rand notes, plus various other denominations. He is astounded. He has never seen this much money before. Just the thousand-rand notes total to more than a thousand U.S. dollars. For the sake of comparison, this is what he would make if he caddied one round a day for the next three years. With the cash now in his hand, he could avoid eighteen thousand holes of golf.

Hearing shouts from "his golfer," he continues to search and is soon successful in his quest. He returns the ball while surreptitiously stashing the red billfold in the golf bag.

Six holes later, he is back in the small outdoor caddies' waiting area. No showers, no fluffy white towels, and no talcum powder for the caddies. They merely wait around for their tips. With time to kill, Stephen reveals his secret to his fellow caddies. Each is incredulous. Like Stephen, they have never seen this much money before.

"How will you spend it?"

"What do you mean?" Stephen asks. "This is not my money."

"It is now! You found it! You keep it! Let's go have some fun!" The voices of his fellow caddies rise up in a crescendo.

"But that's not what I was asking you," says Stephen. "I was wondering whether anyone has advice on how I can get the money back to its owner."

The gang laughs at Stephen. "Don't you understand, *braa* [brother], that this is your chance? You'll never make this much money carrying clubs. And the person who lost it will never miss it. This is"—spitting on the ground—"small change for them. They can't even be bothered to report it."

Stephen is not convinced. Risking the approbation of his close friends, he goes to the dining room–cum–cocktail bar and asks the woman in charge to help him find the woman who has lost her money. Within ten minutes, the grateful golfer emerges from the dining room. She had not even noticed that the billfold was missing. All is well that ends well, yes?

Back home, Stephen tells his parents that the other boys had made fun of him during the long bus ride home.

"Pay no attention to them," his father advises. "You are a good lad, and you did the right thing. We are proud of you."

As is the woman whose wallet was found. Within a week, she surprises Stephen by arranging for him to begin taking golf lessons. The honest caddie has "crossed over" and can now learn to play the game for the first time in his life.

Only later would I learn that the inspiration for this story came from Chris's own youth. His experience as a young black caddie at an all-white golf club had not been blessed with a happy ending. But he is enough of an optimist that he believes that even if he cannot rewrite history, at least he can change the present.

"I don't believe anyone has the right to steal," he told me. "The only way to get ahead is through education, hard work, and being a person of honor. I have not had an easy life. My father deserted us, my mother worked a long way away in the city, and I was raised by my uneducated grandparents. I have always studied, and today I am proud that as the head of Room to Read South Africa I can help our nation's children to learn moral values."

I regretted only that we hadn't found Chris Mothupi earlier. Had he been with us, our launch of operations on the African continent might have been a much less rocky road.

CHAPTER ELEVEN

Sleepless in Siem Reap

I am lucky in that 98 percent of my days at Room to Read are happy ones. But this only makes falling into the abyss that much more terrifying.

"All bathrooms, whatever their minute variations, are over-illuminated at night, just as, at night, all telephones when they ring are too loud."

This quote from Charles Baxter's *The Feast of Love* proves true as I stumble across my hotel room looking for the phone. Its third shrill ring pierces the silence. I have no idea where it is, and come to think of it, I have no idea where I am. The pitch-black room is unable to provide clues. Finally I pounce on the phone. As I fumble for a light switch, I hear a familiar voice.

"Hi, John, sorry, I know it's late in Cambodia." (Now I at least remember where I am.) "But I had to call, because I have some terrible news you need to know about."

Oh God. This is not the way you want to start a phone conversation, especially in the middle of the night. The voice on the other end of the phone is that of Lori, our chief people officer. What disaster is she about to reveal?

Scenarios play out in my mind: Is it about my parents? A traffic accident involving employees? Maoist rebels in Nepal shooting up one of our schools?

None of the above; it's something I least expected.

"It's about the team in South Africa. I am very worried about them, and the evolving situation there."

Gulp—I recall that three members of our senior management team are visiting South Africa to check on our newest Room to Read country. *Oh God, no, please.*

Though Lori is seven thousand miles away, we are connected by the panic we both feel. But somehow she manages to make her voice calm and clear, which snaps me back to immediate attention.

"There is a serious situation there. We need to get our team out of Johannesburg as soon as we can. They've been threatened."

My gut clenches. My colleagues had volunteered to take on what we knew would be a tough mission, flying for twenty-four hours and, upon arrival, firing the recently hired top executive in Africa. There were documented issues of lax management and failure to achieve agreed-upon milestones. Financial controls that should have been put into place had not been. We could not tolerate this underperformance as we established a beachhead for Room to Read on a new continent.

My own suspicion was that maybe there was a reason for this. At Room to Read we were building a culture of GSD—Get Shit Done. The early performance of the leader being terminated indicated that she did not share this trait or commitment. We wanted her to move expeditiously, and the early indications were not good. As always, we would move fast on issues of underperformance. As one of my mentors likes to say, "People problems age more like milk than like wine."

But the regional director who had to be fired wasn't going quietly. Specific reprisals had been brandished. This was worse than sour milk. This was acid.

Ultimately, and part of me is glad we did not know this yet, there would need to be other employees terminated, too, with one particular employee refusing to return assets that belonged to Room to Read. But we'd eventually cross those bridges. For now, there was just one big worry reaching me in the inky depths of the Cambodian night.

I grip the phone harder, and think: *Please, God, let this be a dream.*

It's not; I'm awake and knocked off center here in a tiny hotel room in the middle of the night in rural Cambodia. I'm feeling completely helpless. My brain is not wired to know how to respond.

Lori continues: "The team has already checked into a hotel with high security. Seats out of Jo'burg have been arranged on the next flight out. They will be on a midnight Lufthansa departure to Frankfurt."

It's just past 11:00 P.M. here in Cambodia, so that means it's about five or six hours until midnight in South Africa. From my travels and reading I know that South Africa is among the most violent places on earth. Human beings are often more in danger from one another than they are from wildlife. My stomach is in knots as I think about our team and their safety. I feel like a failure as a leader for not being there.

Lori and I close the call with a mutual assurance that it's all going to be all right. Secure hotel; night drive to airport; quick clearance of airport security. Lori promises that she'll send a text the minute she hears our team has left South African airspace. I hope it's an SMS, not an SOS. Until then, it looks like it will be a sleepless night.

Lying in bed staring at geckos running along the wall, I review the events that got us here. I do not have to look far: Only six days ago, I had one of those days when you wish you'd never gotten out of bed. Maybe I'd have been better off calling in sick that morning, or going fishing, or snuggling up on the sofa with a good book and a pot of green tea.

....

Several members of our management team awaited me as I walked into our San Francisco headquarters on that sunny spring day. They wore pensive expressions.

"We just finished our first surprise audit in South Africa. Money has disappeared. We don't yet know how much, but we think it was about twenty-five to thirty thousand dollars."

Had Muhammad Ali in his prime fighting years hit me in the stomach with his best left jab, it would have hurt less. We were looking at lack of oversight by the very same people we'd hired, whom we had trusted, with whom we had vowed that together we'd help to write a better chapter in the future of South Africa's youth. What hit me hardest was that our regional director in South Africa had so mishandled our affairs that I felt certain the children of South Africa had suffered as a result. Generation after generation, the children who were poor (i.e., the vast majority) had been denied an education. We'd promised them a better solution. And now, had we failed?

"We're on a plane to Jo'burg within the next few days."

I signed a form to instruct the bank to lock down the account. Next were the termination letters, to be reviewed by our lawyers to make sure we were in compliance with South African law.

Back in my office I couldn't concentrate: How had we hired the wrong people? Why had we not listened to the Greek chorus warning us about potential problems on the African continent?

As the self-flagellation continued, I wondered whether we should begin to plan our retreat. Maybe that was an extreme reaction, but I have never dealt with failure very well. I also thought of all those skeptics and wondered whether we now had evidence that they might have been right. The road to success on the African continent might be quite a bit bumpier than we'd experienced in South and Southeast Asia.

Out of the corner of my eye, I spotted a photo of myself with our team leader for southern Africa. We were locked in a warm embrace, with smiles as wide as the Zambezi River. I remembered our conversations on my first visit to Room to Read's headquarters: Together we'd vowed to help South Africa overcome the scourge of apartheid and racism. We'd be part of the building of a new democratic South Africa.

Here was a person I had trusted and welcomed into our family. I wanted to wipe that smile off her face. My grip tightened and the corners of the picture began to crumple. Had she played us for fools? Obviously she had: *Here is John,* she thought, *just another silly, naive white American who thinks he's going to help Africa.*

I tore the photo in half while uttering words my mother taught me never to say, and then ripped the photo again—into four pieces, eight pieces, sixteen, and then thirty-two. I walked the pieces to the trash can and dropped each one in slowly. It was like a funeral, slowly lowering the body into the ground for burial.

But what had died on that day was my optimism.

....

Back in my Cambodian hotel room, I calculate how long it will be before our team is on the flight out of South Africa. The geckos continue to scurry across the walls. It is hard to believe anything can move so fast at such a crazy angle. At least someone is having fun here. I check my Black-Berry: no messages from Lori. Nothing, so I send myself a test message to make sure everything is functioning: affirmative. I walk outside to look at the stars, shining brightly on a clear night. But unfortunately there are no shooting stars on which to make a wish for our team's safety. Thank-fully, I do see something that looks vaguely like a stress reliever. I walk over to the night sentry and, with a mix of bad French and charades, bum a cigarette. The tobacco is local, pungent and harsh, which suits my mood just fine.

I am filled with regret. I felt like a lily-livered CEO who sent our team into harm's way. I get the glory of taking a major donor to meet our students here in Cambodia while my management team tackles the tough stuff.

Back in the room, I grab an Angkor beer from the minibar and lie back in bed, too wired to sleep, too angry to read. Mentally I wander back to the days when we debated taking our organization beyond Asia and onto the African continent.

Going into Africa wasn't an easy move. The talks started in 2005. As our team celebrated our five-year anniversary, we debated what our second half decade would look like. Our Asian teams were doing great work, yet we heard constantly about the need to take our education programs into Africa. Because we had limited resources and a steep learning curve, it was with considerable mixed feelings that we looked at the map of Africa. The prospect fascinated and intimidated us at the same time.

Most of our core team had traveled on the continent, and some had even lived there. We'd met the poorest people in these poorest of nations. We had witnessed what crushing poverty looks like at the village level, and how it robs children of opportunities that our societies take for granted (like not dying of an easily preventable disease or lack of access to clean drinking water). The poverty we witnessed in Africa was different from anywhere else in the world. You'd have to be without a heart or a soul not to want to do something, anything, to help improve conditions for the people—especially the children—there.

Yet Africa is a tough nut to crack. Each of us related stories and anecdotes we'd heard from other NGOs that had gone in with good intentions and a lot of energy, but hadn't accomplished their goals. The list of failures could be stacked up to the sky. Many had gone before us and produced few results. A lot of money had been squandered. How would we avoid doing the same?

I have never stopped being amazed at our team. At a certain point in each meeting, somebody would break through the negativity: "So, yes, we can see the problems. We can talk about the problems until we're blue in the face. But you don't get a prize for identifying obstacles. The question is what are we going to do about it? What is our solution?"

This was GSD at its best. Excitement replaced despair as we rolled up our sleeves to figure out a game plan. The first step was to seek wisdom and insight from our employees and board members. What we got was a veritable Greek chorus of opinions and advice that were just as passionate as they were contradictory.

"I spent a year teaching students in Namibia. Those kids are every bit as excited about reading as the ones in India and Laos. We can't justify continuing to ignore them," said Stacey Warner, who had spearheaded our Africa expansion strategy.

"Yes, but the corruption problems in Africa make South and Southeast Asia look like they're run by Boy Scout troops eager to win merit badges for honesty."

"So we're going to punish the children to make up for the sins of their leaders?"

"I've traveled for months at a time on the continent, and every time I visited a building that was technically considered to be a school, there were no books. Many times they didn't even have a damn chalkboard. Teachers were scratching words into the dry dirt, using a stick, as two hundred students gathered around, squinting as they tried to make out the faint letters. That might look quaint in a Discovery Channel documentary, but we're not in the business of 'quaint.' Our role is to create schools that are so 'normal' and 'boring' that no documentary film crew worth their salt would want to get near them, due to the lack of drama."

I chimed in: "This is a big opportunity. We could change what 'normal' looks like."

One of our board members disagreed: "We're only five years old and we're already working in six countries in Asia. We already have more demand for our schools and libraries in Asia than we can handle. You [pointing at me] are pushing the organization too far, too fast. Now you want to also take on Africa. Asia is not a big enough playing field for you? You must have an ego problem I did not previously know about."

The debate among the staff and members and the board sizzled on. The biggest problem was that everything people said made sense. It would have been so much easier if there were statements of opinion that were obviously "nuts" or "just plain wrong."

A sampling of voices from the various meetings follows.

"Think about this—many of Africa's supposedly intractable problems could be solved in this generation if the world conspired to make just one thing happen: for every child on the continent to receive a quality education."

"The costs of doing business in Africa will be higher because there's less of a competitive economy driving down prices of cement, wood, paper, books, gasoline, etc. If we admit that we have finite resources, we can serve more children by being a 'pure player' in Asia."

"The whole argument that 'the size of the pie is fixed' is a total canard. I'm tired of hearing people argue that when we add on a new country, we somehow penalize our other countries. The data clearly proves the opposite. New countries attract new investors."

"True! When we launched operations in Sri Lanka, so many companies with funds allocated for tsunami relief made their first investments in us. Most of them invested the next year and the next, and not just in Sri Lanka but in our other countries. Rather than Sri Lanka 'stealing' from our other geographies, it actually helped them by bringing new investors on board."

"That may be true, but doing business in rural Africa will make Sri Lanka look like a Sunday picnic."

"You have *got* to be kidding me. Sri Lanka has the longest-running civil war on the planet, and our team is doing great work there. We did not accept 'It will be difficult' as a valid excuse when we made the decision to launch there."

The debate continued for weeks and weeks, and then months and months. Every "pro" seemed to instantaneously attract a "con." Every time an Africa optimist spoke up, he or she would be gang-tackled by a group of Africa pessimists. At one point in the interminable discussion, I read a newspaper story about the new Hadron Supercollider being built on the Swiss-French border. Three hundred feet below the surface of the earth, the collider would accelerate protons to 99.9999991 percent the speed of light. Two protons would follow the twenty-seven-kilometer circumference until BANG, they were smashed together. The power of each collision would reveal something about the nature of matter and the fundamental truths of the universe.

I found myself fantasizing about taking both the pro-Africa and anti-Africa spheres of my brain on a little field trip and accelerating them around that track. Finally a decision was needed: It was time for me to show leadership.

....

Desperate to clear the muddle in my mind, I left work early on a picture-perfect San Francisco afternoon and drove myself across the Golden Gate Bridge to the Marin Headlands. The city has many things going for it, including proximity to a million-plus acres of national park. This trail run would be as much for the mental benefit as for the physical spark.

As you can tell, I spend a lot of my waking hours (and sometimes my sleeping ones) crunching numbers. As I laced up my trail-running shoes, my first thought was that there was a very clear quantitative case for our entry into Africa: more than 100 million children not enrolled in school and more than 250 million illiterate people. In many countries only one in five girls made it to seventh grade. How can a society ever hope to develop if 80 percent of its women don't make it that far in school?

Sub-Saharan Africa had the highest proportion of poor people in the world, with over half of eight hundred million people living on less than a dollar a day. The HIV/AIDS rate was staggering and depressing; school was the primary place for children to learn how to avoid this modern scourge. If they did not go, then they were at all the more risk in a life already full of too much.

Finally, half the population of Africa was fifteen years old or younger: How could there be any hope for the continent if such a large percentage of the population couldn't read?

Moving away from the raw numbers, my mind shifted to the non-quantitative, emotional case. I thought about the kids I had met on my backpacking travels to Zambia and Botswana who had no access to books, and of the schools I had observed in Ethiopia, with one hundred children crammed into a single room, sitting on logs sunk into the muddy floor due to lack of desks and chairs.

I remembered Jimmy, one of the guides from my 1999 ascent of Mount Kilimanjaro: "Because I can speak English, I get to be a guide and make ten dollars a day. The porters, who speak no English, make only two dollars a day, and that's only when they can get work. Because so many people are uneducated, it's very competitive to be a porter, and so they don't get as many jobs as I do. I can afford to send my children to school, but most of them can't."

He said this not to brag. He said it with sadness for his country.

But the strongest voice I heard was that of Nelson Mandela, who encouraged the world to look out for the future of Africa with these words: "Education is the most powerful weapon which you can use to change the world."

What would the world be like today, I wondered, had Mandela not been one of the lucky ones who received an education? The dark stain of apartheid in South Africa has been eliminated thanks to the work of many, but especially because of the educated, articulate, and visionary leader they rallied around.

What if the next Mandela was out there today as a young boy or girl, or the next Wangari Maathai, or Ellen Johnson Sirleaf, or the next Desmond Tutu? Those heroes who'd brought the world all-too-rare "good news from Africa" had education as a common denominator in their lives. While many people think that Africa contains only tragedy, the facts show that there is much about which to be optimistic. In 2010, for example, ten of the world's thirty-five fastest-growing economies were on the African continent. Real strides were being made against malaria. Millions of people with HIV/AIDS were receiving antiretrovirals and living lives that were so close to normal as to qualify as a medical miracle.

It had been clear to me on every visit I'd made to the continent that the "potential energy" was out there, in the brains and ambition of so many kids living in remote parts of the continent. Wouldn't it be timid and cowardly not to try to turn it into kinetic energy?

The case against moving into Africa at that stage of Room to Read's life cycle was also quite strong. First, there was the terrible problem of corruption, one of the albatrosses around the neck of Africa's poor. When people rightfully questioned why so many hundreds of billions of dollars of aid had so grandly failed to lift Africa's masses out of poverty, corruption was always a leading answer. According to the most recent Transparency International survey about perceptions of corruption, seventeen of the thirty-five countries rated most corrupt are on the African continent.

Transparency International estimated that Mobutu Sese Seko had looted Zaire of five billion dollars, with a similar amount being stashed in private banks by Nigerian president Sani Abacha. Mobutu was so brazen about his stolen wealth that he leased the Concorde to fly his daughter to her wedding in the Ivory Coast while simultaneously begging President Reagan for easier terms to service his country's debt. Jean-Bédel Bokassa, for his inauguration as the "emperor" of the Central African Republic, spent an indulgent and disgusting twenty-two million dollars—in a country where the public health systems were so tragically lacking that life expectancy was a measly forty-four years.

The second big issue facing Room to Read was finding a leadership team. Many experts told us that it would be difficult to find a great management team for Africa because there's been such a brain drain on the continent.

"Just look at the shortage of doctors and nurses in some of these countries," they said. "They were trained in Africa but now make their way to Europe for better-paid positions and access to more advanced technology."

The flood of human capital leaving the continent made it that much less likely that we'd be able to find the leaders we needed, especially since we paid less than the private sector and the big multilateral aid agencies. In contrast to Asia, Erin and I did not have a preexisting network of friends and former coworkers we could tap into for help in identifying and recruiting a local team. In Asia we'd also received support and references from leading philanthropic organizations like the Asia Foundation and the American India Foundation. With their help we'd installed new Room to Read outposts quickly. Our limited network of contacts in Africa seemed like another potential nail in the coffin.

Finally, the third big concern was that age-old issue of the green stuff: Sure, we could have another child, but could we afford to feed it?

As I crested a hill on my run, I was greeted by both a cold wind gust and a stunning view of the Pacific. My feet flew faster as my internal debate neared an end point. A launch in Africa would no doubt saddle us with unexpected problems. It wouldn't be easy. Africa had defeated many people smarter than us.

I also knew that a lot of the fund-raising burden would fall on me and that I'd probably be on the road more than ever to support our latest expansion.

My own decision was becoming clearer; there was simply no way I could imagine writing off an entire continent. Until the day I die I will believe that we are all born with the same gray matter, and that talent is evenly distributed around the world. Every kid deserves a chance to unleash his or hers.

We examined the risks and believed that they were worth taking. It was clearly the most difficult decision we'd been forced to make in our first five years.

....

Sleepless in Siem Reap, Cambodia, I continued to dwell on the fact that it was now turning out to be even more difficult than we'd imagined to go into Africa. Maybe, I thought, it's naive of me to walk through life with my "glass half full" perspective. Perhaps the Africa pessimists had been right the whole time.

CHAPTER TWELVE

"I Was in Grade Two When Our School Was Burned Down"

I awake in a panic to the sound of yet another jangling phone in my hotel room in Cambodia. *Oh God, now what?* Light is streaming in through cracks in the curtains. I find the phone and steady myself. "Good morning, Mr. John. This is your wake-up call."

"Thank you, thank you."

I am effusive in my gratitude. My emotions are in such a shattered state that anything not an emergency seems like a gift from heaven. Sprinting across the room to grab my BlackBerry, I see three new texts from Lori, all reporting variations on the same theme: Our team has left South African airspace and is en route to Frankfurt.

I breathe a huge sigh of relief and send her a note of thanks for having stayed up all night to make sure everyone was safe. Looking at the clock, I realize that I have only ten minutes to get ready for a school tour with a major new donor from Japan. I'm not sure how I would have handled this visit had I still been in a panic over our team, on all of three hours of sleep. I'm grateful that I won't have to find out.

Two hours later, we're screeching to a dusty halt in a rented pickup truck in front of Angkor Wat Secondary School. The earthen forecourt of the school is bone dry and hard packed by nature, the result of endless days of punishing sunshine. The gleaming white truck stands in stark contrast to the dirt beneath it and the azure sky above. As we leave the truck's air-conditioned interior, the heat hits us like a blast furnace. It's only 11:00 A.M., and we're already in triple digits.

We notice a buzz of frenetic activity. The young girls are playing games. A girl in her early teenage years coasts her bicycle to a stop as her mother half jumps, half falls off the back. The young participants in our Girls' Education program have volunteered to spend a Saturday afternoon at the school sharing their life stories with our group of donors. These in-country visits for donors are an essential part of showing how we spend our funds as transparently as possible.

At Angkor Wat Secondary School, the headmaster greets our Cambodia team with a broad smile and a friendly wave that guides us out of the sun and into the welcoming shade of the classroom. The headmaster and I share a Cambodian bow and a Western handshake. He then ushers our group indoors.

The classroom is full of teenage girls whose chatter stops as they watch their guests arrive. Some smile shyly, while others drop their gaze to the floor as soon as our eyes meet. All are dressed in their school uniform of crisp white shirt and blue skirt. This day-off dress code may have been at the suggestion of the headmaster in honor of the visitors. Or it could be that the school uniform provided as part of the scholarship package is the nicest clothing they own. Regardless, they look sharper than I do, clad in my favorite North Face canvas trekking pants and a sweat-soaked button-down shirt.

The twenty girls are seated at desks that face forward toward a table in the front of the room, where the visitors are meant to sit. I am placed in the middle, with an interpreter on one side of me and one of the largest donors to the girls' program on the other. The girls range in age from eleven to sixteen. They're excited by our visit, and I wonder if the tiny desks will be able to contain their energy. Along the wall nearest the entrance are a group of mothers. They're also sitting in the small desk chairs. They are not much larger than their still-growing daughters. The interpreter explains that they have come to express their gratitude for our support of their daughters' education.

This support takes many forms, including school fees, notebooks, school supplies, and uniforms. If girls are falling behind their classmates, we provide tutoring. And as girls progress to the higher grades, they have access to what we call life skills training. In most countries, this means they attend a weekly meeting at which five core skills are emphasized, including self-awareness and empathy, communication and interpersonal communication, decision making and problem solving, critical and creative thinking, and coping with emotions and stress. These are based on standards established by the World Health Organization.

As Emily Leys, our global director of the Girls' Education program, notes, "All the girls also get access to a mentor, what we call social mobilizers, to make sure they follow up." (It was the Laotian "mobilizers" who found and supported Inkham the crab fisherman and her auntie.) "The goal is for the girls to complete secondary school and to acquire the tools they need for decision making later in life. We start at junior high, because often there's a big drop-off between the junior-high and high-school levels. In some countries, 60 percent to 65 percent of boys pass the exam required to go on to secondary education, while the number for girls might be more like 50 percent. So far, more than half of the girls who've completed the program have gone on to further education, either college or vocational training. We're also seeing a delay in marriage and a delay in having the first child."

Our current country director in Cambodia, Kall Kann, adds an additional perspective: "Girls attend high school in Cambodia at much lower rates than boys. The cultural norms are changing here: Before, girls were not allowed to go to school. Today culture is no longer a barrier. Socioeconomics is what prevents girls from attending upper-level education or pursuing a university degree. Girls mature more quickly than boys, so the family immediately sees them reaching a state where they can make an income. That's why most girls have stopped school early to take care of their siblings or work in the rice fields. And in the last ten years the Cambodian textile industry, which has grown a great deal, has absorbed females to work in the factories."

The Room to Read Cambodia team suggests to the visitors that they might want to talk to the girls about their lives. To break the ice, I tell them: "Our group is here today because we really wanted to meet you and hear about your experiences in school. We are from many different parts of the world, including Hong Kong, Japan, Australia, and the United States. We're very proud that all of you are coming to school every day and are happy that we can play a small role in helping you continue your studies until you graduate from secondary school."

Small but shy smiles go around. I decide to ask group questions, so that no single girl feels herself to be under the harsh glare of the spotlight.

"How many of you rode your bikes to school today?"

Every hand shoots up.

"Who brought your mother with you?"

Twelve hands: Between mothers and daughters, several glances and smiles are exchanged.

"How many of you live on a farm?"

All of them: Given that they look a bit tense about my questions, I decide to lighten the mood a bit.

"Do you have pigs on your farm?"

As the interpreter translates, I crinkle up my noise and offer up a hearty "Oink, oink!"

The girls break out in laughter. Every hand shoots up in the air. I amuse myself thinking this would have been a funny icebreaker in the good ole days of life in the corporate boardroom.

"How many of you have chickens? *Bawk bawk . . .*"

The laughter is getting louder. A few of the girls are covering their mouths with one hand and pointing at me with the other. Clearly they think I'm a bit goofy, and come to think of it, our donors probably do, too. But the nervousness is rapidly melting away, and the laughter continues as we learn that nearly every girl has *quack quacks* and *woof woofs* on her family's small plot of land—but no *neighs* or *meows.*

The small but comfortable classroom now exudes an esprit de corps that was lacking earlier. The rest of the Room to Read crew begins to ask questions of the girls and to share their own stories.

One of our Japanese donors tells the girls of her struggle to be accepted as an equal member of her own society: "Education has played a role in elevating the status of women in Japan, but still we have to struggle every day for equality. I support your schooling because I want to see the day when every girl is able to finish school, just like I did. Imagine what your country will be like when every child, both boy and girl, gets a full education. You will still have to fight to be an equal member of society, and you must continue to fight, because at least with education you will have more of a chance to be successful."

We ask the girls about their home lives. Typically they live in one-room huts that sit three to five feet above the ground on stilts in order to keep their families dry during the rainy season. The "ground floor" can be occupied by the family's animals. The thatched roof is thick enough to keep out rain on all but the heaviest of monsoon days and overhangs the house to keep the water away.

None of the homes has electricity, a phone, running water, or a toilet. A small pit is dug behind the home, often close to the supply of water used for cooking, washing, and drinking. The families have little or no cash income. They eat what they can scratch out on their small plots of land and engage in some small-scale barter for essentials like kerosene for their lanterns. A few of the mothers make small earthen pots that can be sold in the market for less than a dollar. The girls do at least an hour of chores at sunrise before making their journey to school. At the end of the day there will barely be enough time for evening chores, dinner, and some homework by the dim and smoggy light of the kerosene lantern. Without Room to Read in their lives, none of them would be able to afford the school fee of three dollars per month, nor the school uniform.

As it turns out, there is an alternative to school for these girls—prostitution. It seems unfathomable that in the modern world children of such a tender age could be relegated to this deplorable choice. But this is the reality not only here but in so many other places where abject poverty and antiquated notions of a woman's place in the world force young girls into lives of sexual slavery.

Adds Kall Kann: "If a girl abandons school and goes into the world early, she is also at risk of being exploited. That's why our program is supporting these girls so that they can finish high school."

Interrupting my thoughts, one girl proudly tells us that she and her mother pedaled sixteen kilometers on a shared bike because her mother wanted to personally thank us for her scholarship. Another girl dreams of being a nurse so that she can "help all the sick people" in the poor rural areas where there are no hospitals. One wants to be a flight attendant. In a quick feat of career one-upmanship, her neighbor declares that she would prefer to fly the plane.

Given that the mothers have not yet been brought into the conversation, we begin to engage them with questions to the group.

"I am curious. How many of you were able to complete secondary school?"

Not a single hand goes in the air.

"How many of you finished primary school?"

Sadly, the same result. I decide to ask a similar question, but in a very negative way: "How many of you did not have a single day of schooling?"

Ten of the twelve mothers raise their hand. There is a long pause, broken only when a member of our Cambodian team asks the other two how many years of school they attended. "I had a single year of schooling when I was five years old. After that, my family was forced to leave the city."

"I went to grade two. We were halfway through the year when the school was burned down by the Khmer Rouge."

....

Cambodia is living proof—not that the world should ever again test such a depressing theory—that the fastest way to destroy a country and its future is to decimate the education system.

In power from 1975 to 1979, the Khmer Rouge unleashed the most brutal genocide the world had seen since the reign of the Nazis in Germany. "Red Khmer" was a name applied to a succession of Communist parties whose main political ideology was the hunting down of their supposed enemies, who would be tortured, starved to death, and killed.

In just under five years the genocidal regime of Pol Pot, the Khmer Rouge leader, was responsible for the deaths of at least 1.5 million people. Let's spell that out: one million, five hundred thousand living and breathing human beings, their lives snuffed out for no good reason other than being considered "class enemies." Approximately one fifth of the nation's citizens were eliminated in less than half a decade. The Khmer Rouge had created a landscape of tortured ghosts.

The stated aim of the Khmer Rouge was to return the country to "year zero," in an agrarian paradise untouched by progress. Sadly, it wasn't difficult to be classified as an enemy of the Khmer Rouge. City dwellers were the first to be killed, with many accused of "economic sabotage" due to their lack of agricultural ability. Another telltale sign was a person having "soft" or "nonfarmer" hands. Those with glasses were considered to be educated or literate, and this was enough to send them to the torture chambers. Those of Chinese, Thai, or Vietnamese ethnicity were executed, often by being beaten with a shovel or hammer so as not to "waste bullets." Christians, Muslims, and Buddhist monks were not spared. Teachers were viewed as a threat to the nihilistic ideology of the new leadership and were put to death; 90 percent of the country's schools were burned to the ground, with most of the nation's books added to the bonfire.

As Kall Kann puts it: "In Cambodia overall, education is starting almost from scratch." He "grew up in a family that valued education as a means to tackle poverty and a key to address all issues in life." But like so many Cambodians, his happy memories of childhood were abruptly interrupted. "I lost my parents from the first day, April 17, 1975, that the Khmer Rouge ruled the country." At age twelve, he was instantly orphaned.

The mothers we are meeting today were at least somewhat lucky; they survived against long odds. But the reward for survival was not great, as they now faced a living hell on earth. They had lost grandparents, parents, aunts, uncles, brothers, sisters, and cousins. They live on indifferent patches of earth consecrated by tears. They live in a country that was robbed of those best able to help to rebuild a civil society after the defeat of the Khmer Rouge. The majority of the most educated were killed. Any who survived and who had connections outside the country had every reason to flee Cambodia and attempt to rebuild their shattered lives on firmer ground.

Cambodia was already one of the world's poorest places; then things got worse. By the late 1970s, it was a nation of orphans, traumatized, with no natural resources and no clear path to the future. The survivors inherited a country where pure anarchy met cold, calculating Darwinism. Those left behind were asked to form a government, to establish a police force, to rebuild the schools, and to teach inside them. They faced the Herculean task of building a civil society in a country robbed of its human capital.

....

The twelve mothers we are meeting today were born in the wrong place at the wrong time. Those without the benefit of literacy or even the most basic primary education face one of the toughest existences on this earth.

Noticing the sad looks on their faces, I ask one final question. "How many of you would have wanted to go to school if a program like ours had been available?"

Without even waiting for translation, every mother's arm shoots cannonlike toward the ceiling. As though their arms control their facial muscles, they also break into smiles as they think about what might have been.

....

Our staff at Room to Read can't undo the nation's tragic history. But perhaps the future will be different as a result of the actions we are taking today. The reality for these daughters might even be called hopeful. When the daughters become mothers in turn, their children will benefit greatly from having educated mothers.

The seemingly small progress we have witnessed here today in the form of eighteen girls attending school will pay for itself for generations, like a fertile farm or the shade of a sturdy oak tree. This is a small antidote, but a powerful one, against the crimes of the past. It is one of hundreds of places in Cambodia, and thousands in Southeast Asia, where each and every day the cause of education will be enlisted to help to build a peaceful, prosperous, and civil society.

The Khmer Rouge left one hell of a vacuum. But if they are the past, men like Kall Kann are the future. Once the genocidal government was deposed, Kall completed his university degree. "Having this experience, I always seek out opportunities to bring education to children in Cambodia. Education will prevent the entire younger generations of this country from having a similar experience [to my childhood]. Investing in education is essential for a better future. It helps reduce poverty, social inequality, prevent exploitation and right abuse, as well as laying the foundation for sound governance and effective institutions."

I am grateful not only for these lessons from Cambodia, but also for a few hours during which my mind can drift away from the crisis we've just narrowly averted in South Africa.

Both nations are attempting to rebuild civil society after too many "lost decades" that trapped the poorest of the poor in perpetual poverty. Both societies are suffering from severe underinvestment in human capital. This means that there will be more bumps in the road ahead. But as we drive away from the school, the girls and their mothers waving goodbye, I realize that the children suffering from apartheid's legacy in South Africa are no less deserving of a better future than the youth of post–Khmer Rouge Cambodia. And I recall the words of a trusted mentor from the days of our launch in Sri Lanka: "This is not going to be easy. We're going to do it anyway."

CHAPTER THIRTEEN

"Sorry, but Your Money Has Disappeared"

Walking up New York's Fifth Avenue on a bright, clear morning, I found that my mood was not warmed by the sun. I was as nervous as I can ever remember being. As I dodged tourists gawking at window displays of the latest fashions, my feet beat a double-time tempo toward the location of my breakfast meeting. Allen & Company, also known simply as "Allen," is one of the quintessential power centers of New York. But it is discreet power. There is no name on the door. The firm is not in the phone book. It doesn't even have a Web site. If you need to know about it, you do. If you're important enough in the media or technology or venture capital world, the firm knows about you and may even issue that rarest of invitations to its annual and hypercoveted summer soiree in Sun Valley.

At the front desk I give my name and say that I'm here to see Herb Allen, the firm's CEO and the grandson of the founder. As I take a seat on a firm green leather sofa, a short man in white shirt, black jacket, and black bow tie immediately materializes to offer me a drink. Desperately seeking caffeine, I ask for a double espresso and watch him pad quietly on plush carpet, with one noiseless step after another, down a corridor lined with dark walnut and oversized photographs of Idaho's Sawtooth wilderness.

It isn't being in the corridors of power that causes my pulse to race and my brow to sweat; it is rather the anticipation of delivering the news I am here to share with Herb.

....

After the problems in our newly established South African office had been discovered, our team had made the decision that we owed it to the investors who'd given us seed funding for our African expansion to let them know the awful truth. It was not an easy decision to make, as nobody really enjoys delivering bad news, especially to someone whose money you've managed to lose. Among many for-profit businesses, there is a tradition of viewing fiscal mismanagement as a simple "cost of doing business" in the developing world. As long as the sums involved are not earth-shattering, those problems are swept under the carpet. The mentality seems to be that nobody needs to know.

I felt differently. Just because there is an industry standard or a tradition, that doesn't make it right in my book. The litmus test I used was a simple one learned twice during my school years. In preschool we were taught, "Do unto others as you would have them do unto you." In graduate school the lesson was that ethics demanded that you always place yourself in the position of the other party.

In our case, if I'd been the seed funder of Room to Read South Africa, would I have wanted the charity to tell me what had happened? There was also one benefit, perhaps the only silver lining in this cloud: As the founder, I'd be sending a signal about the kind of organization we were trying to build—one of honesty and transparency, willing to admit mistakes and to try to use every problem as an opportunity to learn and to improve.

I am very fortunate in having a group of mentors who are willing to counsel me during moments of confusion. After I've been "in the cave" talking to myself for probably too long, I find it edifying and clarifying to sit down with someone I trust. Then I can lay out the issues for them, warts and all.

One mentor who has always been generous with his time is Muneer Satter. He is the Goldman Sachs partner who gifted me millions of frequent flier miles and predicted we'd become a twenty-five-million-dollar organization. The only thing wrong with his prognostication was that it turned out to be too conservative! No matter how busy his own professional life was, he always made time for me when I was in need of advice—which was often, given that I was operating way outside my comfort zone. I had never expected to run an education organization operating in ten countries and often found myself walking into his office at Goldman Sachs to lay my problems out on the table and brainstorm the best path forward.

The dilemma of how to best communicate with the donors to our South Africa program was the catalyst for my requesting a meeting at his New York office. Muneer listened carefully as I related the full story. While gazing out at the Hudson River below, I tried to find the words to explain why I thought that sweeping this under the carpet was not the best choice: "I feel as though one can lie by omission. And I don't buy the notion that *everyone does it this way.* What if *everyone* is wrong?"

Muneer assured me that our team had done the right thing both by going into South Africa and by firing the leader who had underperformed and exhibited fiscal mismanagement. He also agreed with our plan to tell the truth to our investors. "Both are tough decisions. They're also the right decisions." He then cited an analogy that came up often in our conversations—that of the rocket ship.

"It's important to remember something about how a rocket ship reaches Mars. When that thing blasts off the launching pad, the NASA engineers are watching everything that is happening down to the fifth or sixth figure to the right of the decimal point. They know that if the rocket ship is off course by one ten thousandth of 1 percent during the first ten seconds, it will miss Mars by several million miles. But within a few minutes they are high-fiving, as long as they can see that the outcome thus far is 99.9999 percent of what was expected.

"This is just like you and Room to Read. If you get the basics and the fundamentals right, then you're going to one day walk on Mars. If you can surround that five-year-old with everything they need to get educated, then twelve or fifteen years from now that child is going to be an educated and productive adult. But you have to get the early part of the journey right.

"You're still a young organization. It would be unusual not to make mistakes. What is important now is doing the slight course corrections—clearing out any of the wrong people and being honest with your investors. Your rocket ship, John, is on course."

The logic was unassailable; therefore the advice was easy to embrace. But now came the gut-wrenching part, actually delivering the news to the donors. Fine in theory. But now, just five miles north of us, on Fifth Avenue, was the office where the next morning I'd do the debut performance.

....

"Look who's here: the guy building libraries for the world!"

Herb filled the small waiting area with his warm greeting and then offered a firm handshake. He guided me to a small guest table at the edge of his office, commenting that he was quite curious about my request to meet on such short notice.

I envied Herb's relaxed demeanor. His suit coat was off. He kicked back in his chair with a smile on his face. He was young, tan, good-looking, with a face free of stress. He looked like a guy who enjoys being who he is; I wished I could say the same right now.

As I began to explain, we were interrupted by my waiter friend. Would I like eggs? Bacon? A bagel? "Yes, please, all three, scrambled, toasted, thank you," I barked, hoping to get rid of him so that we could go back to the process of ruining Herb's chipper mood with my bad news. As I watched the door close behind the nice waiter, I felt bad that I had been rude to him. My mind was preoccupied, my manners those of a caveman.

I took a deep breath. I had rehearsed these words dozens of times. I just needed to press "play."

"Thanks for meeting. I'm here to tell you that I really appreciate your having given us seed funding for our launch in Africa. It was very generous of you to invest in us, especially since you'd only met me twice. You took a risk on a new player."

He nodded. His brow furrowed. Obviously he was wondering where all this preamble was leading.

"Unfortunately, that risk should probably not have been taken. I am here to open the kimono and reveal everything. In short, I need to tell you that some of your money has gone missing."

He looked shocked. I continued, trying to blurt out everything as quickly as possible. There are two ways to remove a Band-Aid—quickly and painfully or slowly and painfully.

"We've been carefully monitoring our new team's efforts to launch in South Africa, and the results have not been good. We found a serious lack of financial controls and much less money in the bank account than there should have been. We've fired the leader who is responsible and we may have to do more house cleaning going forward. The only good news is that we caught the fraud early. That said, about 10 percent of our overall seed funding is gone. You know what you gave, so you can do the math. That's how much of *your* money went up in smoke. I am here to apologize and to take full responsibility."

I took a breath and continued: "When I found out what had happened, it was the worst feeling in the world. Then when I realized that the person we'd fired was also causing the children of South Africa to suffer—children who've historically gotten such a raw deal in life—I got even angrier. Now I have the fun of sharing this bad news with people I greatly respect, people who believed in me and in Room to Read. I am sorry I let you down by hiring the wrong leader. If you choose to never invest in us again, I will completely understand."

Herb offered me a reassuring smile as my waiter friend replaced my coffee with a fresh cup. Herb went into slow-down mode, talking at about a third of the speed at which I had deluged him with the bad news.

"Don't be too hard on yourselves. My first reaction is to say, 'Welcome to Africa.' You're not the first organization to experience this, and unfortunately you won't be the last. The only thing you can do is to audit early, so that if it happens you catch it early. You did, and you did. Also, the fact that you're in here telling me this says a lot about the type of organization you're trying to run. I can tell you that this is the first time I've ever had a meeting like this."

He said this with a slight laugh. But my mouth was still flatlining.

"I'm sure it's not the first time an organization in which I've invested has had management problems, or the realization that their teams didn't put the proper financial controls in place. But it's sure as heck the first time the founder and CEO showed up to tell me the news."

A sense of relief began to break over me. I could feel some of the tension I'd been carrying in my shoulders beginning to dissipate. "But you have to deliver this message to your team, and you can quote me directly. Tell them that they cannot let this experience rob them of their optimism. The children in Africa need for you to be optimists, because if you're not, then you will stop doing your work and there will be even less hope. You've done the right thing, and you need to rebuild from here. Without education, there is no future for South Africa. And since South Africa is the economic engine that pulls along the rest of the train, the other countries in southern Africa also need for you to succeed."

My head was moving up and down like one of those bobble-head dolls you see at the ballpark. I was grateful for Herb's sage advice and his willingness to try to find silver linings in our dark clouds.

I told him about how we were trying to use this as an opportunity to build an even stronger organization. We were recruiting a line-of-business CFO from Microsoft, Craig Bruya, to join our board. He would form a new audit committee and fill it with the types of people who enjoy going to parties and discussing internal controls and procurement guidelines. Here was a guy who had survived working for Steve Ballmer for eighteen years as one of his key numbers guys. This was like a financial vaccine: A guy like him could help us to prevent problems like this.

As I realized our allotted time was drawing to a close, I recounted for Herb the high hopes with which we'd started in South Africa. Because Mandela had said that education was the best way to help postapartheid democratic South Africa, my immediate reaction had been to launch our program there. When Mandela says jump, I say, "How high, sir?"

We agreed that the fall hurts all the more when it starts from such a lofty height.

By the time my artery-clogging breakfast arrived, my blood pressure was dropping. I tucked into the food like a dog that has missed its previous three meals. Herb was a class act. As I walked to my next meeting, I gave myself clear instructions: No more crying about the blow we'd been dealt. We needed to get up, dust ourselves off, and get back into the arena.

I also reminded myself that we would eventually find leadership in Africa who would exceed every one of our expectations. One day we'd look back and see the decision to go into Africa as a pivotal one in taking Room to Read to scale. We'd also recognize that navigating the bumps in the road could teach us just as much as—if not more than—countless joy-filled ribbon-cutting ceremonies.

We had to put the negative behind us now, as one of the most critical moments in our organization's life cycle was looming. The acceleration would be like that of a finely tuned Porsche or my friend Muneer's rocket ship. It would make our already-torrid rate of growth look like a Model T by comparison.

....

It was time for an appraisal on many levels. One of the things I learned from the incident in South Africa was the limit of my ability to oversee operations as the CEO given the amount of traveling I did. I was constantly in "ambassador mode," taking meetings with potential donors, speaking at business and finance conferences, lecturing at business and education schools, and doing media interviews. I had become "Mr. Outside." This was not a bad thing, as the resource engine was firing on all cylinders and our in-country teams were able to approve more projects than ever before. But a growing organization also needs someone at the top to be paying attention to the internals. No organization can scale effectively without the proper delegation of duties.

About a year after *Leaving Microsoft to Change the World* came out, the board, Erin, and I all realized that my touring and speaking and fundraising on behalf of Room to Read was potentially a permanent state of affairs. It was becoming more apparent what my role should be.

One of our board members asked me: "Do you really want to be CEO? You're never in San Francisco. You've got a growing team here."

Every time I came into the office after one of my trips, there were new people. What used to be a big, empty room where we threw a Frisbee back and forth was all of a sudden filled with cubicles and people complaining that they were too close together because we were running out of space. We had done what Bruce Jacobsen had advised—rented a bunch of empty space and then filled it with talented people.

The same board member: "If you want to be CEO, you need to be paying a lot more attention to the day-to-day details."

I had to admit these details had never been my focus.

He went on: "You don't want to run stuff. You want to build what comes next."

Again, I had to admit that he was right. When I took the Myers-Briggs personality test, I wound up being designated as a field marshal type who points to the hill and says, "Let's take it!"

"You seem like you're happiest when you're out building the next empire, as opposed to running the empire that you've actually built," Hilary, our board cochair, chimed in. She was blunt, which was hard to hear. But I appreciated it, because being blunt immediately cuts through the clutter, of which the world has too much. "Just because mundane administrative details don't mean much to you doesn't mean they're mundane to other people. You may not care about dental insurance or a retirement savings plan. But that does not mean it's not important to other people."

We brought in a consultant to figure out what my role should be. There is a chapter in Jim Collins's book *Good to Great* that outlines something called the Hedgehog Concept. Basically it says that if you want to find your role, you should look at three things. First, what are you uniquely good at? Second, what are you passionate about? And third, what drives the resource energy for your organization?

"What are you uniquely good at?" is an interesting question. You can be good at something, but if it's something that's not unique, you can always hire someone else to do it. I could be the best guy in the world at balancing the checkbook or at answering the phone, "Good morning, Room to Read!" I am so passionate about our cause that I'd probably give great phone. But we can also hire someone to answer the phone quite nicely and balance our accounts to the penny.

The question of what I was uniquely good at was pretty easy to solve. I was the top rainmaker in the organization and greatly enjoyed fund-raising. Some founders act as though fund-raising is something that you outsource to a special department, whereas I think it should be in the DNA of the leadership team. I'm also told that I'm a great public speaker, and the market seems to agree, as I always have ten times the number of invitations I can handle. Since my Microsoft days, I've been successful at marketing, PR, and media relations. Finally, a board member reminded me that I seemed to "collect talent"—that the more time I was external, the more we seemed to have great people join us as employees, chapter members, advisory board members, etc.

The second question was about passion. That was easy; I was passionate about sharing the Room to Read story with the world. I was so obsessed with telling people about our organization that I probably risked being a bore. I loved telling our story in one-on-one meet-ups, in small-group get-togethers, on a big stage, on television and radio, you name it! If there was the chance to sell others on getting involved with us, I would never turn down that opportunity.

The third question pretty much solved itself: As long as I was talking to the right audiences, this would clearly drive our resource engine. We were already seeing early signs of this—after all, what other seven-year-old NGO was already exceeding ten million dollars in annual contributions? We could only imagine what might be possible if my role was reconfigured to allow even more focus on ambassadorial work.

At that point Erin was our chief operating officer, internally focused on global operations, developing our programs, and overseeing our worldwide programs staff. She came to my office and told me, "I think I've earned the right to take a shot at this. I've been with you from the very beginning. Every time you've asked me to stretch, I've stretched. I'd like to ask for your support, at the board level, to be named the next CEO."

We used to call her Erin "Never Miss a Number" Ganju. Whatever number she was to deliver, of libraries, school projects, new countries in which to open, she never failed. The target would be hit with the frequency and accuracy of Robin Hood with his bull's-eyes. Now she was proving to be Erin "Not Afraid to Ask for the Order" Ganju.

She had clearly earned the right to be given this opportunity. After I called members of the board to discuss it, very quickly we decided that this made total sense. Her challenge would be to build a deeper management team beneath her, so that she, too, could continue to stretch and to scale.

Her path was clear and well defined. Thousands of chief operating officers have been elevated to the CEO role. There was not, however, as clear a way forward for the founder who had been CEO since day one. I had succeeded in finding "life after Microsoft." Could I pull off this high-wire act for the second time in a row?

....

The hardest part for me was the emotion of stepping aside from a role in a company I'd devoted eight years of my life to starting. Now I was going to wake up and no longer be in charge. I even wondered if it was a first step out the door of a great organization. Was there some hidden message in the board's encouragement to have my role evolve? Was "evolve" a secret code word whose meaning other people understood, even if I didn't? Room to Read was an organization I wanted to be a part of, always; but was there a side conversation going on in a room somewhere to which I wasn't privy?

But I trusted our board, and I trusted Erin. All of us had been through combat together, and every time we'd all been mutually supportive. Even with my newly defined, supposedly narrower role, there was a long list of strategic goals to accomplish, including building out a set of global boards, increasing the fund-raising chapter network, and building our brand to the point where it would be as well known as the big and more-established charities. To accomplish these big goals, I needed the freedom that came with delegating. Without delegation, there is no scaling. To truly delegate, one must overcome the stubbornness of their ego. But this is easier said than done.

As I did before all major decisions, I paid a visit to my most trusted mentor at his New York office. As always, Muneer was spot-on with his advice. "This could be the greatest thing that's ever happened to you. It absolutely *kills* you that Room to Read has to turn away communities that want new schools and libraries, families who want their daughters to be educated. The number one reason you have to say no is lack of funding. So think what happens on day one when you wake up and realize you no longer have the formal title of CEO, no longer have to be in a lot of internal meetings.

"What happens?" he asked again in an attempt to stir my imagination.

"I get my ass on a plane. I fly around the world, make speeches, talk to the media, and go to ten fund-raising events a week. I generate money, money, money—lots of it!"

"Exactly! Go, John, go! You are the best person we have at firing up an audience, at selling them on the mission of education for every child, no matter how poor their country of birth. You'll take this whole fund-raising chapter model to the next level. This will be a cash machine once there are fifty chapters up and running. I saw you at the Hong Kong event this year, and it was magical. You stood on the edge of the stage and you didn't ask the audience to raise their paddles to fund schools and libraries—you pretty much made a friendly and heartfelt *demand* for it. The crowd threw twelve paddles in the air within a minute of your asking them to fund a school. I had goose bumps thinking about that number of new schools being opened within a year. You asked them to fund libraries and got funding for fifty. But what I'll never forget is watching one, two, three, four hundred years of girls' scholarships being funded as the final act of the evening. The crowd, four hundred strong, *gave themselves a standing ovation*. You were grinning like a Cheshire cat as you announced that over a million dollars had been raised.

"Now here's your challenge, and your opportunity. What if you could replicate that event, and do it annually, not just in Hong Kong, but also in London and Zurich, in Sydney and Singapore, Tokyo and New York? If you fly around, on my miles, and make friends with the bankers and the hedge fund managers, they will get behind this big time. They're all too busy making money to think much about charity, and you make it easy, because nobody in their right mind can say that your model of education as the ticket out of poverty, and at a low price, is not a great one. You'll build one of the most powerful networks in the world. And I will help; I can start making more introductions tomorrow."

I looked outside the glass walls of Muneer's office and saw dozens of his coworkers sitting behind Bloomberg terminals, talking on phones, and doing what they did best—making lots of money. And here was one of the most successful and senior leaders in the industry, a man I so deeply respected, telling me that I had it within me to create my own cash-generating machine for a cause I cared deeply about.

"I know you can do this," he said, drawing my attention back into the room. "I can see on your face that you are already fired up. Your mind is already racing ahead with an implementation plan, isn't it?"

I laughed in agreement and then walked out onto Wall Street completely pumped up. Our entire conversation had been not about what I was losing but instead about what I would gain with this change. There was also a more subtle message from Muneer—that this decision should not be viewed through the prism of whether it was painful for me or not. The only thing that mattered was how many more children we could serve if I were completely unshackled and set loose on the world.

CHAPTER FOURTEEN

"We Picked Up the Phone to Call for Help"

Under a blazing Zambian sun, Mr. Tembo is waiting.

Our group is running late. We're making the best time we can as our rented minibus travels east on the narrow ribbon of asphalt across the flat veld. The road is barely wide enough for two snakes to cross paths. We started the day with an early breakfast in Lusaka, which is among the quietest of the continent's capital cities, with little traffic, few skyscrapers, and an absence of construction cranes. The world's real estate and building frenzies have managed to overlook this desperately poor and landlocked nation.

But within five minutes' drive, Lusaka begins to look downright bustling and cosmopolitan as apartment blocks give way to single-family homes, then small makeshift shacks with sheet-metal roofs on small plots of land, and soon enough to vast plains that seem empty of humans, habitation, or anything else. For 150 miles we've gazed out at this beautiful, empty landscape interrupted by an occasional village so small that even at forty miles per hour we appear to blow past it in the time it takes for one beat of a hummingbird's wings. Then, seemingly for no reason, the minibus stops and turns left onto a rutted dirt path—a pathless path. Only then do we notice a group awaiting us at the top of a small knoll.

The headmaster, Mr. Tembo, is the first to greet us, dressed in a white shirt with a worn collar, a blue and white striped tie, and a charcoal suit. The sweat on his brow reminds me how late we are. I apologize, but he assures me that there is no problem.

"The students, they are inside studying, and the choir is practicing their songs to welcome all of you to our school." The "you" is a group of Room to Read investors and employees. Almost all of them have seen the tourist version of Africa, full of game drives and sundowner cocktails. This is their first experience visiting an African school.

Today will be a day of truth and revelation for me. It has been just over a year since the South Africa firings. The team members who had nothing to do with the corruption have stayed on and have performed heroically, launching a new publishing initiative to produce books in all eleven official languages of South Africa. Our team has also hired a new country director for Zambia, who's started to build his own team. Rather than retreating from the African continent, we have doubled down. We have taken a calculated risk; I certainly hope it was a good one.

Like the men with the lights in each hand who guide airplanes into the gate, Mr. Tembo sweeps his hands in the direction of the two school buildings that meet at a ninety-degree angle to form an *L* shape. The path, thirty meters in length, is marked by whitewashed stones so perfectly placed they appear to have had the benefit of a ruler and level. They create some degree of order and a suggestion of progress in this otherwise dusty void of a landscape.

Lukwipa Basic School deserves a better adjective than "basic." The classrooms are relatively large and airy. There are sufficient numbers of desks and chairs. Despite the fact that the school was built over thirty years ago, the infrastructure is solid.

"Do you have enough teachers?" I ask.

Mr. Tembo says yes, they do; and as if on cue, a group emerges from behind the building where they've been setting up for the day's ceremony. We exchange warm greetings and firm handshakes. All are university graduates and have been paid an additional stipend by the Ministry of Education for working in this rural village so far from the big city.

It's always heartening to see evidence that the Ministry of Education is doing its job. It's a more frequent experience than most people assume. There is a stereotype that many government officials are lazy or corrupt. Some are, of course. But as our local teams evaluate new initiatives for Room to Read, the status of the provincial education ministry is a big factor. Will it coinvest alongside both our organization and the community residents by making sure that trained teachers show up at the schools? Will it pay those teachers and the librarians? Unless those questions can be answered in the affirmative, we'll steer clear of that country or province.

My current board cochair and the founding CEO of Yahoo!, Tim Koogle, outlines the process we use to determine which new countries to go into: "It comes down to evaluating the level of need, as well as the existing infrastructure in a country. Is there a sustainable commitment at a government level, a national government level, and at state and regional levels? How much ambition is in that country for the culture of literacy and education? How much of an NGO presence is there?" That last question is asked because the presence of other NGOs may mean there are good partnership opportunities, along with the prior development of a talent base.

"Then you have to take a finer look at the costs of entering and sustaining in an area. Less stable ones that are far more rustic from the point of access, physical access, carry higher costs. One could have a less developed local talent base, with lower costs but less potential for sustainable results. Ones that have a fully developed infrastructure of talent can be competitive enough to drive costs up for sustaining a local country presence. All these things need to be taken into account."

What we find most often is that the local officials want their community, and their nation, to develop. They believe that education is the best path toward that goal. We see that here today, just as we do in so many thousands of other villages around the world. Something must be working, as more than one thousand students attend classes here. Mr. Tembo informs us that many of the students come from homes that require a four- to six-hour walk. For them, two dormitories have been built: one for the girls and one for the boys.

Apparently the only thing Lukwipa Basic School lacked was a proper library.

. . . .

As Mr. Tembo and the teachers lead our group of Room to Read employees, investors, and chapter leaders to the welcoming shade of a giant acacia tree, my mind drifts, focusing on the vacuum we're filling. It's tragic to think of one child without access to books, yet around us stream more than one thousand students gathering for the opening ceremony. I have seen this too many times before: a huge and hopeful aggregation of young minds that have been failed by society. Yet every time it hits me as though it's a brand-spanking-new experience. It's equally depressing each time.

How many thousands of students have gone through this school and not realized their full potential in life? Thankfully, it was not a difficult problem to solve. The Room to Read Zambia team found the school while scouting out locations shortly after the launch of operations in this region of Zambia in 2008. The community and our local team reached an agreement on how we would work together: A single investor put the money in, and an effort by the community, through an appointed library committee, built the bookshelves, desks, and chairs. Voilà—one more library in a world in desperate need of them. But why the heck had this not been done years ago?

This village is a small dot on a very large canvas. There are tens of thousands of villages in southern Africa alone whose situations match that of Lukwipa. What's happened to the hundreds of billions of dollars of government-to-government and multilateral aid that's been showered on this part of the world? What about the billions of dollars' worth of copper exports the Zambian government has sold since independence in 1964? How have they missed something so obvious? These vast bureaucracies do not seem to understand something that every human being gets implicitly. After all, when a person in the developed world announces that he or she is going to have a child, one of the first things his or her friends and family do is natural: They buy books! They know that a child who grows up surrounded by books is much more likely to be successful.

Why couldn't the same thing be done for children in the poorest parts of the world? Perhaps the development "experts" would consider this a naive and simplistic notion and continue their search for a more complicated and labyrinthine aid scheme. But when one takes the time to ask parents what they want most, one of the top answers is always "education for my children."

During the three-hour drive to this school, we witnessed well-intentioned government attempts to help rural Zambia. My coworker Allison Rouse, our regional director for southern Africa, announced that we'd stop at a school halfway between Lusaka and Lukwipa. Room to Read recently agreed to establish a library here. On his last visit, Allison noticed that three cement outhouses were being built with funding from the U.S. Agency for International Development (USAID).

Here, it seemed, was finally a good use of USAID funding; after all, toilets are key for healthier children. Unhealthy children find it more difficult to attend school and to learn. Toilets for girls have also been found to be a cost-effective way to keep girls in school after they reach puberty. If the toilet block also includes clean running water, the effect on health is even greater.

At the school, a group of teenage boys in jeans, T-shirts, and flip-flops wait in front for the school day to begin. Allison asks them to show us to the toilets.

All three are locked. We stand in place, waiting. The boys laugh.

"Are they locked because someone is inside?" I ask.

"No, they're always locked," the tallest boy informs me.

"Why?"

All four boys shrug their shoulders in unison.

"Are there people around who might have the keys?"

"There is only one key."

"And who has that?"

"The teacher who has the key is not here today."

"Is he sick?"

"No. He is never here."

"And so . . ."

The four teenage boys smile shyly and wave toward the bushes. As they accompany the four American men to their preferred spot, we hear giggles from other students, hidden with less stealth than the average leopard.

I have yet to understand why anyone would design a bathroom that locks the students out.

....

Meanwhile, under the acacia tree, there is drumming, singing, and a relentlessly upbeat atmosphere that drags me back to happiness and optimism. Music and dancing are to an African celebration what champagne is to a French one. As I settle onto a bench next to Mr. Tembo, I see one of our scholarship girls, Mulenga, escorting two of our group members back from a tour of the girls' dormitory. In a space the size of my living room (which, by the way, is not that large), eighty girls sleep each night on wafer-thin mattresses atop a concrete floor. How the girls manage to sleep in these conditions is beyond me. And yet they must, because the walk home takes several hours, and most of them go home only for one day on the weekends.

I think to myself that the things in my life I consider problems are so trivial that I should be ashamed of ever complaining.

Mulenga is smiling broadly, holding the hands of both her new friends. She is thirteen years old and lives with her grandmother. Her mother can no longer work due to severe asthma. Mulenga has already signed up to work in the new library. Mr. Tembo proudly tells our small group that when he announced that there was a role for two librarian assistants, Mulenga was the first to raise her hand.

"Her arm shot up in the air instantly, she was so excited."

Maybe she was confused, thinking she would be paid. But that was not the case. She'd heard a rumor that the assistants would be rewarded with extra time in the library. Mulenga told us earlier that she loves being surrounded by books. Some of the work is a bit dull, such as arranging, labeling, and categorizing the books and dusting the floor. The more exciting part of her role is in sales and marketing.

"I encourage all the students to come in here and to utilize the library. 'Why are you not in here learning?' I ask them. 'We have a great library now, with shelves that are full of books. You have an opportunity your parents did not have.' And then I realized that I could do a better job if I

It's not enough to simply open new libraries. We work with the communities, parents and especially teachers to make sure the libraries are living, breathing places, full of kinetic energy. [*Jayson Morris*]

So many choices! As Room to Read reaches the milestone of our one thousandth local-language title published, we hope that one day every child will have a world full of such opportunities to fall in love with books and reading. [*Susie Cushner*]

Girls' Education program participant Inkham, featured in chapter 2, reading aloud to her proud, but mute, parents in Laos.   [*Monty Sly*]

Girls in Bangladesh participating in a language game during a fair promoting literacy. [© *Saikat Mojumder/DRIK*]

Mr. Zaki Hasan and his team in Bangladesh are making sure girls in the most rural areas of the country are able to be educated and learn to read through our Girls' Education program. [© *Saikat Mojumder/DRIK*]

In the schools where we work, teachers encourage the children in their classrooms, like this one in India, to be independent and confident readers. [*Anne Holmes*]

This young chap in India learned about Gandhi at his Room to Read school library. Before long, he was reenacting the Salt March in a school play.   [*Sarah Stewart*]

As Cambodia continues to rebuild after the Khmer Rouge genocide, there is a strong consensus that the best hope for future stability and prosperity is education.

[*Room to Read*]

Yet another low overhead way to travel—by oxcart in Cambodia with Room to Read Asia Pacific board member Ray Zage.   [*Room to Read*]

Busy as he is, former President Clinton has always made time to hear about Room to Read's progress and to sing our praises. One of the happiest days of my life was when he invited me to join the advisory board of the Clinton Global Initiative.   [*Jacky Ho*]

"I have always imagined that Paradise will be a kind of library." —Jorge Luis Borges
[*Peter Stuckings*]

Baby Fish Goes to School, one of our original children's books from Room to Read Sri Lanka—not just a great book but an apt metaphor for a world in need of more "fishbowl" solutions.   [*Room to Read*]

Together with the chairman of Cathay Pacific and president of Scholastic Asia, we announced the Literacy One initiative at a packed Hong Kong press conference.
[*Room to Read*]

Investors tell us their favorite moments have involved visiting Room to Read schools and libraries like this one in Sri Lanka and seeing how much our projects mean to the students. [*Jayson Morris*]

Community participation and coinvestment are keys to the success and sustainability of our projects. Here is a community in Nepal and the building site of a school project.

[*Rishi Amatya*]

One of the highlights of our annual Chapter Leadership Conference is always the Zakkie Awards. It's our version of the Oscars, only with cheap and cheerful statues.

[*Room to Read*]

Room to Read cofounder Dinesh Shrestha addresses the crowd at the opening ceremony of a new Room to Read school library.   [*ThePositiveStory.com*]

One of our first Nepali language books, titled *Mouse House,* is embraced by a young reader.   [*Rishi Amatya*]

Pasupathi Neupane, the man who showed me that first empty library in Bahundanda, was the surprise guest at the launch of the Nepali language version of *Leaving Microsoft to Change the World.*   [*Andrea McTamaney*]

Let the bidding begin! Supporters in Tokyo raise their paddles to fund Room to Read projects, including schools and libraries. Domo arigato, Tokyo! [*Room to Read*]

Sometimes multitasking starts young! These children in Vietnam demonstrate.

[*Peter Stuckings*]

With one of my heroes, Pulitzer Prize–winning columnist Nick Kristof, filming the *Half the Sky* documentary in rural Vietnam. When he wrote about our work, the *New York Times* readers donated more than seven hundred thousand dollars to Room to Read.

[*Peter Stuckings*]

I was thrilled and honored to be presented with one of the first three Microsoft Alumni Foundation Integral Fellow awards, especially since Melinda (my first boss) and Bill Gates were presenting it.   [*Jean-Marcus Strole/Microsoft Alumni Foundation*]

The team members at Room to Read South Africa have dedicated their lives to making sure students like these will find books in their library, not by picking through rich people's dustbins. [*Kim Anstatt Morton*]

With great leadership, all things are possible. My cofounder Erin Ganju with South African country director Chris Mothupi. [*Kim Anstatt Morton*]

In November 2011, Room to Read celebrated the donation of our ten millionth book. Mr. Phong Le, our country director for Vietnam, was the star of the show.   [*Peter Stuckings*]

My proud parents at the closing night dinner after the ten thousandth library opening. They always say they are proud of me. I don't say often enough how proud I am of them.
[*ThePositiveStory.com*]

When I showed my parents the school I funded in Nepal in their honor, I was overcome with emotion while thinking about all the sacrifices they'd made for my education.

[*ThePositiveStory.com*]

"We have never seen such dancing in our village!" (Zambia) [*Allison Rouse*]

Mulenga, the young Zambian scholar from chapter 24, the day we did the interview that resulted in an offer of a university scholarship. [*Room to Read*]

"Keep reading students"— the Burj Dubai acts as the world's tallest fund-raising thermometer for the Million Book Challenge.

[*Room to Read*]

A first grader learning to sound out words. Her school was one of the first in Zambia to implement Room to Read's new literacy programs.   [*Amy Powell*]

could recommend specific books that they might enjoy. So I am reading every book, so as to match up students and the stories they might enjoy."

"How will you know when you're successful?" one of our group members asks.

"I would like to see every student have the same love of reading that I have."

On a prior visit to the school, our Girls' Education program officer, Emily Leys, had asked Mulenga to select and describe her favorite book. Without hesitation she had walked directly and efficiently to a shelf and picked up *Hanan the Peanut Seller.* It's the story of a girl whose family cannot afford to send her to school. She instead works every day and earns a small amount by selling roasted peanuts outside the gates of the local school. As students take their warm nuts back into the school yard, Hanan is envious. She dreams of what it would be like if she, too, could don a school uniform and be inside, filling her head with knowledge.

"Hanan is like me," Mulenga, beaming, told Emily. "If you did not help me, her fate would be my fate. But I am inside the school, learning, not outside of it being jealous of those lucky enough to go."

When I heard Emily tell us this story during one of her high-energy trip debriefs, I made a mental note to try to visit the same school to meet Mulenga. As in so many cases when we invest in education, her story showed the kinetic energy that results when we hire strong local teams and provide relatively small amounts of funding that will be immediately and effectively deployed.

In many parts of rural Zambia, four out of five girls do not make it past seventh grade. And yet again, just as with the lack of books, people act perplexed as to why hundreds of millions of people live in poverty, generation after generation. It's the Mulengas of the world who will change this, but only if we start to be a lot bolder in finding and supporting them.

....

The tempo of the drums is picking up, and half a dozen women have started dancing. It appears that this ceremony will be very different from those in Nepal—e.g., not many speeches. The women begin to shake their bodies playfully; the crowd cheers them on. The louder the cheering, the more forceful and wide-ranging the gyrating, which then causes the drummers to pound out a faster rhythm. Several spectators contribute loud ululations. The women, mostly mothers whose children are students at the school, are large but healthy, vibrant, and full of life. They move so beautifully, as if in one effortless rhythmic heartbeat. Their natural instinct is awe inspiring to watch. The spirit bubbles out in unbridled and energetic dancing as they lift both their faces and their arms to the blue skies above.

Just then, I am confronted by that thing I fear most. One of the women approaches. She is clad in a green dress with matching head wrap that takes her height up by a few inches. Her hands are outstretched, palms up. She is inviting me to be the first man to join the dancing.

I am possibly the world's worst dancer. There are many things I do poorly, including yoga and swimming. But when you swim badly, nobody really notices, with the possible exception of the guy into whose lane you just veered. When you dance badly in this particular Zambian village, over one thousand people are going to witness the train wreck. Since I am the guest of honor, it will be all the more embarrassing.

Then I remember a quote from a college friend that I always channel when I need to be spurred on to get off my butt: "Nobody cares if you can't dance well. Just get up and dance."

Judging by the hooting, clapping, and yelling, this is a first in the history of the village. I reassure myself that they are laughing with me, not at me. With my hands outstretched, I throw my reluctance up toward the heavens and grab the hands of my dance partner. Her face lights up as we swing and sway, faster and faster to match the pace of the drums. A few more in our group join in, which attracts more of the community members. There is a lot of life and positive energy under the acacia tree.

Mr. Tembo shakes my hand as I return. With a hearty laugh, he informs me, "We have never seen such dancing in our village."

"And you never will again," I assure him with a self-conscious chuckle.

Next up is the school choir. Mr. Tembo tells us that they've written a special song in our honor and have been practicing for weeks. The choir is composed of ten boys and ten girls, ranging in age from eight to seventeen. They sing with passion and conviction, their voices clear as a bell. On each upbeat or downbeat they stamp their feet in unison.

"What are they doing with their hands?" The question comes from Stephanie, one of the chapter leaders from Greenwich, Connecticut, who has joined the donor trip I am leading.

I can't tell. Each student seems to have his or her thumb and pinkie sticking out, and each raises the hand to the side of his or her head several times during the chorus.

I relay the question to Mr. Tembo.

"You don't know what they are singing? I thought you were a smart man and could speak many African languages," he says, laughing playfully. "They wrote this song themselves. And when they raise their hands up to their head, they are singing: *We picked up the phone to call for help. And John Wood answered our call.*"

I am overcome. I've never before had a song written in my honor. The pain we've gone through in launching our operations on the African continent is now far, far from my mind, as I watch the choir members stamp their feet, raise those phones to their ears and mouths, and again make that call for help.

I lean over and whisper into Stephanie's ear: "For as long as I'm involved, Mr. Tembo and his school can have anything they want."

....

"I want to welcome you to South Africa." Chris Mothupi, our new country director for South Africa, raises his glass of Meritage to our visiting investors. "We are very excited to show you our new libraries, to have you meet the students using them, and also to see our country's famous wildlife."

Our group has just landed in Johannesburg. Still laughing and reminiscing about our experiences at Mr. Tembo's school, we were told we had just twenty minutes to check in, unpack, shower, and change clothes. The local team was waiting and eager to host us to a *braai*, the traditional South African barbecue. Fires are lit against the night, and a variety of local wildlife—gemsbok, springbok, buffalo, and even warthog—sizzles on the multiple grills.

Just over a year has passed since our corruption problems and house cleaning in South Africa. Thankfully, two of our most talented and dedicated early hires have ridden out the chaos. They've rolled up their sleeves and helped us to get on with the process of rebuilding. We've assured them that despite the early problems, we remain very committed to the African continent in general and South Africa in particular.

"This is the right decision," they've told us. "We cannot punish children for the sins of the adults."

They are now publishing inviting children's books in all eleven official languages of South Africa. They are opening beautiful libraries in remote provinces and training a large number of librarians.

After the previous debacle, I was very interested to meet our new leader. All of five feet six, Chris Mothupi wears khaki pants, a blue button-down shirt, and a stylish brown leather jacket. His welcoming countenance is every bit as warm as the South African sun that kissed the vines that produced the nectar now dancing slowly across the back of my tongue and down my throat.

"In the Setswana language," Chris tells us, "*mothupi* means 'warrior.' And the only weapon this warrior had was education. I am living testimony to its power. There is a saying in South Africa that if you educate a woman, you actually educate the nation. It's quite true, because here I am. I had a single parent who worked in Johannesburg cleaning houses and cooking for rich people. I lived with my gran and only got to visit my mother on school holidays. With her meager wages my mother managed to pay for my school fees. Now, in turn, one of my own children is at university, and the other is in high school. From one single parent we can see real progress in terms of educating South African kids."

Room to Read's gospel of self-help fits very well with Chris's personal philosophy: "We cannot continue to blame apartheid, the segregation that we suffered in the past. The time has come for us to do for ourselves. The onus is on us to prove that as South Africans we are willing to help ourselves. We have to take the lead. Then other people will come and join us. This is our message to communities out there: 'Do things for yourselves, and there will be other organizations like us who will come on board.' I like what other people refer to sometimes as 'self-help and other help.' You have to help yourself first, and other assistance will come your way. But you have to make a start."

Then he tells us a story that has us riveted to our seats, of a young

caddy passed over because he didn't offer half of his small payment in order to be chosen to go out on the links—a tale later related in Chris's own
children's book.

"If he'd been chosen, this young man would have made a lot of money
on a busy day. I tell you this story because I will be talking to you during
our trip about why I am so adamantly opposed to corruption. It is a can-
cer that affects the health of this nation of South Africa that I love. Having suffered from it myself, I understand how these daily indignities can
sap the morale and work ethic of many who want to get ahead in life.
Just one corrupt person in the right place can do a lot of damage. When
the entire system is corrupt, it strips away people's faith in that system. It
is an attack on their dignity.

"I could have chosen to go out and steal from rich white people because that would be easier and more lucrative. Or I could have decided
that, contrary to myth, hard work does not pay. The other alternative
was to play within that corrupt system and start to offer bribes myself.
We would then have one more person taking part in a system that is already pervasive and endemic."

Relief swells in me as I realize that this time around, we've hired the
right leader in South Africa. Our management team picked up the phone
to call for help, and Mr. Chris Mothupi answered our call.

We were knocked down; but we've gotten up again.

....

Despite the raw deal he's gotten in life, Chris does not seem to have a
negative bone in his body. I want to learn more about him, so we book
time to have a quiet lunch together. But with Chris, nothing is ever really
quiet. He loves to tell stories, and over the next two hours I sit back and
let his personal biography wash over me.

"Growing up black in South Africa in the 1960s and 1970s pretty
much guaranteed you were poor. I lived in a rural village with my grandparents. My father left the family when I was three, and my mother went
into the city to find work. Her visits were infrequent. But my gran and
gramps took good care of me. I was surrounded by a lot of love. It was
difficult for them to take me in, as they were already living on the edge.
The food that had barely fed two of them was now divided into three

parts. Every day I would go to school hungry. During lunchtime, I would hide in a field behind the school building. I did not want the other children to know that I could not afford lunch. I was ashamed.

"But I still went to school every day. I knew that I had to study and get good grades and read as much as I could. Only by understanding how the world works could I hope to find my place in it. One day at lunchtime I noticed another student who was also behind the school. I recognized him. He was smart, always one of the top two students. I was the other one.

"Why was he also behind the school and the outhouses? He couldn't afford to eat, either. But we told ourselves that we are as good as everyone else, because on the one thing that could be objectively measured—our grades—we always came out at the top."

A driven personality, Chris was not content to rest on those laurels. He tells me how he would do everything in his power to read as many books as he could get his eager young hands on.

I ask him how this was possible. If his grandparents were too poor to afford a meager lunch for him, could they buy books? He says they could not. Perhaps, I venture, his school had a library? Again, he shakes his head with a forlorn look that seems to say, "If only."

The situation faced by the young Chris Mothupi is one common to hundreds of millions of young people across the globe who have parents who want their kids to read. In Cambodia, the majority of children still don't have access to books several decades after the Khmer Rouge burned down the libraries and schools. The world has managed to find ways to get soft drinks, beer, and chocolate bars to thousands of rural villages, but not books.

"How did you do it, Chris?" I ask him. "I understand your love of books—I grew up with it, too. But I was lucky."

"You were lucky, but I was innovative." He laughs.

During his infrequent visits to his mother, he looked forward to Thursday nights. "I only visited my mother once or twice a year. It was a long journey to the city where she worked, and there was not enough money for bus fare. I also looked forward to Thursday nights because that was garbage night."

"Garbage night?"

"After dark I would sneak around the neighborhood going from dustbin to dustbin, knowing that some would have books in them. Those white people had long driveways." He chuckles. "The house was far enough away that they couldn't see a young black man digging through their garbage.

"I couldn't believe that white people would throw away books and magazines. It was inconceivable to me that something so valuable could be making a one-way journey to the dump. I came home with five or ten books every time. In this way I even taught myself math and learned concepts like angles, and 'pi R squared' and geography. I always wondered where these places were that I'd heard about on the radio: Egypt, London, America. Thankfully, a local family had tossed out a world atlas, so this became my way of playing Magellan, exploring the globe.

"Eventually, when I was fifteen, I even taught myself to drive from reading a book. I'd study how the car worked. One holiday I went home and told the preacher at my church that I had learned to drive from reading a book. He laughed and said, 'No, Chris, that is not the way you learn how to drive. You can only learn it by doing it.' He was white, but unlike many white men, he was very kind to me.

"Then, with a look of, 'Why not?' he let me get behind the wheel of his Ford. I was nervous but reminded myself of everything I'd read. As I pressed the accelerator twice to get some petrol into the engine, started the engine, and shifted the car into first gear, the preacher looked on in total surprise. And then we were off! I was so excited to show him my skills. I was like a proud son showing off to his father. And I think it was on this day he decided to help me to find as many books as possible, and to continue to develop my education."

Chris may have drawn a different number in the lottery of life. But he didn't let his vastly different circumstances come close to stopping him. I think of how different our childhood realities were—Spalding Memorial Library versus Thursday nights scouring the dustbins. But now it is the best of all possible worlds: Chris and I are united as teammates in a quest to reach millions of children, young versions of ourselves.

CHAPTER FIFTEEN

Nine Books Last Night

A jet zips along at seven hundred miles per hour, covering an entire time zone and three states in an hour. A bullet train exceeds two hundred miles per hour, and a taxi to the airport might hit seventy if traffic is light. A ferry plying the waters of Vietnam's Mekong Delta, however, is a tortoise compared with the modern world's hares. It offers a rare chance to slow down and watch the sights slip by in slow motion. The ferry moves at a speed that says: *Enjoy the journey, as you may be here for a while.* I believe that any day that starts on a ferry is bound to be a good day.

Along with a group of our investors, I visited Vietnam during the summer of 2007. This was my fourth trip to the country, and from the moment the Cathay Pacific jet touched down in Ho Chi Minh City (named Saigon in prewar days), it was utter bliss to be back. The chaos and cacophony of the city's streets imbue a simple walk with drama. Sidewalk vendors ply everything from spicy *pho* noodle soup to ice-cold 333 beer, while entire families zip by on single 100 cc motorbikes: Was that really a mother, father, son, and two daughters all on one bike? Yes, it was; and exactly one of them, the father, is wearing the only helmet.

The next morning the scene at the rural ferry dock is similar. Our group competes with chickens, local farmers, bicycles, and motorbikes to board the flat-bottomed ferry. Our water chariot is rusted, hulking, and ancient. It does not inspire confidence, but the water is shallow, and there are local people in longboats everywhere who would probably be willing to fish us out.

With its yellow star and red background, the Vietnamese flag snaps sharply in the wind as the last passengers board. Mostly local people, they're caught in a battle between the captain, dedicated to a punctual departure, and the deckhand, even more dedicated to revenue maximization. The latter wins and makes his best last-ditch effort to shove and cram on board every last paying client, whether human or animal.

I scramble up a ladder to the upper deck to better enjoy the view and the breeze that provides a bit of relief from the intense sun. Our group talks about the day ahead, with two big activities planned: a visit to a school to see one of our libraries in action and a home visit with some of the young scholars in our Girls' Education program to meet their families and gain insight into what their lives are like outside school.

The ferry engine rumbles and belches diesel smoke into the sky. We're soon puttering up the delta. All seems right with the world. The entire day stretches out in front of us, as only a day of travel can, offering long hours and little pressure. My eyes drink in the busy river traffic, with aqua farmers hauling up catches of catfish and shrimp in their nets and kids rowing makeshift boats to school. On one, the older brother paddles while the younger sits in the back hunched over a book with fierce concentration—a floating library.

....

On the rapidly approaching shoreline, the teachers from Dien Hong School are lined up. They scramble out of the way as the ferry begins to unload. A dozen motorbikes roar down the gangplank, as if annoyed at how slow we've been traveling and eager to make up for lost time. Women on foot carry four upside-down chickens, two in each hand, feet bound.

Our Vietnam country director, Thuy Pham, introduces the groups. The teachers' countenances are as warm as the equatorial sun. There are handshakes, photos, and a small welcoming gift from the school committee. The headmaster, Mr. Nguyen, tells us it will be a ten-minute stroll to the school. As we walk, I learn details about the school and the community. The people of this area are poor, most working as farmers on land, growing rice, or as aqua farmers, growing and processing shrimp: "The parents, they might make fifteen thousand to thirty thousand dong [one to two dollars, at the time] a day if the harvest is good and there are no natural disasters like cyclones or floods. Most of them have very little education; maybe a few years if they're lucky. But for their children they want education. Not just a little bit—all of it, as much as possible."

This passion for education means that enrollment at the school has increased to 1,500 students. Mr. Nguyen says proudly that the school now teaches grades one through ten.

The belief that education is a way for children to live a better life than their parents is a common thread connecting dozens of countries where I've traveled. In Vietnam, it's magnified by the strong influence of Confucian thought, which stresses the importance of education and intellectual development. Confucius wrote that a country can only be strong if the family is strong and that the family can only be strong if each individual is strong. Central to the character of the individual is intellectual development. Educate the child, Confucius advised, and the entire nation will benefit and live in harmony. These roots, two thousand years old, remain deep and sturdy.

Unfortunately, this desire to learn could not always be realized. The nation of Vietnam, and its rural schools like Dien Hong, faced an imbalance between the desire to learn and the lack of educational materials. From Mr. Nguyen I heard the sad reality that the village was too poor to afford a library: and what hope did they have of developing economically if their children were illiterate?

This thesis was depressingly familiar. Yet again, I was hearing it paraphrased: "We are too poor to afford education. But until we have education, we will always be poor."

....

By the time we stop in the town's small market to buy water, the temperature is already above ninety. As I watch Mr. Nguyen scramble to be helpful—making sure that everyone gets what he or she needs and is given a fair price—I reflect on the facts of our respective lives.

Forty years earlier, war raged here in the Mekong Delta. My country's leaders took sides in a civil war, sending in hundreds of thousands of troops. There was so much pain and suffering for nine long years in this region: death by machine-gun fire; jungles scorched by napalm; entire villages burned to the ground; teenagers facing off across a firing line. Neither set of soldiers understood the other's culture. All they knew was that their government had ordered them to kill the enemy.

Millions of Vietnamese were widowed and orphaned. Parents endured the horror of burying their children. There was little income to sustain broken lives or rebuild communities.

This all occurred during my lifetime and that of Mr. Nguyen. We were too young to be combatants, yet the scars from that war were a prevalent part of the history we'd both learned in school. In U.S. history books, it was called the Vietnam War. In Vietnamese history books, it was called the American War.

Had we both been born fifteen years earlier, we might have met under very different circumstances. I feel fortunate to be here today, during an era of peace, rising prosperity, and cross-border cooperation.

....

BOOM! BOOM! BOOM! My thoughts are interrupted by the loud and incessant thumping of a giant bass drum. The school band strikes up its song of welcome, and a giant dragon sways to the rapid percussion. I count sixteen legs in all and wonder how hot those students must be. A snare drum joins in. The girl playing it is less than half the size of the beefy fifteen-year-old pounding away on the bass drum, his face red with effort. "Put the biggest kid on the bass drum" seems to be standard operating procedure for school bands worldwide.

The students scramble to greet us with a chorus of handshakes and "hellos." Their red kerchiefs are bright against their crisp white shirts and blue shorts. The drum cadence gains strength as students, parents, and teachers gather and our group begins the long walk through the crowded receiving line. Video cameras roll, Nikons snap, and smiles are exchanged.

Soon we're in the shadow of a sight every bit as beautiful as the children—the new library building. Painted in a fresh coat of mint green, with white trim on the windows, the library occupies six hundred square feet adjacent to the two-story school building. A banner in Vietnamese welcomes us and announces that today is the official opening day. A buzz of activity surrounds us: students finding seats in the courtyard, the headmaster testing the microphone, teachers stretching out the red ribbon and amassing a collection of scissors that will allow everyone big and small to participate.

I am happy that as a group of Americans, we are in this small village for a positive reason. I am also reminded that it is not just one nation or nationality that is helping Room to Read grow so quickly. We've rapidly globalized our fund-raising base, and by now, in 2007, our team is raising significant funding in Australia, Canada, Hong Kong, Holland, Japan, Singapore, Switzerland, and the United Kingdom.

Thuy and I sit together and listen to the speeches by Mr. Nguyen and the local government officials. When it's my turn at the podium, my first reaction upon facing the audience is shock: Where have all these students come from? They are shoulder to shoulder in the courtyard, hanging out the windows of classrooms on both floors of the school building, and lined up along the school-yard fence. Some have even climbed onto the high branches of trees.

It is always a humbling experience to address a community. The celebratory spirit and high energy always hit an emotional chord that inspires me.

"Thank you for making our group so welcome in your community today. I wish to start by saluting the parents for working on the construction of this beautiful building. Students, you should know that what your community has given you is a treasure. It's a place where you can learn about yourself, your country, and the whole wider world. Education is a blessing, as is reading.

"Our group has traveled here in the spirit of friendship and cross-border cooperation. My own nation has caused problems for Vietnam in the past. We can't change that, but we can change the future by the actions we take today. So students, all of us want to remind you that you must make the most of the opportunity. It is in your hands. I share the conviction, along with your government, that education is the best path to a hopeful future for Vietnam. You now have opportunities your parents never had. You should honor them by studying hard and reading frequently. By doing so, you'll also contribute to the continued development of your great nation, and you will be part of Vietnam's reengagement with the world."

With that, it's time to cut the red ribbon. I encourage the four teenage girls in our group to take my place and represent us. They're along as part of a new initiative we're testing, which will eventually be branded the Teen Trek. The idea is for parents who are donors to Room to Read to bring their teenagers overseas to see how their investment is paying off and to meet the young students who are benefiting.

Room to Read has been so successful at raising money not just because of the tremendous work of our staff and of the chapter leaders but also because of our ongoing efforts at transparency and our follow-up. We're always looking for ways not only to allocate resources effectively but also to monitor the results of programs and to show donors how their money is being used. Treks are an ideal way for major donors to see concrete results of their donations.

Stephanie Scott, who has been promoted to become a major gifts officer, describes the benefits of a new program like Teen Trek: "To see the projects on the ground is the most amazing experience the donors have. We work with high-level donors who have teens who are interested in learning more about what we do and what reality is like in places like Asia and Africa." In addition to the educational aspect, this is "also about creating an opportunity for the parent and their teenager to bond."

The teenagers are thrilled to have a starring role. A fifty-year-old teacher, looking completely comfortable coaching the American students, guides them to their place. Together with teachers and community leaders, our teens choose from the dozen pairs of assembled scissors.

Meanwhile, I continue to marvel at the number of students in the school. Mr. Nguyen told me that the total was close to 1,500 and that it cost sixteen thousand dollars to build this spacious library building, to train the librarians, to provide desks and chairs, and to fill those shelves with books in both Vietnamese and English. The cost per student was about ten dollars. I run the numbers again: Is it really possible that less than the cost of a pizza back home had been the financial equivalent of this barrier preventing the school from having a proper library?

A cheer goes up as the ribbon is cut in twelve different locations, and dozens of people plunge inside to tour the library. On my way to the door I am intercepted by a student who looks about fourteen years old. He offers a self-confident smile and a firm handshake that make me think he's about to sell me a life insurance policy. With his other hand he slaps my shoulder and then proceeds to hit me with rapid-fire English.

"Hello, Mr. John Wood. I wish to welcome you to our school and thank you for our new library. My name is Thanh. I have a simple goal, Mr. John Wood. I wish to read every book in this library. First I will read every book in Vietnamese, and then I will read every book in English. What do you think of my goal, Mr. John Wood?"

"Thanh, I think that is a great goal. I encourage it. But there are a lot of books in this library, over one thousand. Do you think you can read that many?"

"It is no problem. I have already started. I came to the library last night, even though it had not opened yet. I asked the headmaster if I could come in early. He said yes, but I could not take the books out yet. So I came in last night and brought a flashlight with me.

"Mr. John," he tells me with great pride, "I read nine books last night!"

....

This is the best part of my life on the road for Room to Read: feeling the connection between the Spalding Memorial Library in Athens, Pennsylvania, and the Mekong Delta. The library always welcomed me, fed my brain, and fueled my imagination. Now Thanh and his fellow students have a similar opportunity. A week ago 1,500 kids here had very few books; a week later everything has changed. One more pin on the world map I keep in my head; and in Thanh we clearly had a young man worth keeping an eye on.

He reminded me of a young boy near the famous Angkor Wat temples in Cambodia who was so eager to read that he held a red box and stared at it, slowly reciting the words. He'd found the empty Colgate toothpaste box along the side of the road. "This, Mr. John, will help me learn English, and then I can get a good job as a tour guide."

In my earlier book I told the story of meeting Vu, a fifteen-year-old boy who worked as the night desk clerk at a tiny twenty-dollar-a-night hotel in Hue, Vietnam. Over the course of my three days there during a 1997 backpacking trip, he asked me each morning to help him to practice his English: "If I study technology, and of course English is the language of technology, then I can go to university. We will sit and have coffee, and as you sip, you can help me to learn your language."

Vu's English was surprisingly proficient, as was his grasp of technology. Impressed, I asked him to show me the books from which he was learning.

"I have just one," he said, as he reached into his well-worn dark blue canvas briefcase. He handed over the dog-eared and well-loved book.

I examined the book's cover and then quickly flipped through its pages. "This is a guide to a programmable Casio calculator."

"Yes, you know about it? Do you have one of these? This one is the CX-753 model."

I didn't have the heart to tell him that the programmable calculator on which he was learning technology was at least ten years out of date: "I have one that is, errr . . . somewhat similar. But I do most of my calculations and programming in Excel."

"Yes, you work for Microsoft; you are very smart. Today, you will teach me Excel, yes?"

"Maybe, but I was planning to go visit the Confucian temple this morning; how about later today?"

"Later today is good. But if you start now you can teach me all day."

"Okay, you drive a hard bargain. One more coffee and we will start on Excel."

"And then you will also teach me Word, and Access. I want to learn about databases." It was a command, not a question.

"Yes, Vu, I will quit my job and just move here to Hue."

"Very good, then I will learn a lot. You will be the master." Smart kid, but no sense of irony.

"But first, can you show me this CX-whatever-it's-called device that you've been learning on? You seem to have a good grasp of how to program it. By understanding how you do that, I can better explain the formulas and commands in Excel to you."

"I would show you, but I do not have one. I could never have enough money for such an expensive device."

"Then how did you get the owner's manual? And more importantly, how do you know so much about programming?"

"A Japanese tourist was here at the hotel four months ago. He left it in the trash. I guess he had finished his learning. So I picked it up and have read through it many times. But now I have learned this; it is time for you to teach me Excel."

The number of books Vu would eventually read would be substantial, and he'd one day know more about computer science than I did. Over thick and viscous cups of Vietnamese coffee, a long and fruitful friendship began. This was only the first chapter in what would become a unique, productive, and lifelong friendship.

CHAPTER SIXTEEN

On Her Narrow Shoulders
Rest a Family's Dreams

W hen she heard the news that her family would be hosting our home visit, she jumped up and down with excitement, clapping her hands.

Anh is ten years old. She is the recipient of a long-term scholarship for promising but economically marginalized rural girls in Vietnam. When her school's headmaster announced that fifteen of the program's supporters were interested in visiting the girls in their home environment, she begged her parents to take part. The family had never hosted guests from outside the Mekong Delta, let alone from outside Vietnam.

So as not to overwhelm any one family and its limited financial means for entertaining honored guests, we planned to split into five groups of three. From Anh's perspective, that meant there would only be five "winners." She was determined that her family would be one of them.

Though she didn't know how the decision would be made, she was confident enough to begin thinking about what she and her family would do if they were chosen. They'd sweep the dirt floor of their open-air bamboo hut even more thoroughly than usual. Their only animal, a hog, would be moved out back to clear the entrance path for the guests. They would use some of the family's scarce dong to buy half a dozen ears of corn. By breaking each ear in half, the offering of this afternoon snack would appear less paltry. Once the guests arrived, she would bring her notebook out from its hiding spot and show off her art work, free-hand sketches done with her precious and treasured colored pencils and crayons.

....

Anh's family was indeed chosen, and our group (especially the teenagers) is excited to meet them. Our Vietnam team tells us that Anh is excelling academically, despite the fact that her parents had little education and that the family has no books.

The teachers at her school have put us on the backs of their motor-bikes and driven us for twenty minutes to the rural hamlet where thirty of our scholarship girls live: fifteen teachers, fifteen tourists, and fifteen motorbikes. They ask nothing from us in return. The subject never comes up; to them it would be insulting to even raise it. In Vietnam, teaching children is a revered profession. Since we are helping them to educate more children, they would probably do anything we asked them to, in-cluding driving us all the way back to Ho Chi Minh City, 120 miles to the north.

Once the road ends, we walk along raised earthen dikes. Each is tight-rope narrow, topping out six to nine inches above the rectangular water plots. Some contain rice, while others are home to fish, shrimp, and tur-tles. If we are served a snack, let's hope it's one of those first options. I had a turtle growing up and could never imagine practicing "Myrtle-cide."

Each family has a small hut somewhere along this patchwork of water and hard-packed dirt. The walls and roofs are made of straw thatch. They look to be no bigger than they need to be; there are no McMansions in the Mekong.

Anh waits outside the hut, eager to welcome us. All four and a half feet of her stand proudly erect and ramrod straight. Her parents offer us handshakes and nervous smiles. This is obviously as big a deal for them as it is for us. I feel as if we were imposing ourselves—that I am a big buf-falo of an American stumbling clumsily through their village. But I re-mind myself that our aim is true: We have seen these girls in their school and in their library, and we want to know what their lives are like at home. If we're invading, it's only because we're hungry for this knowledge.

Says Emily Leys, global director of the Girls' Education program: "Now we have what we call an 'enhanced approach' for girls' education. We're working with individual girls, assessing their circumstances. Our teams get to know a lot of what's happening with girls in their families. Drawing that line between what we can have an effect on and where we can or cannot get involved—most importantly, how we refer girls and families to the other support networks in a community—becomes really, really important."

To break the ice with Anh and her family, I pull out my trusty Polaroid camera and begin snapping portraits. This trick has overcome language barriers in places ranging from Burma to Bhutan. Anh stands close to her older brother, her smile beginning to loosen. Then I snap a photo of her parents, who appear healthy but rail thin. Watching each photo develop over the course of sixty seconds provides time for us to bond.

Even in rural Vietnam people know how to, in the immortal words of the musicians in Outkast, "shake it, shake it, shake it like a Polaroid picture." As the colors and hues emerge slowly, there are "oohs" and "ahhs." Anh scoots over to her parents' side to share her photo. Her mother points proudly at the image of her daughter, then at that of her son, and says something in Vietnamese that makes Anh laugh.

There is never any question here of family support for Anh. We have been invited inside the home of parents who couldn't be prouder of their daughter.

The ice has been broken.

The house is a room, and the room is a house. Its centerpiece, and the only significant piece of furniture, is a bamboo bed. Though it's roughly the size of an American queen, there is no box spring, no mattress—nothing except for a frame holding up a thin bamboo base. All four family members share the bed each night. Thankfully, there is a mosquito net. My first thought on seeing the stagnant water in the surrounding rice paddies was how potentially lethal the insect population must be. The toilet is outside. Or, more accurately, outside *is* the toilet. Next to the bed is a small single burner. The kerosene flame flares loudly underneath a boiling pot of corn.

The three foreign guests are invited to sit in the place of honor. Carefully we balance on the side of the bed, and by squeezing close we make room for our interpreter. Anh's mother sits on one of the two minuscule woven stools, so small that it looks made for a cartoon mouse. Anh perches beside her mother, pressed tightly to her side. Showing respect for his father, the son, Bang, remains standing.

Through the interpreter, we learn that the family scratches out a meager existence from this small plot of earth. It must not be much, because seventeen-year-old Bang looks twelve. A male teenage frame should be filling out, not looking deflated. The parents did not enjoy more than a few years of schooling. As in too many parts of the world, war and its aftermath got in the way.

Experts often define "postwar" countries as those that exited a conflict three to five years ago, as though time were capable of waving some magic wand and then, presto, the country were suddenly *post-postwar* and all were for the best in this best of all possible worlds.

The reality is that wars annihilate educational opportunities for children. You may as well define the postwar period as lasting for five decades. I ponder this because a number of foundations have told me that if Room to Read is working in "postconflict countries," we do not meet their funding criteria. They say this with a straight face. In their Western minds, they may have already moved on, along with their funding dollars. That is a nice luxury to have.

Yes, I think, *you should go tell that to the children of postapartheid South Africa. Explain that to the child in Cambodia whose village school was burned down, and the teachers bayoneted by the Khmer Rouge.* "If only your country's conflict was more recent, then we could help you." I am sure they would understand.

Bang would not. He had to drop out of school in the eighth grade. His parents just did not make enough to pay for food, school fees, books, and school supplies. When I ask what he does now, I'm told he lives here at home and does what he can, patching the dirt walls of the dikes and helping with rice and shrimp cultivation.

Does he have dreams?

He does for his sister, but not for himself.

He is not the only member of the family who has invested hope and optimism for the future in Anh. The mother tells us about how well her daughter does in school: "She is always in the top of her class. Were it not for your support, Anh would have had to drop out after grade four. I am appreciative; we are all so appreciative," says her mother, her coal black eyes blazing. She reaches out to touch my hand.

"We know that Anh will finish school," she says. "She will make us proud. She will always be in the top of her class."

Her father interjects: "Even if I die now," he says, emitting a cough that I hope is not a harbinger, "I know that Anh will do well and will support our family going forward. My wife and I know we'll be looked after in our old age."

All eyes turn to Anh. She looks so young and fragile, and perhaps a bit overwhelmed by this sense of responsibility. I wish I could hug and reassure her that we are with her on this journey—that whatever obstacles she runs into, we will help her to overcome them. I hope she realizes that our Girls' Education program is not a short-term thing, not one of these dreaded Band-Aids that the world always seems to offer the developing world. She should not be crying now, during what was supposed to be the happy day she'd been plotting for weeks.

I promise her: "You will be the first member of your family to finish school." Then I add a caveat to let her know that we cannot offer her equality of outcome, only equality of opportunity. "We will be with you to the end, as long as you study and pass to the next grade."

"She *will* study, and she *will* excel."

The mother's interjection, although abrupt, is not a rude or disrespectful one. It is said with pride. During the last rainy season, she tells us, the entire family told Anh that she didn't have to go to school. After all, the walk—which takes forty minutes on a dry day—would now require two hours in each direction while negotiating ankle-deep mud along many parts of the dirt road. Anh stomped her foot and cried. She had misunderstood her parents, thinking that they had ordered her to stay home, rather than simply offering her that option.

It was an option she chose not to exercise, her mother proudly informs us.

"Anh told us that she loved school, loved her teachers, and would be sad to miss a single day in the school's library. Your local team had bought the girls boots in preparation for the monsoon. And every day she got up earlier than usual and pulled on her boots and then her backpack. She put her rain poncho over the backpack to keep her books dry. Nothing was going to stop her." (Wherever possible, we "layer" our programs. As an example, when we build a primary school, we also establish a library within it. The participants in our Girls' Education program receive supplementary books to help encourage them to read outside school hours.)

By now Anh's tears have been replaced by a proud smile. There is no warmer moment in a child's life than sitting at her parent's knee, listening to a story in which she is the hero.

"Look at all she's done," her mother exclaims as she points to the hut's main wall: awards for her art, for her grammar, for her penmanship. The wall is lined with academic awards stacked in a four-by-three grid. And Anh is only in fifth grade.

Then I realize that these academic accolades are the only things hanging on any wall in the hut, period. They are the sole adornments. There is a fierce pride here. But along with that, for Anh there is intense pressure. To take the pressure off and to allow her to revert to being a ten-year-old for a few moments, I ask Anh about her artwork. Letting her know that our local team has praised her skills, I ask her to show some of her work to Alex, a seventeen-year-old from Seattle who is part of our travel group. Perhaps sharing student to student, girl to girl, will be less intimidating. Anh's eyes light up as she scampers off to liberate her notebook from its secret hiding place, though there aren't many secrets in a one-room, open-air hut.

Meanwhile her father has drained and salted the corn and now offers it to the guests. Realizing that none of the family members has tried the corn, I make a "Please, eat" motion with my hands. They refuse. The food is for us, the honored guests. Through the interpreter, we point out that the honored guests would be honored if they would join us. Again they say no.

I'd like Bang, who could gain fifteen pounds and still look thin, to have my last two meals and then my next five.

Thankfully, the Room to Read team in Vietnam has taught us how to handle this situation. The only thing we can do is act as though we are satiated. If we feign being filled up and then leave, the family will finish the food we have not consumed. In other words, we should eat enough to not insult them, while also leaving as much as possible behind.

I think of how often I've been blessed to experience this level of hospitality shown to the traveler. From Burma to Morocco to Turkey, people living on the economic margin have shown extraordinary generosity. "Eat, eat," they encourage, refusing to take no for an answer. "This is all for you, our guest," they say as they point to heaping plates. It is the best and worst of all worlds. One is always touched by selfless magnanimity, especially while being a stranger in a strange land. But there's also the painful realization of knowing that one's hosts can't afford the gift one is being encouraged to receive.

Meanwhile, Alex and Anh are hitting it off big time. They have gone through the entire book, at least fifty drawings in all. Anh asks her new friend, "What is your favorite?" Alex thinks for a moment, leafs through the book, and points to an illustration of a Vietnamese princess clad in bright red. "This picture is the one I love best."

In a flash, there is the sound of paper ripping. "No, no," Alex insists, "please don't." It is too late. Anh is proud that Alex liked her art and is insisting that she go home with a reminder of her visit. Alex is in tears. We are being called back to our two-wheeled motorcade. There is only time for a few more Polaroids. As I snap away, I am overwhelmed with happiness that we are here but also in awe of the challenges this family is trying to overcome. Its hopes for a brighter future are high risk, entirely on a ten-year-old set of shoulders—a very narrow set of shoulders.

....

Stories like Anh's inspire our team to never stop moving forward on two fronts: finding ways to get more girls in more places into the program while simultaneously raising enough money to pay for it all. We are painfully aware that every day more than one hundred million girls wake up and don't go to school. More than four hundred million girls and women lack basic literacy, which is the cornerstone of a solid education. This is a massive system failure. Every day, this reminder drives me to stay in high gear and fast motion. One of my mantras is that every day we lose is a day we can't get back.

My hope is that one day we will have built a movement that is so large that we will have a million girls like Anh in our program, with two million proud and supportive parents urging them on.

After meeting Anh's family, I thought often about her father. In contrast to many adult males in the world, he was supportive of his daughter being educated. In many places, the main barrier to the Room to Read education program for girls has been economic, but with a gender twist that works against girls.

Observes Emily Leys: "In some countries, girls are held back for economic issues, coupled with bias; the family may not have the resources to send all the children to school. For the most part, they'd rather support their son. The daughter is going to be marrying into another family. Why water your neighbor's lawn?"

Once these challenges are overcome, it's a somewhat straightforward process to get the girls into the classroom and to provide them with the after-school tutoring and mentoring that will help them succeed. Yet in many other places there are serious attitudinal barriers to gender equality in education. The men are often in charge, and their resistance can run the gamut from the benign (simply ignoring the issue so that the status quo never changes) to the shockingly evil (burning down girls' schools).

Emily adds: "Working with girls in isolation is not enough. We've redoubled our efforts to work on their environment, to make it as conducive for their ongoing education as possible. Some of that involves engaging men and boys." I'd personally seen some of these sessions taking place in which parents were asked, "Why is it assumed that the girls should be cleaning the house and cooking while the boys play soccer?" or were told that in most parts of the world, it's become the "new normal" for women to attend university, so why not have similar goals for their own daughters?

As I thought about these attitudes, I found myself wondering if absence of education for men might be a factor in their desire to rob women of the same opportunity. Might their own lack of schooling be contributing to male insecurity and misogyny?

I had no way to prove this, but I had a gut feeling that there might be a certain irony at work. The brutal logic (or lack thereof) that often strangles any hope of human or societal development in the poorest parts of the world could once again be revealing its ugly face.

In order to fight the scourge of gender discrimination, I had to understand it. Study it. Debate it. It was necessary to stare the enemy in the face. To start, I asked myself a simple question: Was it educated men who tried to deny this basic right to girls, or was it the uneducated ones?

I tried to get inside the minds of those who stood in the way of progress. How was it that they'd become convinced that women were ignorant and inferior and not deserving of an education?

"Stupid woman!" I'd heard this curse in too many parts of the world.

Nobody is born thinking this way. I am way too much of a Pollyanna to believe that humans are that mentally bankrupt at their core. What child thinks that as his mother greets his birth by holding him close, feeding him, responding to his cries in the middle of the night?

Stupid. Woman. It has to be taught.

I grew up in classrooms where I witnessed girls and later women routinely kick my butt academically. Little Katie won the spelling bee I'd spent weeks cramming for, completely nailing the word I had misspelled: "serendipitous." Just my luck! In grade nine, Andrea always had the right answer during biology class. As she proudly answered our teacher's questions, our gang of young male "scholars" was busy mutilating the corpses of previously dissected frogs while hatching an after-school plan to blow them up with firecrackers. During college, I survived a week in Spain without starving only because my girlfriend would whip out flawless restaurant *español*, while I meekly asked for the only menu item my peanut brain was capable of ordering. As my *cerveza* arrived, I would offer our waiter my best "*merci*."

While I'd never stereotype to the extent of saying that girls are de facto smarter than boys, I'd certainly witnessed sufficient evidence to opine that we men would be getting a good deal if we agreed to call it a draw.

Unlike some other men, I'd been fortunate enough to be educated through high school and beyond and had never been in a classroom that was not close to gender equality. But not everyone was like me. There were two other types of men out there: those who had not received much, if any, education and those who had been educated, but in an all-male environment.

What about the boys and men educated at madrassas that excluded girls? If their teachers had told them that girls were ignorant, inferior, and unworthy of education, they might just believe it. After all, there was no evidence to contradict this claim. The boy sitting in front of you might be smarter, and the boy to your left dumber, but there was no comparison set that included girls. They were pretty much the unknown in the equation. Bigotry is almost always most prevalent in those who don't know the people against whom they are biased.

I thought about how different things could be. Were the Katies and the Andreas of my childhood sitting in the same classroom, calmly nailing the reading-comprehension questions and the math equations, the boys would have a ubiquitous presence giving them daily evidence that the misogynists are wrong.

And what about those who'd received little or no education: How can a man who dropped out after second grade even begin to understand what an educated mind looks like? Are we to trust a person with a fifth-grade education to define the structure of an ideal society?

I tried to avoid judging these men too harshly. Who was I to say that I was somehow superior to them? They were the products of their childhoods and their environments, just as I was. Perhaps I had simply won the lottery of life in a way I had not previously understood, having grown up in an environment that taught me to respect girls and women.

As I thought more about this issue, I also wondered if there was evidence of yet another catch-22. During my first trip to Bahundanda, I'd heard a headmaster say that his village was "too poor to afford education" but that "until we have education, we will always be poor." Now a second paradox presented itself: There were many societies that believed girls were ignorant and not deserving of education. But if the vast majority of the girls didn't ever go to school, didn't this just become yet another self-fulfilling prophecy in a world that already had too many of them?

Our belief that boys will benefit when they learn alongside girls is one of the reasons Room to Read has never opened an all-girls school. We believe that communities and indeed entire nations will be better off if men and women grow up in proximity. A child who completes twelve years of coed schooling will have spent at least 2,500 days in the company of the opposite gender. Girls and boys will have spent their most formative years in each other's company, literally growing up together.

Could this become the new normal? How different would the world be if this vision were to become reality? We were likely to find out one day, as we raced through 2007 opening schools at a rapid rate. There was a substantial backlog of communities requesting our support and willing to eagerly embrace our challenge-grant coinvestment model. We were on track to open our thousandth school by our ten-year anniversary in 2010.

In every one of those locations the boys and the girls would be in the same room, every class, every day, learning together. They'd be not only receiving an education but also learning the lesson of tolerance and peaceful coexistence—in a word, equality.

This is one more way education has a ripple effect. It's the one issue that affects every other issue. Done right, it might even produce a generation of men who deeply respect women, and vice versa.

CHAPTER SEVENTEEN

Mr. X

Two months after my visit to Vietnam in the summer of 2007, we've planned a big night in San Diego to help more kids like Thanh and Anh. Inspired, three of the investors who went on the Vietnam Trek have spent months planning a big Saturday-night fund-raising party. One of them, Renee, has offered up her beautiful home in the hills north of San Diego, just east of the famous beach at Del Mar.

It's a perfect October night. The sun is setting over the Pacific. The crowd has formed early, and a cool breeze caresses them. As darkness descends, the stars above twinkle like a mirror image of the candles lining the pool.

I am in the kitchen with Renee when our friend Marshall bursts in with news. "Guess what?" His voice is loud and insistent. His timing is off, as I have just shoveled two duck buns into my mouth.

"Mr. X just sent me a text message. He's on the way to our event. He's flown down from San Francisco in his jet. He just landed and said, 'Tell John—since I know he will not be shy about asking—that I brought my checkbook.'"

Our trio is giddy with excitement. We have been pursuing Mr. X for a year. It looks like, in Rod Stewart's words, "tonight's the night" and "it's

gonna be all right." I celebrate with two more duck buns. "To build up my energy stores," I explain to Marshall.

Mr. X is a legendary investor with more money than God. Long ago he quit working for investment banks, as it was more profitable for him to be out on his own. His reputation was of being brilliant at math and a very tough negotiator.

Knowing that he was thirty minutes away, we break camp in order to mix and mingle with our guests. We know that once Mr. X arrives, we'll need to feed his not-insignificant ego by paying a lot of attention to him and making sure he has a jolly good evening.

....

As I present my brief slide show, Mr. X paces in the back of Renee's living room. Bearded, tanned, fit, and dressed in jeans, loafers, and an Armani blazer, he looks like the definition of success. He also resembles a tiger trapped in his cage at the zoo, striding back and forth, his cup running over with boundless energy.

Am I boring him? Apparently not: He does several "air punches" when I present our results. He nods vigorously when I make the case for running a tight ship. He appears to be paying attention, to be captivated by the presentation. He is just running laps in the process.

As always, I close with a direct appeal. You can't grow an NGO if you're shy or if you beat around the bush. I've heard too many people apologize when asking for money or say, "Even if you only give a small amount, that's okay, too." I don't give people that easy an out, especially with a wealthy crowd like this.

"All of us who've done well in life have education to thank. Without education, few if any of us would be in the position we're in today. We're amongst the luckiest 5 percent of the world's population. If you've benefited from the lifelong gift of education, the best thing you can do is to pay it forward and give that same gift to a child in one of the most resource-deprived parts of the world. Tonight we are offering you that opportunity. Not to donate, but to invest. Not to give a hand out, but a hand up."

There is another hand up; Mr. X's is flying in the air, waving like he's trying to hail a cab in Manhattan at 6:00 P.M. on a Friday. "I have an announcement to make," he shouts. All seventy-five well-coiffed heads turn 180 degrees. The room is silent. Mr. X plays it out skillfully. In the time it takes for a phone to ring three times, he moves to the front of the room and stands next to me.

There is a continued hush. The crowd waits.

This guy is good, I think. He could add "thespian" to his CV.

"Okay, everyone, I'm aware that nobody at this party knows me. But I want to challenge all of you. These guys are doing really great work, and they deserve our support. So I'm going to make you an offer I hope you won't refuse. If you write a check tonight, I will match you—with no limit. You can go as high as you want. I can afford it."

What an offer! The group gives the new guy a spontaneous and sustained round of applause. He beams, turning his face both ways to bask in their affection like an actress at the Oscars.

It takes people all of two seconds to begin making public declarations.

"I'll sponsor a school."

"Count my wife and me in for a library."

"I'll also sponsor a school. I wasn't planning to go that big tonight, but I've been looking for a way to honor my deceased husband, and since you're matching . . ."

Marshall and his fiancée, Darah, declare that instead of buying thank-you trinkets for their wedding party, they'll sponsor twenty years of girls' education at $250 per year, $5,000 total. Knowing that they are saving their money for Marshall to begin his MBA studies, I am inspired. Every dollar they donate will mean a dollar of additional student loans.

So I match them with my own five-thousand-dollar pledge. The spirit of generosity is flowing through the room. There is an electric current moving from guest to guest. Everyone wants to do something, and I commit to myself that I will give away twenty scholarships as wedding, holiday, and birthday gifts. Also, that is a lot easier than a trip to the crowded mall.

As each new declaration of support is made, the person raising his or her hand looks directly at Mr. X. He is beaming with pride at all the activity and energy he has catalyzed. His marketing director, who has flown down with him on his private jet, pledges five thousand dollars and tells me later that it is the largest charitable donation she's ever made.

Our hostess, Renee, despite already having given generously earlier in the year, also makes a commitment—as does her boyfriend, after feeling her sharp elbow hit his midsection.

And then Mr. X pledges twenty-five thousand dollars to build a school.

"Wait," I say, always the guy needing data and seeking clarity. "Are you going to match yourself?"

"Hell, yes!" he roars. "My son's twelfth birthday is next month, and I will do this in his honor."

More applause; some of the attendees, preferring to be a tad more discreet, make their way to the donation table. Renee and I wrap things up by thanking everyone for coming and for their generosity. We give Mr. X a final round of applause.

All seems right with the world. No one wants to leave. As we tally up the final total, guests continue to mingle. Mr. X is playing Chopin on the piano. A foursome takes over the pool table.

Then Renee appears with a bottle of champagne. We have raised $141,000, she announces. With Mr. X's matching gift, we'll be at $282,000. That's a lot of money. But take it to the developing world, where money goes so much further, and it's a heck of a lot. This is enough funding to sponsor education for more than 1,100 girls or to open seventy libraries, serving nearly thirty thousand children. Our mood is ebullient. The postparty is bound to go on for a few hours.

....

I wanted to take Mr. X out for dinner to thank him for his investment. Unfortunately, it never arrived.

....

"Hi, it's John Wood again. I know you're annoyed hearing from me so often. But I need to know whether you're planning to pay your pledge."

"I thought I already did. I sent you guys a check a few months ago."

"Yes, you did. And you probably received my thank-you note. But unfortunately the check bounced."

"It didn't bounce. We had closed that account. We're always moving money around. We move money with speed, all over the world!" the master of the universe explained.

"Uh-hmm, so you're aware that you still owe us the money."

"Uh, yes. My finance guy screwed up. He is supposed to be sending you a check from another account."

"We've followed up with him five times. He doesn't return our calls or e-mails."

"Let me check into it and I'll get back to you."

I thought he intended to honor his words. Sometimes I can be quite naive.

....

We played a little cat-and-mouse game. I would call and be told, "He's in a very important meeting."

I would e-mail but get no response. I'd ring again, only to learn that he was on his jet going to Cabo San Lucas for the weekend to sail. The next time I called, his team would tell me, "Mr. X and Sammy Hagar [the singer for Van Halen] are on the way to open a new tequila bar in which they're coinvesting."

Clearly his nonpayment was not due to a lack of liquidity.

I had become Ahab chasing the whale, even as people on our team told me to give up. But I was stubborn, though after a year it felt like I was throwing good effort after bad. The children we serve needed him to honor his pledge. Not to mention all the people at our event who had been inspired by his "generosity" to donate more than they had planned. Didn't he owe it to them—in addition to our students—to make good on his very public pledge?

Back in San Francisco after a fifteen-day business trip to Europe and the East Coast, I was reviewing our financials when I saw once again that the Excel revenue-forecasting spreadsheet had a big zero next to his name.

I dialed his hedge fund's main number. His receptionist answered on the first ring.

"Hello, this is Mr. Gerhard von Tromp. I am calling from the private wealth office at Bank Julius Baer in Zurich. One of our biggest clients—a very prominent family whose name I am *not at liberty to disclose at this time* [try to say this in a fake Swiss German accent—a really snobby old-money one—for full effect]—is quite interested in investing up to fifty million dollars—*perchance more*—in your new Middle East fund. Would it be possible to speak immediately to Mr. X? It's quite late here in Zurich, and I am hoping to go home soon."

Within fifteen seconds, Mr. X was on line one.

"Hi. It's John Wood, calling about your pledge."

"What the . . . ?! I thought you were calling from Zurich."

"No, sir, I'm just across the Golden Gate Bridge from you. Want to have lunch? If you bring your check, I'll treat." I laughed, hoping that humor could do its trick and loosen the tension.

"Hang on—I must have picked up the wrong line."

In the background I heard screaming barely muffled by his mitt covering the mouthpiece. The F-bomb was dropped more than once. Someone was in Big Trouble. I hit my speakerphone's mute button as I emitted an evil chortle worthy of Snidely Whiplash.

"Mr. X, please—can we talk?" I pleaded to be heard over the cacophony at his end of the line. "I promise that I only need two minutes!"

He came back on the line. I resolved to be diplomatic but firm.

"Why are you calling me?"

"I'm just calling to ask if you can fulfill your generous pledge. It's now been more than a year that we've been asking."

"Are you sure? You need to check your records. I think your people are incompetent."

"I have checked. Our team is good. They pay close attention and have been really patient in trying to work with your team to get the donation paid."

He began grasping at straws. "You're probably looking for a check. We're now paying all of our invoices by wire transfer. It's more efficient." The self-proclaimed paragon of efficiency said this without noting the irony as he continued to waste both his time and my own.

"Great, we accept wire transfers—as your team would know, because we've sent them the instructions at least half a dozen times."

"I'll wire you the money today or tomorrow. I am between assistants and my last one obviously screwed this up."

He continued to throw gorilla dust in the air, as I pictured his nose growing longer. I tried to appeal to his human side.

"Do you understand how humiliating this is for me? I don't enjoy begging for money. It's the worst part of my job. I'd like to also respectfully point out to you that Room to Read is now out this money. We built schools, established libraries, and added girls to the program, assuming that you'd make good on your very public and effusive pledge. That money is gone."

Silence.

"If you're having cash-flow issues, maybe we could break the amount into four installments, and you could pay a quarter of the amount every three months?"

"I don't have any cash-flow problems. All of my funds are doing really well," he said with utter self-confidence.

"That's good news. From our side, we have done everything we promised to do. We even sent a report to your son at his mother's house showing him the school that was built in honor of his birthday. He saw the dedication plaque with which his father honored him."

His side of the line was still quiet.

"You'd never tell my son, would you? Or"—a note of panic seeped into his voice—"my ex-wife?"

"I'd certainly prefer not to. But can you just promise to get this over with in the next five minutes, be done with it, take the tax deduction, and go back to your day job? I promise to never ask you for funding again."

He agreed to wire the money that day, or the one after. "Or maybe next week—this week is really busy."

You won't be surprised to hear that this story ended badly. Mr. X turned out to be Mr. Zilch. Yet on his Web site he continued to list himself as a "major supporter" of Room to Read.

....

As difficult as it is, I try not to let myself get too frustrated when dealing with situations like that of Mr. X (and am thankful that he is a rare case). I admit to finding it impossible not to be angry. Patience has never been my strong suit. But there is a certain point at which anger is counterproductive. To me the key is to get it all out as quickly as possible. Hit the gym. Go for a run. Leave all the bad stuff out there, and then get back to work.

I can't control whether people like Mr. X make promises that they have no intention of honoring. The only thing I *can* control is how I react to it. And if the anger lingers, it will spill over and cause further harm. There is much to be said for moving on.

Fortunately, there are many people out there whose word is indeed their bond. For every Mr. X, there are thousands of people making small donations that—ten to twenty dollars at a time—collectively add up to game-changing amounts. For every Mr. X, there are hundreds of successful executives who have strong ethics and have gone out of their way to help us.

In fact, one of our biggest moments of 2007 came as a result of one of these business leaders proposing, and then executing, one of the most breathtaking ideas we'd ever heard.

CHAPTER EIGHTEEN

Now Departing for Cambodia: *Literacy One*

Our team was racing through 2007 in hypergrowth mode. The global economy was strong, and the financial markets were booming. Communities across the developing world were embracing our challenge-grant model. Literally thousands of communities in the eight countries where Room to Read was working were in the queue to build new schools and libraries. Our network of fund-raising chapters continued to grow in both number and effectiveness. As a result, we were able to approve many more projects than in prior years. Only seven years old, we were achieving a scale I could never have dreamed possible during those first days back in Bahundanda.

We were hiring employees as rapidly as possible. But this took time. There is a downside to being superselective about whom you hire: It means a lot more time spent screening applicants and putting them through lengthy interviews full of tough questions.

On many occasions, by the time candidates got to the final round with me, they would comment that this had been the most intense interview process they'd ever been through. They had not expected a "small nonprofit" to be so dogged and thorough. I'd smile inwardly, recalling my own seven-hour interview at Microsoft in the early days. One of our executives had once shared his personnel strategy: "No matter how smart your coworkers are, you can't hire any candidate who is not above the average of those already within the company. If you do that, it starts an inevitable downward spiral."

Erin had cut her corporate teeth at two companies that, like Microsoft, placed a premium on finding the right talent: Goldman Sachs and Unilever. We agreed that this was one of those critical "rocket ship" issues. The next person we hired would be involved with hiring the next ten, and those ten would hire the next hundred—and so on. Like ripples in the pond from a dropped stone, their influence would radiate outward in ever-widening concentric circles. If we hired B players, they'd hire other B players. But if we got the right people on the bus (a mantra borrowed from Jim Collins's management bible, *Good to Great*), we could grow with quality without losing our core values.

Says Tim Koogle, former CEO of Yahoo! and now my cochair of the board of Room to Read: "There's a real uptick of people who've been lucky enough and fortunate enough, and have worked really hard enough, to get to a place where they can give back with their time and capital. Many of them come from a business environment where they've been trained to think in terms of return on investment. A lot of what it takes to build and scale an organization on those fundamentals is very like scaling a business. I agreed to be on the board because Room to Read operates more like other really well-run organizations in the for-profit world than what I've seen in the not-for-profit world."

Our fund-raising growth was surging ahead at a torrid pace. We'd raised a record $9.3 million in 2006 but were tracking to exceed $17 million during 2007. Our revenue growth of 70 percent was actually faster than that of either Apple or Google during the same period (albeit off an admittedly smaller base).

With the increased funding, we made plans to add more than 1,700 scholars to our Girls' Education program during 2008 and to open 155 schools. We were also on track to open more than 1,600 new libraries in just twelve months. I was astounded by the implications of these numbers: We were opening a new school every two and a half days and establishing more than four libraries per day. A new library was opening every six hours.

By the middle of 2007, we realized that our little start-up was approaching a major milestone. We were on track to open our five thousandth library by the end of the year. Ironically enough, we had all been so busy that nobody had really noticed this impending large round number. It was the Room to Read way to think about what came next, rather than celebrating today's accomplishments. But once we realized that we'd soon be opening our five thousandth library, we began brainstorming on a creative way to celebrate this accomplishment. I wanted something that would help the world pay attention to us and inspire people to join our "caravan."

Thankfully, the answer was about to find us.

....

"I have this idea I'd like to run by you. You'll have to hear me out, because initially it will probably sound a bit crazy."

Crazy is not what I normally expected from Martin Cubbon, the group finance director for Swire Pacific, the parent company of Cathay Pacific Airlines. His forty-fifth-floor office in Hong Kong's Pacific Place skyscraper had the wide-open spaces, the hushed quiet, and the commanding views that remind the visitor, intentionally or not, that he or she is in the seat of power of one of Asia's oldest and most successful companies. Swire dated back to the days when not just Hong Kong but also large swaths of China were in British hands. This was clearly not new money.

Martin was dressed in standard CFO garb: pinstriped charcoal gray suit, crisp white shirt, Bordeaux red tie. His face was both thin and tanned from long-distance trail running. As I gazed upon a wall-sized antique map of nineteenth-century Asian trade routes, I assured Martin that we were always open to crazy ideas.

"Good. This one qualifies. I had this idea while running the Dragon's Back Trail this weekend. Would you be able to make use of a Boeing 777?" he asked.

"Come again?"

"We're taking delivery of eighteen new extended-range 777-300 jets from Boeing. I'm thinking that maybe there's some creative ways Room to Read could make use of one of them."

"As in, make use of it *permanently*?"

Martin flashed me a lopsided smile that said, "Nice try." It was a look I saw with increasing frequency; but at least it indicated that I was doing my job, "making the bold ask."

"No, John, you might find it rather amusing that when we spend hundreds of millions of dollars on wide-body aircraft, our business model requires that we fill them with revenue-paying passengers," he said with his best British understatement. "But here's what I'm thinking. We take delivery of these planes from Boeing Field, outside Seattle, and they fly practically empty across the Pacific. So I'm wondering if there's some way Room to Read could take advantage of a delivery flight?"

"Martin, wow! That sounds like an amazing opportunity. We have to come up with something big."

Robin, our development director for Asia, asked Martin what differentiated the extended-range 777-300 from other jets in their fleet.

"The 777-300ER has the largest cargo hold of any plane in the sky. It's designed to allow an airline to make money on each flight from both passengers and cargo. It allows airlines to diversify their sources of revenue. And as the name implies, it has an extremely impressive range. It can fly nonstop from New York to Hong Kong or from Los Angeles to Dubai."

Hmm: big airplane, flies long ranges, has a huge cargo hold. Duh!

"Martin, here's my big idea," I blurted out. "By year-end, we're going to open our five thousandth library. It's a big milestone—in fact, it puts us in Andrew Carnegie's territory. We've been trying to figure out a way to celebrate and to recognize this milestone and then blow beyond it. But how do we make that number real to people? Everyone is constantly bombarded by large numbers. How can we make our five thousandth library stand out?

"Here's one idea: What if we convince a bunch of publishers to fill that massive cargo hold with books that will stock these libraries, and the next five thousand also?"

"You'd need a lot of books," replied Martin. "It's one hell of a cargo hold."

"That's true," Robin opined. "But everyone who works with us knows that we're never afraid to think big. By now people are used to being on the receiving end of John's crazy requests."

Martin laughed as I blushed.

"Hold on, I've got it!" I yelled a little too loudly, shattering the tranquility of the carpet-lined offices. "Let's call the plane *Literacy One*."

"Like *Air Force One*, only with better leadership," quipped Robin, who wasn't a big fan of the then American president.

"Wait, I have another idea! Martin, could we invite some of our most loyal donors to come along for the ride? It would be a 'money can't buy' experience. You know, kind of like American Express has their 'membership has its privileges' campaign? I think this would be a fantastic way to thank some of our investors, and even our volunteers, for their dedication to our cause. They'd fly on this awesomely large and luxurious private jet from Seattle to Hong Kong, and on arrival we could have a big party."

"Great idea! I imagine we could allow that. I'd just have to check with catering to make sure we could feed everyone."

"Martin," I said with a chuckle, "if we have to pick up a case of beer at the 7-Eleven and a bucket of fried chicken at KFC, I'm sure it would still be a very fun flight."

The bookish CFO remained in creative brainstorming mode. "We have a plane being delivered in December. What about doing a holiday theme—you know, sharing with those who have less than we do, in places like Cambodia?"

We knew Cambodia was near and dear to Martin's heart, as he had supported the opening of two schools there.

"We should plan press events on both sides of the Pacific," suggested Robin. "This will be huge. Let's start working on a *Literacy One* logo and T-shirts."

"Brilliant!" I threw out an idea for a story line: "Room to Read started with one man and one yak. Now we've gotten so big we need a 777!"

Martin then put the cherry on top of the sundae: "We can position this as the ultimate free upgrade!"

The meeting ended with an excited round of high fives. Our creative juices were flowing, and we were already envisioning *Literacy One* lifting off as it headed west across the Pacific. Like Santa's sleigh, only bigger and more comfortable, it would fly through the night with the promise of books for tens of thousands of children in Cambodia.

One week later, back in San Francisco, euphoria was replaced by reality. Martin had sent the dimensions of the cargo hold—the rather cavernous cargo hold.

"Dang! Where and how are we going to come up with 250,000 children's books on short notice?" I asked our team.

"Let's start with Scholastic," suggested Laura Maestrelli, the Room to Read team member responsible for soliciting large donations of English-language books from publishing houses. Prior to working for us, she'd been in the publishing business, and she was a perfect fit for her role. "They've always been hugely supportive. We could even offer to have Clifford the Big Red Dog be the guest of honor at the launch event and invite media to cover their donation."

This quick attempt to find a win-win situation was a sign that our hiring was going well. Laura was not just going to beg for a book donation for "charity": She was instead going to try to find ways to make this initiative also accrue benefits to Scholastic.

"Great, why don't you call and tell them we're looking for three publishers to each commit seventy-five thousand books? That gets us close."

Two hours later I was eating a microwaved burrito at my desk when Laura walked in.

"Hey, you didn't call any other publishers yet, did you?" she asked.

"No, that's your job. I was combing through my contacts, though, and have a few ideas. But wait, why are you smiling like the cat that ate the canary?"

"Carol [Sakoian, Scholastic's VP of international business and a Room to Read advisory board member] just called. They are over-the-top in love with the *Literacy One* idea, so much so that they want an exclusive. They've asked for one week. She's going to start making calls to gather enough internal support to hit the 250,000 target."

"Wow, that didn't take long."

"It's a great idea. And it's fun. I'm not that surprised. If I were them, I'd want to be part of this."

....

Three days later I was interrupted in the middle of an internal meeting. Carol was on the phone and had told my assistant that it was urgent.

Urgent? Uh-oh, was that the sound of an echo in a cavernous but empty 777 cargo hold?

"Hi, John, how are things?"

"You tell me. Whatever news you have for me will most definitely make or break my day. But no pressure." I laughed.

"Don't worry; you are going to love me."

"I already do. But please, tell me what's up."

"We pitched the *Literacy One* idea all the way up the food chain. When we told [CEO] Dick [Robinson] about the idea, he approved it immediately. In fact, he upped our donation. Instead of getting 250,000 books, you'll be getting 400,000. Can you ask Cathay for *Literacy Two*?"

"Well, Cathay also buys planes from Airbus, so maybe we can get them involved, too."

"Given the level of English comprehension in Cambodia, we've picked a lot of early readers. These smaller books are thin, so hopefully they'll all fit. Listen, all we want in return is one seat on the plane. Carra, who works for me, is your biggest fan, and she takes care of logistics on our donations to you. If you knew what the bureaucracy is like to ship books to South Africa and Vietnam, you'd realize what a hero she is. She'll be thrilled when I tell her she'll be on the flight."

"Carol, we can bring you along, too, if you like—and Dick! Please tell Carra that we have the authority to upgrade her. For the first time in my life, I've been handed a seating chart for an entire airplane. I'm like Julie McCoy the cruise director, only with a 777-300. Oh yeah, and Cathay Pacific's business class is quite deluxe."

"Fantastic! Now I just have to go hunt down books from all of our warehouses. I don't know how we're going to find you four hundred thousand books, but I've rarely seen Dick so excited, and so it's definitely going to happen."

Upon hanging up, Laura and I exchanged a hearty high ten. We immediately knew what had to be done. We jumped up and sprinted across the office in search of the official Room to Read yak bell. We have a custom of celebrating our wins by ringing a yak bell from Nepal. If you hear it clanging, you hit "pause" on your meeting, take your hands off the keyboard, and come out to the open bullpen to hear about the latest victory.

As our team gathered around, Laura announced the news. *Literacy One* not only would fly but would fly with the cargo hold stuffed to capacity.

We had the plane. We had the books. Now came the fun part: calling our key supporters to invite them onto our private 777!

....

Four months later, Boeing's Museum of Flight was packed with a raucous and high-energy group. As volunteers wearing *Literacy One* T-shirts moved through the crowd serving drinks, I surveyed the room and took in the joyous sight of all the Room to Read employees, board members, chapter leaders, and donors. Five thousand libraries was a significant milestone, and I loved that they could help us celebrate it. Executives from Cathay Pacific and Scholastic had flown in from Hong Kong and New York, and a large contingent of Boeing executives were playing host. Not to mention the two most special guests.

I had not expected Carolyn and Woody to be passengers on *Literacy One*—not that they hadn't asked. Just two months earlier, I had visited Denver to speak at a fund-raising event. Later, over a quiet three-way dinner, I shared all the recent news with my parents, including the plans for *Literacy One*.

Woody not so subtly smiled, put down his fork, and stuck his thumb into the air.

"Dad, what are you doing?"

"I'm hitchhiking. I just need a cardboard sign that says 'Hong Kong or Bust.'"

I said nothing.

"If there are seats available, your mother and I would love to join you."

Rarely the silent one in the relationship, Mom simply nodded her assent.

I thought to myself, *Woody must really want to go on this trip. He's never this direct.* With my father, you usually had to guess what he was thinking. Not this time.

I played my cards very close to my chest. Probably a bit defensively, I told them that we could only bring along twenty guests and that our management team had agreed that the first priority was our largest donors.

They looked a bit disappointed. I tried to convince myself, *Of course they totally understand*. But it gnawed at me, and whenever we spoke by phone, I hoped the subject would not come up. Proactively I would steer the conversation in a different direction. When they asked about my upcoming travels, I talked about everything but *Literacy One*.

Then one day it hit me. I was on an afternoon run through San Francisco's Presidio National Park, thinking about the upcoming trip. We'd received word just a few hours earlier that all production on the jet was on schedule; there was 99 percent certainty that Cathay could give us the flight day. I was elated, but at the same time there was a pit in my stomach. Why?

During the run, it hit me that the situation was very similar to the one in 1998 when Woody had asked, humbly, whether he could join the trek to Bahundanda. I had responded by telling him all the reasons this was a bad idea. Thankfully, I had realized my error eventually. In retrospect, I'd never once regretted having Woody as my travel buddy. We'd had a unique father-son experience that had permanently tightened our bond.

Here we were nine years later. In the words of Yogi Berra, it was déjà vu all over again.

I thought back to my childhood and how airplanes had always played a role in my relationship with my father, who worked at Boeing when the company was designing the 707. Some of my earliest memories were of my father walking me through airports, hand in hand, as he pointed out how to tell the different planes and airlines apart: "You can tell that's a 727 because it has three engines, all on the tail. That jet over there is a 747-400, the only plane with the big upper deck. It's made by Boeing. Over there is a DC-10. How did I know it's a DC-10?"

"Because it has one engine under each wing and one big one on the tail?"

"Correct. Do you know who makes it?"

Silence.

"McDonnell Douglas. That plane at gate 12 is a 707. That's the plane I helped design. It has two engines under each wing. Do you remember what other plane has that same engine configuration?"

"Yes, the DC-8."

"Very good. Over there is a North Central Airlines plane. They're the only airline that serves Duluth, where your grandparents live. We flew them last year. You probably remember the city we had to transit through—it's one of the Twin Cities."

"Minneapolis."

"Do you see the plane that just landed, the Allegheny Airlines DC-9? It's probably arriving late, as they are *never* on time. Do you know what their nickname is?"

"Agony Airlines!" I yelled in celebration not only of my recall, but the shared father-son geeky humor.

Back then Woody had taken my hand and walked me through numerous airports and onto countless planes. Forty years later, our situation was reversed. I controlled one of the newest high-tech planes in the sky. He was simply asking for me to do the same thing for him and take him along on the adventure of a lifetime.

How in the world could I have been so clueless and self-centered?

I needed to stop thinking of myself and to view this from the vantage point of my parents. Eight years after opening that first library, my father would be with me to celebrate our five thousandth. Even better, my mother would be joining us. Just as Hewlett-Packard had been started in Dave Packard's garage, Room to Read had started in theirs.

It was time to correct my mistake. I sprinted the last two miles to my home in the Marina at the fastest pace I could manage. The only thing faster was their acceptance of the long-delayed invitation.

....

Oh my God!! It's here! Check it out!!

An excited yelp went up from a group of our employees as we raced to the window. Outside under a patchy blue Seattle sky was one of the most beautiful sights I have ever seen—a gleaming white and exceptionally large 777-300ER being towed toward the building: $150 million worth of aircraft, and for the next fourteen hours, it was ours, all ours!

I looked around for my parents and saw only my mother. I wanted to share this moment with Woody, too, but he was nowhere to be found.

Mom told me that earlier he had been wandering the Boeing flight museum "like a kid at Christmas." She hugged me and with tears in her eyes said, "You have no idea, John, how much this means to him. At our age, all we want is not to be forgotten, to be expendable. To be included by your kids in their adventures is the best gift you can give us."

I was reminded of a quote from Matthieu Ricard, the Buddhist monk: "the immutable simplicity of a good heart." He could have been talking about my mother.

Our conversation was interrupted by a commotion. Woody had decided to "sing for his supper" by dressing in the official Clifford the Big Red Dog suit that Scholastic had shipped in for the occasion. He's always been willing to be the life of the party.

Woody the Big Red Dog had a woman on each arm, guiding him.

"Dad, usually it's the dog that guides the humans. How did you manage to get two women to guide you?"

"I'm just lucky. You're jealous you're not in the suit!"

Crystal, one of our Seattle fund-raising chapter leaders, offered some impromptu advice. "Woody, you might want to think about going to the bathroom before you go out there to work the room and have your photo taken with everyone."

"Why's that? Is it hot in the dog suit? I feel fine so far."

"No, because if there ends up being photos in the media of Clifford the Big Red Dog lifting his leg on *Literacy One,* that would be what they call very bad publicity!"

My mother had a suggestion. "John, will you stand next to your father and Crystal? I want to get a picture to send to Lindsey and Greg [my older sister Lisa's two children]. They asked that you send photos from your BlackBerry so that they could post them to their My Face pages."

"Their what?"

"Their My Face pages. Haven't you heard of it? It's the site all the young people are on."

"Mom, you are mixing up two separate things. There's Myspace, and there's Facebook. They're two different sites."

"Yes, that's what I said, My Face. Now quit arguing with me and stand next to your father."

We were interrupted with the welcome news that the plane had passed final inspection. Now boarding for Hong Kong, *Literacy One!*

As the opening bars of U2's "Beautiful Day" blasted throughout the room, the floor-to-ceiling doors slowly peeled back to reveal our gorgeous airplane. Clifford led the charge onto the tarmac. At the back of the plane, the numerous pallets of books were being loaded into the cavernous cargo hold.

I've never seen people board a plane so quickly. The *Literacy One* passengers were running up the stairs like Rocky on the steps of the Philadelphia Art Museum. They were greeted by Cathay Pacific flight attendants who were already pouring the champagne.

My boarding was delayed for five minutes, as an e-mail arrived asking that I call a major potential donor immediately. We'd been nurturing a relationship with a young couple from the San Francisco Bay Area for the last six months and had even tried to get them to join us on this trip. Not knowing what to expect, I called back immediately. She answered on the second ring.

"I know you're about to leave on your flight. Before you do, I wanted to share some good news with you. We've finished our due diligence on Room to Read. We're impressed, so impressed, in fact, that we're making a five-million-dollar commitment to your library program."

I am speechless. I tap-dance as we talk. Goose bumps march up and down both of my arms. Five. Million. Dollars. Enough to set up more than one thousand libraries. With a single commitment, we could begin outreach to an additional four hundred thousand little people who yearned for their first library. We've just barely gotten the party started on celebrating five thousand libraries and here comes a huge slug of capital that is saying, *Do more. Think bigger.*

It felt like the best of times. We had the single largest commitment in our history—one that was game changing. We had a fully fueled, gleaming white Boeing 777, its cargo hold stuffed to capacity with children's books. A team of our friends, supporters, and chapter leaders were ready to meet us in Hong Kong in fourteen hours. As I walked up the steps, I slowed my pace, giddily anticipating sharing this news with our team of fellow travelers. I pictured the looks of pride on the faces of my parents, who had been so supportive on every step of this journey.

Thank God they're along on this trip, I thought; there were no two people with whom I'd rather have shared this moment of victory.

The year 2007 had almost killed me. I had never been busier, taken more meetings, or traveled more miles. If I was not waking up in a strange hotel room, it was only because I was sleeping on the plane. I was ecstatic that a globe-trotting year was now destined to end on the highest of high notes. In a terribly crowded field of more than one million NGOs in America alone, Room to Read was building a brand. The donors who were able to ride on a private 777 were given a "money can't buy" experience, which helped deepen their loyalty to Room to Read. Besides the incredibly generous contribution from the San Francisco donors, we also received a $250,000 commitment shortly afterward from another donor who said she was happy to be "along for the ride." *Literacy One* also made a big splash in the Hong Kong media.

You build a brand not by sitting at a desk and playing it safe. You have to go out, take risks, and sometimes have the guts to do crazy things to get noticed. Richard Branson immediately comes to mind. Not all of these risks work out, but it's a bit like skiing: If I don't fall a few times each day, I know I'm not skiing hard enough. And with *Literacy One,* we had dared to take Martin Cubbon's crazy idea and run with it.

The most obvious benefit was the books for the children of Cambodia. There were now four hundred thousand books in circulation there that would not have arrived had *Literacy One* never flown. Our investors were inspired by their "membership has its privileges" trip on the private 777. We'd been on the Seattle morning shows, and over the next two years our big events there set new fund-raising records for any U.S. city.

But the biggest result lay ahead. The publicity around *Literacy One* continued to build our brand in Hong Kong. The local chapter took full advantage of this. During the next four years, we raised an incredible twelve million dollars of new commitments from this most generous of cities. With metronomic regularity, Hong Kong remained the number one fund-raising chapter. Not content to stop there, it also helped to incubate the successful launch of our Singapore chapter, which quickly became . . . you guessed it . . . number two!

CHAPTER NINETEEN

Frantic Footsteps in the Night

The elation I'd experienced in late 2007 was replaced by the opposite emotion early in 2008 while leading an investor trek in Nepal.

The conversation in Nepal in 2008 had started out happily enough. Reema Shrestha, a strong and self-confident Nepalese woman who ran our Girls' Education program in Nepal, was telling our group how proud she was of the girls who were staying in school with our help. "Last year, I was particularly excited," she told us as we formed a circle around her.

The members of the group were all people who'd invested substantially in Room to Read's growth as investors or chapter leaders, and in some cases both. They came from all over the world: Hong Kong, Los Angeles, San Diego, San Francisco, Seattle, Tokyo, and Toronto, and ranged in age from fifteen to sixty-five. It was a nearly even mix of men and women. What united them was an excitement at seeing Room to Read's programs across Nepal. We'd attend several opening ceremonies for schools and libraries, visit scholarship girls in their homes, and meet some of the local people who were writing and illustrating our Nepalese-language children's books. But for now, everyone was gathered around Reema.

"I was excited because we'd had a really strong year financially, and as a result I was given the budget to add five hundred girls to our program.

I was so surprised and so happy." Her brown eyes lit up at the memory. "So we put the word out to all our contacts—to Ministry of Education officials, to headmasters, to other NGOs—letting them know that we were looking for girls we could help to be the first in their families to complete secondary school."

"That must have felt great, Reema," said Susan, one of the cofounders of our Tokyo chapter.

"It did! I was really inspired. I thought about how many young girls we could welcome into the program. But what happened next was really sad. We had four thousand girls apply. Do you know how it feels to realize you have to turn away thirty-five hundred young girls—to say no to their dreams?"

Suddenly I felt like a failure.

Our group was subdued and speechless. Thinking about the girls made us contemplate how much more there was to be done. What were these girls doing as we sat here talking? At age six or eight or ten, they were being sent the signal that they'd be yet another generation of women not to get educated and to be treated as second-class citizens.

Personally I felt that I had let Reema down while simultaneously doing the same to those 3,500 girls. What if we'd persuaded an additional 3,500 people during the prior year to donate $250? Or 350 to each sponsor ten girls by investing $2,500? Reema and her team could have said yes rather than no.

The story we'd heard yesterday, that of a young girl named Sunita, was as vivid a reminder as we'd ever heard that too many children live in a unique form of hell on earth.

....

In rural Nepal there is not much noise at night: no cars, no hum of streetlights, and no business that stays open past 7:00 P.M. Unless, of course, it's a business the proprietors don't want you to know about, in which case they stay quiet anyway. From time to time a stray dog barks. Tree limbs rustle slightly due to light winds coming off the Himalayan foothills. Inside a small hut, there are only two sounds: the hiss of a kerosene lantern that sends thick obsidian smoke toward the unventilated ceiling, and the rapid scratching of a pencil against paper as a girl named Sunita does her math homework.

She has not looked up for nearly an hour. The look of concentration on her face is that of a chess grand master. Not wanting to disturb their accomplished young student, her mother and grandmother also sit in silence. They'd rather be asking Sunita about her school day and her playmates, but they know better. She does not like to be disturbed, especially when she's doing math puzzles. The near silence inside the hut is interrupted by three loud and urgent knocks against the paper-thin front door. The three women—old, middle-aged, and young—look up simultaneously, alarmed. The knocks mean only one thing. Nobody moves to open the door.

Sunita interrupts her studies, slamming her math book shut, and hastily crams her notebook, ruler, and pencil into her book bag.

The knocks mean he is on the way.

The neighbor who has knocked on their door does not stick around long. As soon as her message is delivered, she moves swiftly away. Her next destination is four houses away. Similar door, same set of three knocks. This time the door opens instantaneously. She runs in and looks at the family: father, mother, two teenage sons, and a ten-year-old daughter.

"*Namaste.*" Even in an emergency, there is still a need to greet the God within her hosts.

"Get ready. Sunita will need us again tonight."

Four houses away, Sunita finishes stuffing her school supplies into her bright red backpack and then grabs her jacket to protect against the cold night. She leans over to kiss her grandmother good-bye.

"Stop, child. There is no time for this. Go now, *chito, chito.* Fast."

Sunita's father always regrets hitting her. He says so the next morning to anyone who will listen—not that any of the three women in the house wants to. His eyes are bloodshot. The family makes a very small amount of money from their teahouse. Customers drink tea, and the man of the house drinks the profits from that tea: input, output, cause and effect, with metronomic regularity.

He'd never hit his only daughter while sober. But the problem is that most days he is not. His wife has actually debated whether they'd be better off closing down the tea shop. No tea sold, no alcohol consumed.

"He gets in a rage when he's drunk. If he 'catches' our daughter studying, he will knock her to the ground. He has kicked her. He has ripped her schoolbooks into pieces and lit her math homework on fire."

The metamorphosis is scary. Though he's proud of her during the day as she goes to school, at night he sees the world differently. He likes to drink. She likes to study. And now he is less than fifty meters from home.

In conjunction with a "social mobilizer" working for Room to Read, Sunita's neighbors have devised their own solution. They pretty much assume her father is drinking every night. Some nights he's a happy drunk; but on others it's clear from his red-faced rage that darker forces have taken over.

One of the regulars at the small and unlicensed bar who holds his liquor well slips out to "use the *charpi*." But his destination is not the bathroom. Instead he walks the thirty meters to his home and informs his wife that it's a "bad night."

She moves quickly to knock three times on two different doors: once to initiate the escape and once to alert the sanctuary.

Sunita's mother cracks open the front door and peers out. A look of panic overtakes her face. Sunita moves to the back of the living room and lifts the curtain covering the window as she climbs into the chill and darkness of the night on the feet of a ballerina.

One, two, three, four houses; she's there safely.

Three more knocks, no less urgent, but this time less ominous. She is welcomed inside. Sitting down next to her friend Lakshmi, she pulls out her math text, her notebook, her ruler, and her pencil. The look of concentration returns. It's almost as if the last five minutes hadn't even happened.

....

Because of stories like Sunita's, I will always be fanatical about scaling our programs to reach many more millions of children. My desire for Room to Read to be a huge organization is driven by a burning desire to get this right—and by the realization that you can't just build buildings and then walk away. Scaling up, followed by monitoring and ongoing support of the kind we provide in our Girls' Education program, is the only way to have a real impact in young lives.

Girls like Sunita benefit from the strong, educated, and self-confident women who form the crux of our local Girls' Education teams and serve as ideal role models for the Sunitas of the world. Like me, those local teams spend a lot of time thinking about how we can bring as many girls like Sunita as possible into our program.

My obsession with scale comes from what I've seen over and over—things that have robbed me of every iota of patience I've ever had.

In rural Cambodia in 1994, after noticing the charred remains of a building alongside the rutted and potholed road, I asked the motorcycle taxi driver what had happened.

"That was our village's school. The Khmer Rouge burned it down."

"When did that happen?"

"Fifteen years ago."

"Why has nobody done anything about it? I thought Cambodia was now in a rebuilding phase."

The driver looked sad, his face drawn and forlorn, his eyes dull. "Many people have told us they will help." He flashed a smile that was without hope and dismissive of the wider world. "But none of them ever come back."

Then, on a cool fall day in 2003, my friend Hilary and I trekked in the Simien Mountains of northern Ethiopia, close to the Sudanese border. As we ate dinner around a small campfire, our guide told us about how local men go about getting married, via the "acquisition" of a bride. A man identifies a girl whom he'd like to be his wife. Then he recruits a few friends and leaps into action. What follows is the antithesis of romance, as they kidnap the unlucky "bride" and rape her—several times. She's then abandoned to walk home, humiliated, in tears, at risk of both HIV and pregnancy.

Within a few hours or perhaps a day, the "groom" will then approach the father of his intended bride: "Your daughter is now spoiled. The entire village already knows, and now no man will want to marry her. But I will do you a favor and take her off your hands."

Already dealing with the trauma of being raped, the girl of perhaps eleven or twelve or fifteen soon learns she is now a child bride, with the expectation that she will soon begin having children of her own. She is attached for life to the man who raped her. She will cook for him, clean his house, sleep with him, and bear him children. It must be a terrible form of hell on earth to realize that your fate has been decided so capriciously and unfairly at such a young age. If she follows the norm, she will give birth to six children. The odds that she will complete secondary school are less than 10 percent.

The things I have seen and heard have made me fairly obsessed with the idea of reaching as many children as possible as quickly as possible. Thankfully, not all of those things are negative. Many are extremely positive.

Just the previous day, in a tiny hovel in a village close to the one we're in here in Nepal, a group of us listened as a grandmother told us how every man in her life has been abusive. The entire family lives under one roof. Grandmother, mother, and daughter live alone. The man of the house ran away fourteen years ago, never to be heard from again.

Though the grandmother was only sixty, she looked two decades older. Deep crevices lined her face. Her hands were gnarled, and she had few teeth left. We knew this because she was smiling widely as she opined that "the only men in our lives who keep their promises to us are the ones who work for Room to Read." She had not a day of schooling. Her own daughter went through grade three.

"But now, my granddaughter is in grade eight, and she is near the top of her class." There were tears forming along the shores of the cloudy lakes of her eyes. "I can die now that I know my granddaughter will finish school."

In rural India, an illiterate mother has a face lit up with hope and fire. Her day of backbreaking labor on the family's small plot of land is finished. Now she is inside their tiny one-room shack. She has pen in hand, and on a dusty notebook page she writes her name, over and over again.

Neema Chettri.

Neema Chettri.

Neema Chettri.

"My daughter taught me this," she proudly reports. Nearby, her nine-year-old stands ramrod straight in a school uniform so squeaky clean it could be in a laundry soap commercial. "Until a week ago, I had never written my name. Now I can. It means better things are possible for me and for my daughter."

Across large swaths of the developing world, it is common for 40 percent of the population to be under the age of fifteen. Nature abhors a vacuum—and vacuums get filled either with positive forces like education or with the stuff that makes for the usual depressing headlines: child soldiers, prostitution rings, recruitment by Al Qaeda.

A fourteen-year-old girl might spend the majority of her waking hours in an urban brothel, taking off her clothes for a man twenty years her senior, who uses her as a piece of property. She might encounter ten or twenty of these men per day. Or she can spend her time reading in her village library, preparing for the day when she might become a teacher, shopkeeper, or doctor in her village.

A young boy in East Africa can pick up an AK-47—or he can pick up a book.

A teenager can walk into a crowded market in Colombo or Dhaka or Delhi with a bomb strapped to his body. Or that large lump being hoisted over his shoulders could be a backpack filled with books.

If we dare to dream big and execute flawlessly, we have the ability to influence the choices and opportunities these children have. Or we can just decide it's someone else's problem and let the status quo perpetuate itself.

I view every decision I make about how I spend my time through one lens: How can we reach more children, in more places, more quickly? How can we fill the vacuum before something else does?

I tell our ten country directors that even though on the official organizational chart it looks as though they report to the CEO and then the board, I view it differently, and that the reporting is reciprocal and runs both ways. "I report to you and to your teams. It is my job to get you the money and the resources you need to get the job done. You, in turn, report to the children, to their parents, to the teachers. Your role is to get them everything they need to be sure the youth are gaining a quality education."

Constantly I remind our teams that we must make the best use of every moment and every dollar; we are playing for very big stakes. Girls like Sunita can give in to the pressure to quit their studies, not to attend school, or they can be guided and encouraged by positive role models. Another whole generation of children in Cambodia or Ethiopia or Laos can remain illiterate, thereby stumping the "development experts" who wonder why people stay poor. Or they can gain literacy and the habit of reading from a young age and thereby have the foundation and cornerstone of a solid education.

I'm frequently asked how I am able to travel so constantly, to be always "up" for meetings and presentations. There are times when that can be tough, but most times I manage to convince myself that there is really no other choice. Having met so many thousands of these children and their families, I know what's at stake. Some armchair psychologists in my life (usually partners in romantic relationships that aren't going particularly well) have opined: "It seems like you're running from something."

No, not at all. Most often I am running *to* something: our big annual wine gala in Sydney or Tokyo; a school-opening ceremony in Laos with major investors in tow; a meeting with the staff of a bank in London or New York that supports our work and could be persuaded to do even more.

This is one of my rules of fund-raising, as borrowed from Sir Isaac Newton: An object in motion tends to remain in motion.

The perpetual activity is not something that it takes a psychology PhD to figure out. It's simply a result of stories I hear, like that of Sunita, and the desire to do better. Even as I write these words, the battle is being lost in thousands of places. I constantly rack my brain with the urgent query: How can we persuade more people to care?

We'd soon find a unique and inspiring answer to that question—one that involved helicopters, several sheikhs, and the world's tallest building.

CHAPTER TWENTY

The World's Tallest
Fund-raising Thermometer

E ven with sunglasses on, I am blinded by the white helicopter gleaming brilliantly in the desert sun. It's one of three identical choppers, side by side and neatly aligned, parked outside a cavernous hangar. I peek inside and see a Gulfstream V in the shadow of a Boeing 757, each proudly bearing a "UAE" logo on the tail. The floor has the shine and cleanliness of an Intel chip factory.

The chopper pilot's muscular body is shoved into a military green jumpsuit that looks two sizes too small, as if it had been washed in salt water, then dried in the desert sun. He barks at us, as though we were his soldiers, that it's time to go. Eager to be up in the air, we pile into the embrace of air-conditioning, sandalwood scent, and the tush-gratifying comfort of well-tanned leather seats. A bottle of Evian, chilled to mountain-stream temperature, resides next to each seat. My first gulp spills on my shirt as we lift off, straight up, at warp speed.

To our left a parched and sun-bleached desert stretches south and west for hundreds of miles across the Arabian peninsula, places I've seen on maps but have never visited: Oman, Saudi Arabia, and Yemen. To the right rises a seemingly never-ending vertical wall of glass and steel. The highly polished buildings of green, onyx, blue, silver, and obsidian stand in sharp contrast to the flat nothingness that surrounds them, in silent testimony to the power of architecture. A rabid fan of *The Fountainhead* and its protagonist, Howard Roark, would weep at the sight.

As we rise and point west, I see the roof deck of my hotel, where just ninety minutes ago I was enjoying fresh-squeezed orange juice and the morning edition of the *Gulf News* poolside. The pilot has promised us a tour, and within minutes we are buzzing the Burj Al Arab Hotel. Its fifty-eighth-floor helipad was made famous as the site of a great publicity stunt—the world's highest tennis match. Andre Agassi played Roger Federer on a specially constructed court. Over two hundred meters off the ground, it floats apart from the building, hanging in space. Its ability to defy gravity makes it the perfect metaphor for all that we see around us.

The helicopter host is His Excellency Dr. Hanif Hassan Al Qassimi, the minister of education for the United Arab Emirates. He's invited me to spend the day with him. We started with a private meeting in his oversized office. A legion of employees appeared out of nowhere to serve us tea from long-nosed silver pots. His bearded face lit by a radiant smile, Dr. Hanif told me that his daughter Maria had insisted the entire family read my book. During their summer holiday, he recounted, there were six copies of *Leaving Microsoft to Change the World* strewn around their rented home in the Swiss Alps. Room to Read's work had become a constant topic of conversation. When Maria had heard from the Dubai-based foundation for which she worked that I was about to pay a visit, he had suggested that we get to know each other better.

We talked at length about the importance of education, not just for the developing world but also for countries like the United Arab Emirates, which is composed of seven semiautonomous nation-states. Some, like Abu Dhabi, are swimming in oil and will be for decades to come. For others, including Dubai, there is either no oil or a dwindling amount. To continue to prosper, these nations need to rely on an economy built on intellectual capital.

The majority of the workforce in cities like Dubai comes from neighboring nations like Bangladesh, India, Nepal, and Sri Lanka. The illiteracy problems and the lack of education in those countries affect the UAE. An illiterate guest worker might pour cement or hammer nails. One who is literate and speaks English could instead program computers, work in the burgeoning tourism industry, or get a job with Emirates Airlines (which now has one of the largest fleets of wide-bodied aircraft in the world). Our conversation reminded me once again that our generation lives in a borderless world. There are few, if any, places where problems can be isolated or quarantined: They spill across the artificially demarcated boundaries of the nation-state, whether we want them to or not.

Dr. Hanif then announced the day's big surprise: We'd be taking a helicopter 120 kilometers down the peninsula southwest to Abu Dhabi. Waiting for us at the other end to host a lunch was the minister of higher education and scientific research, His Excellency Sheikh Nahyan bin Mubarak Al Nahyan. It would be a two-sheikh day.

Beneath the window, the land disappeared, replaced by the crystal clear and cobalt waters of the Arabian Sea. Seventy-two hours earlier I'd been on the sun-drenched plains of rural Zambia, one of the poorest countries in the world. Out in the Chongwe district, things had looked pretty much the same way they probably had in the eighteenth century, with farmers working their small plots of land with ancient hand tools and goats tethered to trees. The only buildings in sight had been small shacks made of thatch. Our small bus had moved at forty miles per hour down a narrow highway so primitive it lacked even a dividing line.

Now I soared among skyscrapers in the most modern and vertical of cities.

Within minutes, we were over the world-famous Palm Jumeirah. Like much of this part of the world, this enormous man-made island started with an ambitious idea: to create additional coastline via a massive dredging and land-reclamation project. One hundred million cubic meters of rock and sand had been quarried from the UAE's interior and trucked to the coast. We learned from Dr. Hanif that the island would hold thirty-two hotels and more than four thousand houses and condominiums. More than eighty kilometers of coastline had been created.

Five minutes later I was hit with a sense of déjà vu. Below us was another palm-shaped island, this one appearing even larger than the first. "Dr. Hanif," I asked, "am I seeing things, or are you guys actually constructing a second palm island?"

"I can assure you, you are not seeing things." He laughed. "This is indeed the second palm island. If you like, we can have the pilot divert the helicopter and visit the third one, also."

"You're trying to fool the foreign guest, right?"

With a radiant smile lighting up his animated face, he assured me that the third palm would be bigger and better than the others. The first one had used one hundred million cubic yards of sand and rock. The third one would use a billion, to create an additional two hundred kilometers of coastline.

I imagined my childhood summers on the shores of Assateague Island in Maryland, accumulating a large pile of sand to shape into a castle with fortifications and moats, only to learn with dismay halfway through the construction process that the high tide threatened destruction. It moved in on the little castle of my dreams without stealth: When you have the luxury and the joy of brute force, you don't need to bother disguising intentions announced with a defiant roar or actions that speak for themselves. Dumping sand in the ocean to create land seemed like a Herculean struggle.

And yet beneath me was this newly created land. Abracadabra!

Clearly, nobody in the UAE lacked for ambition.

············

It was for an equally ambitious project that I was here, one with an "only in Dubai" twist. It had all started with very persistent stalking.

In 2007 our team learned of a newly formed foundation named Dubai Cares, created via a fund-raising drive during the holy month of Ramadan. Citizens were encouraged to mark the holiday by donating funds to help the poor, in addition to the usual practice of fasting from sunup to sundown. The money raised would be used for education projects in the poorest parts of the world, many of which were close to the UAE.

As with all things Emirati, the campaign leaders decided to go big.

The electric traffic-sign system broadcast real-time updates on total funds raised. A daily update was posted prominently in every newspaper on the front page above the fold. Two weeks into the campaign, Sheikh Mohammed bin Rashid Al Maktoum, the constitutional monarch of Dubai, announced at a press briefing that he knew who'd made a lot of money on significant deals over the last few years, as many of the business and finance leaders had been coinvestors in his own successful projects. At the same time, he was following who'd pledged money to this campaign. He announced disappointment not to see the high degree of correlation he expected: "I am not asking you to support the formation of Dubai Cares with a generous endowment. I am telling you that I expect this of you."

That opened the floodgates. In just three weeks, an incredible $476 million was raised. At a press conference to announce the result, Sheikh Mohammad then demonstrated his personal commitment to having Dubai Cares be one of the world's leading foundations supporting education in the developing world. He planned to contribute to the fund a nice round number, twenty-four million dollars, to take the foundation's size to five hundred million.

But wait, that's not how they do things in the UAE. He doubled down and took it to a cool billion.

To me this news was a hell of a lot more interesting than all the reports in the media about Dubai's identification with indoor ski slopes and the world's largest shopping mall. In a flash, less than the time it takes Mercury to make one revolution around the sun, the citizens of the UAE had created the biggest foundation in the world focused on one of the most important and overlooked issues.

Naturally, we had to meet the Dubai Cares people. Their unhelpful Web site said in so many words: "Don't call us, we'll call you." An alternative approach was needed. So I simply started telling anyone and everyone I talked to that I was trying to get into Dubai Cares: Did they know someone there, or know someone who would know someone?

Sometimes if you state your intentions and goals to enough people, eventually enough seeds will be planted so that some bear fruit. Two of my coworkers at Room to Read once finished a perplexing meeting with the words: "We don't know how to solve this problem, but that doesn't mean we can't get it done. It's highly likely that someone in our networks will know how to solve it. We just have to get the word out to them."

We put out the word and hoped for the best.

. . . .

Two weeks later, on a blustery and foggy morning in the Presidio, my morning scan of the in-box yielded this intriguing subject line: "Call me, you're going to love me." It was from Carol Sakoian at Scholastic—the same Carol who had been so helpful with *Literacy One*.

Intrigued, I dialed her immediately and was greeted with inspiring news delivered in her heavy New York accent: "I was just over in Dubai, and I met with the team at Dubai Cares. The woman who spearheaded the campaign is named Chris Tight. She's originally from California, and she reports to Reem Al Hashimy. Reem is the minister of state for the UAE—very young and smart. Reem is also the chairwoman of Dubai Cares. Chris has read your book and really enjoyed it. I've given her your e-mail address and she's going to reach out to you. Try to get her on the phone as soon as you can, as she has some interesting ideas."

This global diaspora of Room to Read fans is critical to our success. Every week, they make hundreds of introductions and connections on our behalf. Never in our wildest dreams could we have afforded to hire so many superstars who didn't quit their high-powered jobs to change the world: They just added it to their list of responsibilities. One volunteer once joked with me that the title of *his* memoir would be *Not Quitting Cisco, but Still Changing the World*. Their employers were paying them to work in Amsterdam, New York, Sydney, San Diego, or Toronto. We leveraged that investment to our benefit, as those volunteers used their phones, computers, iPhones, BlackBerrys, and meals with clients to discuss their involvement with our young and growing organization. And very often they even beat down the doors of their corporate philanthropy departments on our behalf.

My musings were interrupted by the delivery chime of incoming mail. Chris, like Carol, was in GSD mode.

Dear John,

I understand from Carol Sakoian that you are open to discussing a potential partnership with Dubai Cares. We have some big—Dubai-like—ideas for a program in the fall. As such, I was hoping to speak to you ASAP. May I suggest that as a first step we set up a time to speak. Please let me know what works for you.

> *All the best,*
> *Chris*

It was the first of many times over the coming months that the word "Dubai-like" would be used.

....

It was an early morning when we patched in to Dubai on speakerphone. Fueled by the largest latte I could find at Chestnut Street's Coffee Roastery, the official "founding office" of Room to Read, I had come to work excited and eager to hear Chris's big idea. Four people from our headquarters team were on our end of the phone. On the other end it was just Chris, driving home from the office at the end of her workday. Wasting no time, which we came to learn was her standard operating procedure, she dove right in.

"Here in the UAE, we are trying to promote a culture of reading. The kids have video games and iPods and four hundred channels on satellite television, but they don't read enough. We're also trying to convince people to be more philanthropic. So our idea is to combine the two. We're planning to launch a big initiative this fall, just after Ramadan ends, called the Million Book Challenge. We will challenge the children of the UAE to read at least one million books during a sixteen-day period—two weeks, plus an additional final weekend. We will tell them that for every book they read, we will fund one book in the developing world. Read one, give one."

Sounds great, we enthused: Let's talk numbers. How many students were there in the UAE?

"A hundred and forty thousand, grades one through eight. So this is totally doable. I'm really impressed with your local-language publishing program, so you guys came to mind as a potential partner."

We cheered Chris on, as I told her that we would indeed be the perfect partner. We were planning to publish as least a hundred new titles over the next year, and for each book we would print ten thousand copies. It was almost too good to be true; her goal was exactly in sync with ours.

"I'm also thinking that it would be good for us to fund some libraries. I figure that it's not enough to just print books, as those books need to have a home. They need to reside in a library that has adults who run it and encourage the children to read and to take the books home and read them at night and on weekends outside of school hours. So I'd also be interested in talking to you guys about that. I'm thinking that maybe we could fund something like a hundred libraries?"

In our small conference room, I waved my hands at my team, indicating that we should remain silent.

"Hello? Are you guys still there? I think I lost you."

"No, Chris, we're still here," I answered. "That long pause was because from this end, we were a bit perplexed."

"Perplexed? Why?"

"Because you led off the call telling us that at Dubai Cares, you guys are thinking big. So our confusion was why you'd pick such a low number of libraries."

She laughed. Obviously she saw me throwing a line in the water, trying to land a bigger fish.

"Okay, Mr. Big Thinker, what number of libraries would impress you?"

"How about five hundred or a thousand?"

"Can you really do that many?"

"Yes, in fact, we're hoping to open around two thousand libraries this year."

"Okay, I'm game to talk about a larger number. Why don't you put some thoughts down in an e-mail and send them my way?"

....

My coworker Jayson Morris and I have a favorite scene from the David Mamet play *Glengarry Glen Ross,* set in a Chicago real estate office full of desperate agents. A harsh regional manager (played in the film by Alec Baldwin) yells at an underperforming agent who is pouring himself a cup of coffee: "Put that cup down, you SOB."

The agent, played by Jack Lemmon, has not closed a deal in months. He looks perplexed. And he then hears immortal words from a man two decades his junior that hit him in the solar plexus: "That coffee. Is for closers."

It was a tradition for Jayson and me to treat each other to coffee when we dared to be a closer and succeeded. We'd hang up, exchange a war whoop and a high five, and head out to the nearby Peet's.

But a lot has to happen before that. Closings don't just magically happen. They have to be imagined, plotted, and then willed into existence. But we'd taken a critical step in daring to ask a potential funder to think big.

············

Both organizations moved with GSD speed toward a Dubai-sized goal. None of us had ever met in person, and yet we communicated on a daily basis as we planned an ambitious agenda: an October launch of the Million Book Challenge with Sheikh Mohammad; a media tour introducing Room to Read across the gulf; a still-to-be-negotiated implementation of Dubai Cares–funded local-language books and libraries; and a *Leaving Microsoft to Change the World* event at the Virgin Megastore, Dubai's biggest bookstore.

Two weeks into our conversations, I surprised myself. I had been thinking about the importance of relationships in the Middle East and was debating whether I could fit a trip to Dubai into an already-packed travel schedule. Sure, we could continue to negotiate and plan by phone and e-mail, but was that really optimal? Relationships are not built on the phone. There is no better way to build both trust and a relationship than in face-to-face meetings and over chatty meals or endless cups of tea.

Obviously it had to be done. Nagging at me was the fact that I had just returned from a whirlwind five-day trip to Japan and had spent twenty-two of the previous thirty days on the road. The idea of a week or two in San Francisco in perfect June weather was quite tempting.

But here was potentially the most game-changing deal in our organization's history. The short term had significant upside potential, but the true value lay in the long term, as well as the instantaneous access we'd have to business, government, and thought leaders across the gulf.

Just three weeks ago, hadn't I been dreaming about being introduced to this brand-new, billion-dollar foundation? And now I was debating gaining a face-to-face meeting with the key decision makers? Going online to look at flights, I groaned: a thirteen-hour flight to Hong Kong, a six-hour layover, and then six more hours to Dubai. Door (nice comfy home that I miss) to door (hotel room door, yet another hotel room) would be twenty-seven hours. Total round-trip time in transit would be fifty-four.

I could send Jayson. But it was obvious to me that if I showed up, that said everything. If I did not, that said even more.

Was I a closer or a poser?

What would the parents and children we serve want me to do? Stay home in San Francisco and be comfy? Or get my ass on a plane and close the deal?

"Don't think. Act. GSD." That was my succinct advice to myself. I fired off an e-mail, before I allowed myself time to even think about it or talk myself out of it.

Dear Chris:

I'd love to check your schedule for the next week. I am thinking about dropping by Dubai. Can we grab lunch?

....

His Highness Sheikh Mohammad is sitting on the stage, surrounded by children. His flowing white robe is pristine, his beard dark and neatly trimmed and, dare I say, even a tad sporty. As he holds a five-year-old girl's hand, an ivory smile even more brilliant than his robe crosses his face. His left hand is clutched by a seven-year-old boy who looks slightly terrified. The poor kid is with a man he's seen only on billboards, the television news, and ubiquitous photos hanging in a place of honor in every public place, be it an office or a small business.

Meanwhile, the entire room of journalists and honored guests is as quiet as the ocean floor. All eyes are locked on His Highness.

Without any preamble or introduction, Sheikh Mohammad speaks: " 'Read.' That is the first word in the Holy Koran. 'Read.' "

Cameras snap: This guy knows how to deliver a clear-as-a-bell message. Later I look up the opening verses of the Koran and see it indeed focuses on reading:

> In the name of God,
>   Mericiful to all,
> Compassionate to each!
> Behold the Book!

Sheikh Mohammad's comments are brief. His first words really said it all. And with those words, the Million Book Challenge is launched, leading to instantaneous, ubiquitous, and unrelenting media coverage. Now it's up to the children of the UAE, who have the power to put one million books into the hands of kids across the developing world—as long as they *read*.

....

The next day every newspaper in the UAE has a photo in full color of Sheikh Mohammad with a coterie of adorable kids listening to his every word. Few things can be better than sitting at breakfast with five newspapers and seeing your little start-up on the front page of all five of them. When I show Sahlim, my favorite waiter at the hotel where I'm spending the week, his jaw drops and he touches his heart. Now he understands my late hours and why I was ordering coffee from room service at 10:00 P.M. last night as I cranked out e-mail and media requests.

In my own country, with three days to go before our election, our president's popularity is at a historic nadir. After eight years, at least 78 percent of the nation is voting thumbs down on W's performance. Here, the ruler has brand rub-off that any organization would die for. Today that brand rub-off is all ours.

....

We have one more brand rub-off in store, one that will be truly historic and serve as a beacon of progress to let the UAE know, each and every night, how its children are doing at accomplishing the goal of one million books read and one million donated.

The inspiration struck during Jayson's and my spontaneous trip to Dubai just four months ago. During the first meeting we had with the

Dubai Cares team, we were struggling to come up with a metaphor that would make "one million books" a concept students could relate to. It was a big number, but without any context.

"Let's do the math," I suggested. "If a stack of ten children's books is an inch high, how tall is a stack of a million?"

Jayson and Chris both searched for the calculator function on their BlackBerrys.

"Ten thousand feet," Chris reported.

"Wow, that's cool—nearly two vertical miles of books," Jayson added. "That should get them excited, yes?"

"But how do we put this into a perspective kids can understand? I mean, two miles is a distance their family can travel in two minutes."

"Not with our current traffic jams, they can't," Chris joked.

What would excite them? What would they want to post on their Facebook page or tell their parents about?

My gaze traveled out the window of our eighteenth-floor conference room. The answer was sitting in plain view right in front of my eyes. I just had to open them.

"Jayson, can you go online and find out the height of the Burj Dubai?"

He tap-tap-tapped his keyboard.

"They're keeping it secret until it's completed. But the estimates are for it to be between twenty-five hundred and three thousand feet high."

"Excellent," I said, moving toward the whiteboard to sketch out my idea. "So we have clarity of message, and a damn inspiring one at that. The books that the kids in the UAE read will be the equivalent of three Burj Dubais. The books we put in circulation in other countries will be three more."

"This sends a great message about teamwork," interjected Maria from Dubai Cares. "An individual's action may be small, but collectively the effort is really significant."

The energy level in the room was on the brink of thermonuclear, and about to go higher. Chris lit the fuse. Her idea brought to mind a quote from a Room to Read board member, who had said he joined our board because he liked that we were so entrepreneurial: "An entrepreneur is a person who does things with resources he does not yet have."

Chris was about to take this concept to an entirely new level, with resources that we most definitely did not have.

"I've met the CEO of Emaar, the property company building the Burj. What if we can convince them to light it up, floor by floor, to track the students' progress? It would be a visual reminder, updated on a daily basis, of our progress towards one million. We could also have a big electronic ticker at the base of the Burj. I can visualize families going at night to check on the progress on a big billboard with scrolling messages. Every hour we could update the total number of books read, along with encouragement like 'Keep Reading, Students! Don't Stop Until We Reach the Top.'"

We exchanged a round of whoops and high tens. This was as bold as entrepreneurship got: We would take control of a resource, the tallest building in the world, one that we didn't (yet) own.

I told Chris I regretted ever questioning whether she was thinking big.

"Don't congratulate me just yet," she said. "Ideas are worthless unless they're put into practice. I still have to close the deal. And I will either do so or I will die trying."

....

I've requested a window seat on the right-hand side of the plane. I am hoping, hoping, hoping. The 747 accelerates through the pitch-black night. We lift off, and my eyes are locked on the window: Will it be there?

Seven minutes after takeoff my wishes are granted. I can see in the distance the green glow. As we climb higher, we are still not above the Burj Dubai. Green lasers run up and down its 2,800-foot face. More than half a mile of light illuminates the sky.

We have successfully converted the world's tallest building into the world's most exciting fund-raising thermometer! I never could have imagined a more awe-inspiring way to tell the world that every child deserves access to books. The message will be heard across the United Arab Emirates and way beyond: Those of us who have won the lottery of life and have prosperity also have an obligation and an opportunity to help others, and to do so in a big way.

As the plane further ascends and we leave the Burj Dubai behind, I think about all the kids in the UAE who will be more motivated to read than ever before. It's equally inspiring to contemplate the other end of the chain: kids in South Africa, Cambodia, India, Nepal, and Sri Lanka who will receive one book for each one read by students in the UAE.

I also think of *Literacy One,* another seemingly crazy idea that we dared to dream into existence. There are literally millions of charities in today's world, so one critical and perpetual challenge is always this: How do you stand out, differentiate yourself, constantly refresh your story and give people something new to get jazzed about?

It's quite certain we have just done something that fits the bill! I ring my call button and persuade the flight attendant to start the drink service early with a celebratory glass of Shiraz. Eager to capture every moment of this unique week, I pull out my journal. I sip, I write, I smile.

"It's been well worth the sacrifices. We've got Sheikh Mohammed on our side. We're on a path to 10,000 libraries. We've got airlines offering us 777s. And now the world's tallest building is lit up in a celebration of literacy that will raise millions of dollars. I have the best job in the world."

In a short time the euphoria would end abruptly. But for now, seat 15A was celebrating.

CHAPTER TWENTY-ONE

Whose Version of the Future Will Win?

"This is the worst possible news you could be delivering. I really hope you are not serious about this. It could have incredibly negative ramifications on the entire organization. I think you need to seriously think twice about your decision."

I try to avoid raising my voice in the office, but this morning my frustration echoes off the walls of the conference room.

She is stoic and says nothing.

"Seriously, I'm really saddened and shocked that you could show up in our office out of the blue and on virtually zero notice and spring this news on us."

I can feel my blood boiling and my heart pumping in a panic mode that must go back to the early stages of evolution. This is primal: I feel threatened in some existential way. Or, more accurately, I feel that our children are at risk.

Having been backed into a corner, I lash out again.

"I think this is an entirely irresponsible decision. I don't agree with it, and I most certainly don't respect it. While you keep talking to our team, I am going to leave so that I can run the numbers. I can come back to you with a list of the projects we can draw a big red X through. We can cancel the building of two hundred schools, or maybe go tell twelve hundred villages that when we said yes to their requests for libraries, we really meant no. Or we can tell a lot of girls that they have to drop out and abandon their dreams of finishing secondary school. Although come to think of it, even that would not be enough to close the resource gap you just created."

....

She was always a bit flighty.

She reached out to us a year earlier, in 2007, saying that she'd heard great reports about our work in Cambodia. She hinted at the large investment that her family foundation would make "as soon as we get to know each other better." She was quite adamant that each meeting be at her home, usually late in the afternoon or early in the evening.

For several weeks, we'd get together, with each encounter involving a fair bit of alcohol consumption—more on her part than on mine. Champagne would be opened on the flimsiest of excuses: "We have to celebrate getting to know each other. There's a special bottle of wine I think you'd enjoy."

I'd try to say diplomatically that as much as I love red wine, I don't usually drink it at 4:00 P.M., especially when I have a big night of work in front of me. Insert sound of cork popping here. I'd have a glass to be social and watch the bottle be drained to empty: four for her, one for me, in the course of a one-hour meeting.

Having married into a family with a net worth in excess of a billion dollars, she knew that she had us. She was in the *Forbes* 400. We were one of a million charities. She knew we had to play her game.

"I am just doing my due diligence, learning more about your organization, and nobody can tell the story like the founder." This was said as she opened a second bottle of champagne and suggested that we move from the kitchen to in front of the fireplace.

"Since we're going to make a large commitment to your organization, why not begin toasting it now?" It was at this point that I vowed to bring a staff member with me to all future meetings.

Thankfully, it seemed to pay off. This was the donor who reached out by phone while we were boarding *Literacy One*. After pledging five million dollars, she told me to get ready to "grow, grow, grow" the organization. Now that inspiring and soaring commitment was crashing down to earth in a fireball.

....

"Our assets are not what we'd thought they would be at this point of the year. We are pulling our commitment."

"But . . . you made a promise to us and, more importantly, to all the kids we serve. You're not just going to rip that away, are you? Everyone is down in the current stock market, but does that mean you have to go from five million dollars to zero?"

She says nothing. She's surprisingly emotionless considering the severity of this news.

"The markets have contracted by about 20 percent from the time you made the pledge. So can you look at reducing the commitment from five million to four?"

She is sphinxlike. No concern, no remorse, just merciless indifference.

"Also, you threw out a big challenge to our donors—your pledge was in the form of a challenge grant. We told thousands of our closest friends that if they helped to make our campaign to reach ten thousand libraries a success, you'd match them. Hundreds of people stepped up their commitments because they knew, or at least they thought they did, that their money was being leveraged by your matching funds."

She shrugs. I keep trying.

"I can't even begin to stress how much we've aligned our entire organization around your pledge. We've hired dozens of new people, following your advice to get ready for growth. It will be crushing to them when they hear this news. As of course it will be when we tell hundreds of villages that we're not going to make good on our promise to help them build new libraries and schools."

She would not budge. The best she could give us was this: "Today is not like yesterday. Everyone is hurting in this economic climate." I resist the urge to point out that her family's net worth is estimated to be $1.3 billion. If they've lost 20 percent, they are still worth over a billion. Their total commitment to us is a drop in that ocean.

Alas, the largest gift in our history will instead be the largest withdrawn pledge in our history. Defeat snatched from the jaws of victory. I slam the door hard upon exiting and take the most direct route to my office, hoping nobody on the team will notice that I am already choking back tears.

....

Given Room to Read's proven track record with donors, it was dispiriting to acknowledge in the fall of 2008 that it was not a fun time to be raising money. Or to state it more accurately: It was not a fun time to be *not* raising money.

The failure of Lehman Brothers (a Room to Read donor), the implosion of AIG, and the midnight fire sale of Merrill Lynch in September and October could not have come at a worse time. For American charities, the fourth quarter is the biggest fund-raising season of the year. Our team had historically raised 50 percent of our annual budget during Q4. Financial market Armageddon, circa 2008, came at the worst possible time. We predicted that our growing and still-young organization would face the toughest test since the aftermath of the September 11 terrorist attacks in 2001.

Having continued to scale the size of our local in-country teams, Room to Read was on track to achieve an aggressive slate of projects in 2008. Nearly seven thousand young scholars were now enrolled in our Girls' Education program, a growth of 67 percent over 2007. More than 250 communities were opening new school buildings with our support—an average of five new school groundbreakings per week. The most torrid growth was in our library program. Our local teams were on track to open two thousand libraries during the year—or one every four and a half hours!

Dreams are wonderful, but they cannot move from concept to reality without a funding mechanism. No money = no mission.

The global financial markets had just placed a big CLOSED UNTIL FURTHER NOTICE sign on their front door. It was not a good time to be showing up at anyone's door with your best salesman's handshake and Boy Scout's smile.

....

To shake out of my five-million-dollar funk (not the only *F* word on my mind), I wanted to leave the office immediately. We had just been pushed off a cliff and, upon landing, had salt rubbed in our wounds. I felt a deep sense of regret that I no longer worked at Microsoft, where I had usually felt a greater degree of control over my destiny.

But I could not leave without talking to my team. They had seen me lose my cool with our so-called major investor. One of my core beliefs is that a leader can never let his or her team witness panic. Even when things look exceptionally dark, the message from the top has to be positive. When a plane hits serious turbulence, the pilot goes into his best *calm voice* mode and assures the passengers that *this is a temporary condition we will get through.*

That's not to say that the leader can ignore the cold, hard, brutal facts. If he or she sweeps the bad stuff under the carpet and instead gives a rah-rah speech, the team will wonder which planet they're living on. My belief is that you acknowledge the bad stuff but then tell the team you believe in them enough to know that together you will find creative ways to get through the crisis. Victory will be all the sweeter for having been hard won.

I gathered the key players and started by apologizing for having gone ballistic on our now-former donor: "That was wrong of me, and I can only chalk it up to the yin and yang elements of my psyche. I have a passion for helping kids to get education, but I also have a temper. That was not one of my better meetings. Sorry."

I moved on quickly.

"Look, I realize this totally sucks for all of us. We're already severely overworked, and now there is a sword of Damocles hanging over our head. We either find five million additional dollars in an economy that's imploding, or we start determining who to lay off and which projects to cancel. That language is actually a bit tepid. I should say we'll have to determine to which communities and parents we will send our in-country teams to say, 'Sorry, but we're going to have to renege on our commitment to help educate your children.'

"None of us want to cut staff or cancel projects. That being said, I have no idea where we can find five million additional dollars. It will no doubt be either impossible or tough. But we've found our way through past challenges. I'm confident that together we are a team that is smart and resourceful enough to figure it out. But not today—let's lick our wounds and sleep on it."

....

Arriving home, I noted the diminished light, even at 4:30 P.M. The onset of winter is one of the things runners dread most. I was determined to get in a run, hoping that would pick up my mood a bit before I began working the night shift. But this afternoon it wasn't destined to be. As I laced up my running shoes that evening, my heart wasn't in it. The fire in my belly had been replaced by a cold vacuum, my usual optimism by what Winston Churchill once described as the dark dog of depression.

During twenty years of passionate dedication to the sport, I'd never uttered the words "I am too depressed to run."

Until today.

Five. Million. Dollars.

The house felt empty. I thought of calling a friend but knew that I would clearly not be good company. The best alternative seemed to be my home away from home, Chestnut Street's Coffee Roastery. It was only three blocks away, and there I could be near other people while still being alone. I stuffed my computer, several back issues of the *New York Times*, and a stack of news clippings into a duffel bag. With a hangdog countenance and a slow gait, I shuffled past Christmas shoppers and holiday lights that failed to produce any internal "fa-la-la-la-las."

....

A warm greeting from Tha, the Coffee Roastery's friendly owner, lightened my mood a bit. Beethoven's Fifth Symphony and the smell of freshly roasted beans added to that special feeling the Germans refer to as gemütlichkeit. This was the cozy and friendly place this wounded warrior needed.

Tha is originally from Cambodia. He fled the country shortly after the Khmer Rouge takeover, escaping across the western border into Thailand. An industrious man always willing to put in the effort required to land on his feet, he secured work immediately as an interpreter at a UN refugee camp.

"I speak Khmer and a little French. I know some Thai. And although you might not be able to tell, I also speak some English." He'd laughed as he filled me in on his background when we'd first met eight years earlier.

"I felt lucky to have made it to the camp, because the Khmer Rouge had come to my village. They put a machine gun in my hands and told me to kill anyone who looked Vietnamese. I did not want to kill or be killed—I just want peace, brother. So I had to get myself across that border. I walked for five days with no food through the forest, and then thick jungle, always worrying that some Khmer loyalist would find me and have me arrested for deserting, or more likely put a gun to my head and kill me on the spot.

"But after a few weeks I wanted to get out of there. Refugee camps will kill you if you stay because there's no hope for the future, no reason for optimism. Nobody has to work, so they become lazy. What is the English word—lethargic? They have no incentives. I had to get out because that isn't me.

"I came to America. I have family in Seattle, and where I come from, family looks after family. So I went and started working at Starbucks. After a few years the big boss for the region said I was ready to manage a store. He sent me to a small town in the middle of nowhere in Washington. It was remote, and nobody there had ever seen a crazy Cambodian before, especially one offering to make them a café mocha! So I memorized every customer's name and their favorite drink. *Hey, Fred, how are you—you want a medium-sized black coffee, the usual, right? Hi, Susan—medium-sized latte, yes?* I thought that if I did that and remembered every detail, maybe they'd be nicer to me—not hate me because I'm from Cambodia and look different and have to struggle with pretty much every word of the language.

"After seven years, I was ready to go out on my own, so my wife and I came here to the Bay Area. Now we have three shops: one here in the city and two in the East Bay. We're very lucky to be here in America. Sure, I have to work hard. Every day I wake up at four-thirty, and by five o'clock I'm in the store roasting the beans and making coffee for the first customers, who are waiting for me to unlock the door at five-thirty. Some love my coffee; others are just insomniacs.

"My son, Alex, says, 'Daddy, why do you have to wake up so early?' I tell him, 'Son, don't get soft. You owe it to America to make an effort.' While I'm cleaning and opening the store, he is required to study and do his homework."

As I recalled our first few encounters, I was reminded that America is a nation built on immigrant success stories like Tha's. He may not have finished seventh grade, but with his work ethic and devotion to customer service, he and his wife have carved out a solid middle-class existence. Alex and his younger sister, Natalie, live in a country that can guarantee twelve years of free schooling, after which they'll have access to the best university system in the world.

The hissing of the milk steamer interrupted my meditation. "I'm making it extra hot, just the way you like it." Tha's memory for detail never failed to amaze me. My cold hands greedily wrapped the mug in a cobralike grip. His friendly face turned to a glare as I paid for the drink.

"What is this?"

"Sorry, I hit the ATM and all they had were twenties. Do you not have change?"

"Of course I have lots of small bills and some big bills, too, now that I'm a successful American businessman." He laughed. "Your money I won't take. You help the people of Cambodia. You do more for my homeland than I do."

I protested that he has a business to run. This was something like the tenth coffee he'd bought me in the last month. He reached out to shake my hand and then clasped my right hand in both of his. "Brother, you keep doing your work, and I will keep making the coffee. You help those kids in Cambodia who are not as lucky as Alex. That is your role."

The day had just gotten better. The unreliable billionaire might have screwed us over, but the struggling small businessman believed in us and continued to do his part. On that note, I resolved to put the pains of the day behind me. I knew that tomorrow would hit us with the sad reality of making difficult choices of where to cut budgets. Would it be new schools in Nepal, libraries in South Africa, or the launch of our Girls' Education program in Bangladesh—or potentially all of the above?

"Tomorrow," I vowed, "tomorrow," trying to banish these images to some kind of mental Siberia. For the moment, couldn't I simply focus on my adopted family member, my Cambodian American brother, believing in me and helping me to lick my wounds?

My spirit lifted, I grabbed a *New York Times* from my backlogged stack. I hoped to spend the next couple of hours reading, free of outside expectations.

The internal quiet lasted for perhaps ten minutes, maybe fifteen. Sandwiched between articles about financial-market meltdowns and predictions of sustained global recession, one story leaped off the page.

The human brain freezes while trying to process concepts and words that should not be together: The story reported that two men on a motorcycle had used water pistols to spray acid into the faces of girls who were walking to school in the Afghan province of Kandahar. At least twelve girls were attacked and risked being permanently blinded and of having scars that would eat through the skin to expose bone. The men were believed to be Taliban followers who opposed the education of girls and women. Three teachers were also attacked, in a warning to those who dared to educate girls.

I had to read the article three times to begin to comprehend it. I had heard stories in the past about this barbaric method of intimidating women; and yet each time some dispatch arrives from the front lines of misogyny, it's gut-wrenching in its own unique way.

In too many places, a man seeks revenge on a woman who has rejected his courtship by permanently scarring her with sulfuric or hydrochloric acid. *If you will not marry me, then I will ensure that no man will ever marry you. You think you are too beautiful for me. You will now be ugly, scarred for all eternity.*

These horrors occur in Bangladesh and Pakistan, as well as Afghanistan. The forces of darkness continue to find ways to up the ante.

I thought about some of the very smart and promising young women I'd met during my years of travel. Anh, on whose narrow shoulders her family's dreams rested; Mulenga, the young girl in Zambia who was motivated to work extra hours as the librarian's assistant so that she could have extra time with the books; Sunita, who was being protected from her abusive father by her mother, her grandmother, her community, and our Nepal team.

These girls could have what we offered or be abandoned to nefarious forces like the Taliban. That may sound simplistic; but reality often is.

....

In life there are two ways to respond to unimaginable and horrid tragedies: Like a turtle avoiding danger, you can pull your body into its shell—lock the door, draw the drapes, and isolate yourself from the wider world—or you can resolve to respond, immediately, with all your energy and passion, full force.

As Tha dimmed the lights in the coffee shop and began his final sweep of the premises, I pulled out my journal and opened it to an empty, snow white page. I began drafting an open letter not only to these two cowards on the motorcycle, but also to the wider forces of darkness.

> *Dear Bastards,*
>
> *I read about your cowardly act. Do you really want to keep alive a set of beliefs that comes straight out of the eighth century, and do so in a barbaric way? You want to tell little girls that they don't belong in school?*
>
> *Guess what? Our team is going to engage you in battle on this issue. We are going to send the exact opposite message. And we plan to use a much louder megaphone. With every fiber of my being I vow that Room to Read will embrace young girls around the world. We will tell them that we believe in them, that we will support them, and that they belong in school and they will stay in school. We will do this not just today or this year, but every single day until that glorious moment when they become the first member of their family to complete secondary school.*
>
> *Inaction in the face of tyranny is cowardice. Reading about your despicable acts convinces me to oppose you. One of the immutable laws of physics is that for every action there is an equal and opposite reaction.*

Looking up, I stopped talking to the bad guys. I had reached a point of clarity and made a simple vow: *Financial crisis or no crisis, whether donors are flaky or not, Room to Read will stick with our 2009 growth plan. We were debating delaying the launch of our Girls' Education program in Bangladesh. But no; it will be given the green light to launch with our first two hundred girls. The team in Zambia will be told it can triple the number of girls from two hun-*

dred to six hundred. The program in India, in which Muslim girls are a primary focus, will stick with its plan to add more than one thousand girls. Worldwide, we will grow the program from seven thousand girls to more than ten thousand.

Where would the money come from? I did not know. I reminded myself that back in 2000 when I had launched Room to Read, I'd also had no clue. It had been the same when we launched operations in Sri Lanka within a week of the tsunami. We'd had no money for Sri Lanka. And yet we had opened more than one hundred schools within three years.

What I did know was that the one constant of the last seven years was an infinite supply of goodwill. It would take getting my butt out on the road and providing people with an opportunity to take action. We reminded people that they didn't need to be paralyzed by the forces of darkness. With our encouragement, they could exhibit the action-oriented optimism that is the source of all human progress.

I wasn't finished talking to the cowards.

Here's my vow. My team and I will work harder than ever to convince people everywhere in the world to join us in this battle. If I have to personally fund those girl scholars in Bangladesh, I will do so. Nothing could make me happier than writing that check. The financing mechanism is unimportant. What matters most is this: We will oppose you, 24/7. Make no mistake. Our team is larger, and our team is smarter. We will win.

With that, I asked Tha for a cup of coffee to take home as I continued to work the night shift. There were e-mails to send and calls to make.

That event in Sydney? Count me in! The proposed donor meetings in Hong Kong? Ditto. I'm sending an e-mail to Muneer's assistant, Leslie, who always manages to find me frequent-flier tickets. The backlog of New York meeting requests? Let's get every one of them booked by noon tomorrow.

During all the whirlwind travel, I hoped that there would be time to fit in a stop in Bangladesh. I couldn't wait to meet those first two hundred girl scholars.

CHAPTER TWENTY-TWO

Boat to Read

The strong and unpredictable currents are making it extremely difficult for Zaki Hasan to pilot his small boat in tricky tides due to the continued rise of the Jamuna, the largest river in Bangladesh. It is flood season, and a perpetually wet country is once again at risk of drowning.

Upstream the monsoon rains have been both torrential and perpetual. For eighty consecutive days at least two inches of rain have fallen every twenty-four hours. Downstream the effects of the deluge are devastating to the local people.

On this hot afternoon in 2003, the river is wide. Zaki's goal is to visit a local *char,* or river island. The Jamuna, hundreds of miles long and with a width of up to eight miles, is home to hundreds of *chars*. Because the overcrowded country is desperate for land, the majority of the islands are inhabited.

Much of the water lapping the side of Zaki's boat was originally Himalayan glacier. Sometime in the late spring or early summer, the sun began to bake the normally frozen peaks of southwestern Tibet. Once dislodged, the snow and ice begin a journey of nearly two thousand miles. As these melt waters spill into India, they are officially designated part of the Brahmaputra River. The Brahmaputra becomes even deeper and wider as the summer monsoon rains soak large swaths of South Asia.

Upon crossing into Bangladesh, the river is once again renamed the Jamuna. The metamorphosis is now nearly complete. What was once a tiny Himalayan stream has become one of the world's top three rivers in terms of total discharge: Up to one hundred thousand cubic meters per second flow past these sand islands. With the force of an inland tsunami, the river constantly reshapes the *chars*. On a good day, huge deposits of Himalayan silt will become part of the *char*, providing more land for the local people to farm. But on a bad day, thousands of acres of this marginalized land will be washed away.

And on a really bad day? Zaki is about to find out.

....

Life is tough if you grow up in the developing world. It's really tough in Bangladesh. Every year, the United Nations researches and publishes the Human Development Index (HDI), which examines how well governments have done at providing their people with the things that make life worth living. The idea behind the HDI is to aggregate a number of quality-of-life factors into one composite rating. Factors that are considered include availability of clean water, immunization rates, access to health care, school enrollment rates, and life expectancy. A hundred and sixty-nine countries receive rankings. Bangladesh comes in at number 143.

This level of development is akin to that in Benin, Burma, Cameroon, and Yemen. The day-to-day reality for the people of Bangladesh is shocking. Nearly half the children under the age of five are classified as underweight. Less than half the population has access to a phone. The gross national income is about two dollars per person per day. The typical adult has had 4.8 years of schooling.

As difficult as life is for the average Bangladeshi, it is worse for those who live on the *chars*. The river islands are the most marginal land, so only the people with the fewest options will live on them. The areas are highly vulnerable to sudden and forceful flooding, causing erosion and permanent loss of land.

A farmer can witness his field being washed away in less than an hour. During the second hour, he watches his home be taken down by the rising waters. As his tears mix with the river, he then has to decide whether to load his children or the family's livestock onto a small and unstable boat. For many families, this horror is not a once-in-a-lifetime experience. It happens with metronomic regularity every year, along with the monsoon rains. Life on a *char* is an unpredictable and dangerous existence; and yet for five million people it is their day-to-day reality.

The problems for these "sandbar people," as some of the local elite deride them, are exacerbated by a lack of basic government services. Some of this is no doubt due to snobbery, but there is also a pragmatic element: Why build a hospital or a school in a place that's at serious risk of being washed away?

No schools, no roads, no health care, and a small plot of land that can be washed away at a moment's notice make for one of the most tenuous of existences on this sometimes-cruel earth.

Zaki views another boat moving in the direction of his. It appears to be loaded with all of a family's possessions. In the back of the boat, a man paddles his single oar. As he gets closer, Zaki observes that the boat is crammed with bamboo, most likely salvaged from the family's home. There is a small table and chairs, a rusted bicycle, and four chickens. Not used to being on water, they squawk clamorously.

Zaki's voice is barely heard above the din as he tries to get the other man's attention. "Excuse me. I am trying to find the local school to check in on it. This flooding seems like it's even worse this year than last."

The other man laughs morosely and replies: "It is here."

"Really? Where, exactly, is it?"

"Right here."

Zaki, perplexed, asks again for clarification. Years later, as he tells me the story, his face is tinged with the same melancholy it wore back in 2003: "The man laughed again, but it was not a mirthful laugh. It was more of a helpless, existential one. He pointed to the bottom of the boat on which I was traveling and said, 'The school is right there, under your boat. It was underwater as of two days ago.'

"Ever since that day, I have been saddened to think of the conditions faced by the people living on the sandbar islands. I term the situation 'consistent inconsistency.' These are my fellow citizens, millions of them. They have some of the most difficult lives in this world. It was on that day that I vowed to do more to help them."

Zaki found himself back on this same stretch of river just seven years later. This time, it was destined to be a much happier experience.

....

Zaki joined Room to Read as "our man in Dhaka" early in 2009. The experience described above occurred during his tenure with the British NGO ActionAid. Later he worked for Save the Children. In late 2008 he applied for the newly created position of country director for Room to Read Bangladesh. Having opened South Africa as our seventh country and Zambia as our eighth, it had taken us a few years to bring those operations up to speed. With their leadership teams now in place, we were once again in expansion mode.

Zaki's mandate was to launch our operations in Bangladesh. When I met him at our global headquarters in San Francisco, and then at the annual country directors' conference in Sri Lanka, both times his first question to me was: "When are you coming to Bangladesh? I am trying to build a cohesive team. I need your help. The team has read your book. But what will really help me to inculcate the Room to Read history and culture is to have you there. Please, I know you are always traveling already, but tell me, when can you visit us?"

I was a bit nervous to share my trepidation with Zaki. I had never been to his country. The only images I had were the ones from the world's news media. And most of them were negative: a bloody civil war in 1971; the mass starvation that led to George Harrison's famous Concert for Bangladesh; one of the highest poverty rates in the world. It was not the stuff of tourist brochures.

But of course, my job is not to be a tourist but to go instead to the places where our work is most needed. On top of this, I was really impressed with Zaki. He was extremely well read and intelligent. By the age of thirty-five he had earned three different master's degrees. "Studying is my most time-consuming hobby," he told me in our initial meeting.

He was also thoughtful and humble. During his first visit, he attended a fund-raising event hosted by our long-term board member Hilary Valentine and her husband, Don Listwin, in their beautiful home in the Silicon Valley community of Woodside. Zaki spent most of the evening walking around her sequoia-filled backyard with a Flip camera, talking to our investors. "I want my team back in Bangladesh to know why you support Room to Read. If you tell them in your own words why you are willing to invest your money in a country that is ten thousand miles away, it will motivate them more than ever to make sure they spend it wisely. I want them to feel like a custodian, who has to be both efficient and ethical at putting your funding to work."

He had indeed put together a great team. During my first conference call with them, listening to their well-thought-out questions, I was ready to accept Zaki's offer to visit Bangladesh. As if she were reading my mind, the final question came from Ruksana, our Girls' Education program officer: "John, we read the e-mails you send out about your experiences visiting our work in South Africa and Cambodia and Zambia. When are you going to pay us the honor of a visit? I'd like for you to meet our girls and see our first school libraries."

It finally happened in August 2010. The record monsoon rains had recently ended. As Zaki and I shook hands in my hotel lobby, he told me that he'd waited for this moment for two years. Then he peered over the tops of his glasses. His sincere eyes met mine, and I immediately knew that this signaled his intention to ask a very serious question.

"Do you mind if we eat here tonight, at your hotel?"

"Okay by me. Why—do you want to keep things expeditious?"

"No, anything but. I have been asking you to come to Bangladesh for two years, and you are finally here. I want to make this a long meal."

"Good. We have a lot to catch up on. But to be candid, I'd rather soak up a little of the local culture. Nothing against the Dhaka Westin, of course." I laughed.

Again Zaki gazed over the top of his glasses with eyes that could launch a Hollywood career.

"We should stay here. It is Ramadan. During this period, it is considered a bad thing to drink alcohol in public—unless you are in an establishment that caters to foreigners."

"Are you worried about me? I don't mind not having drinks with dinner."

"No, it is not that. I promised to buy you a beer when you came to visit. I want to honor my word. I have been looking forward to this. Tonight," he said with a laugh, "I am a bad Muslim. My observance is usu-ally faithful, but this evening will be an exception."

As my bad Muslim friend and I sat at the bar, he told me more about the work our team was doing to help the education situation on the river islands.

"John, you will see tomorrow that the *chars* are the extreme example of poverty, of villages that have literally no facilities: no roads, high schools, electricity, water supplies, or hospitals. The people are completely mar-ginalized. When I worked with ActionAid and first visited the *chars*, I became convinced that a lot more needed to be done. The image of that school being washed away never left me. When working on my second master's degree, in economic development, I found out that this was a depressingly common occurrence. So when we brought Room to Read to Bangladesh, I became convinced that we should first work with the river islands.

"We went out to do our research, which included visits to thirteen dif-ferent *chars*. We visited on multiple occasions, so that we'd gain the trust of the people before asking them too many questions. What we found in all of the villages was a lack of educational uplift. We asked around to as many people as possible, and we could not find a single girl who had ever finished secondary education. Not one. Can you believe it? Is this 2010 or 1810?

"There are also no libraries. Finding a 'library' in any of these islands would be like finding a living organ floating in outer space. Every com-munity we visited needs our intervention. There are also very few books for children in the Bangala language, so we are launching the local-language publishing program.

"Our team talked to a lot of people in government and at other chari-ties. Many people told us that such areas are difficult to work in. They talked all about the obstacles—lack of roads, entire villages having to fre-quently relocate, long and inefficient travel by slow boat. There were also no other groups doing education work in these regions, so we'd not have anybody to help show us the way. We were told that we would definitely fail."

"Definitely fail?" I interjected.

"Yes, that is a verbatim quote. That made us even more convinced that we should go into these islands, to prove that just because people lived on these silty islands didn't make education for their children any less a priority than anywhere else in Bangladesh."

Now it was my turn. I was a bad Buddhist and waved down a second round.

Not missing a beat, Zaki continued. "I told my team to invest as much time as possible getting to know the people. Only by meeting them on multiple occasions could we develop a respectful and symbiotic relationship. We'd then have at least a chance of convincing them to be part of the eventual solution. If we showed up out of the blue and immediately started asking difficult questions, we would not learn the truth—we'd only get the answers they thought we wanted to hear.

"Our team had to walk miles in blistering heat during the dry season. It was worse during the monsoon, as they'd get soaked by rain and be forced to rely on an inefficient and unpredictable boat taxi system to get out to the islands. I requested that they bear the pain for three months. *If we don't help these children, nobody will. So yes, our job is difficult. But the lives of the children on the* chars *are tougher, and for them we should be willing to make a sacrifice.*"

I reminded Zaki that when the going gets tough, as when we had our South African calamity, I would tell our team, "Stick with it, and don't get discouraged. If this stuff was easy, it would have been done by now."

"Yes, I said something similar to my staff. And tomorrow, John, when you see what we have done, I know that you will be very proud of our Room to Read Bangladesh, the new kids on the block!"

....

The next day, as our team drove east out of Dhaka, I noticed with a great deal of panic that Bangladesh had failed one of my own personal litmus tests for a nation's development: Does the country's national highway have a dividing line? Ambiguity in this regard can, of course, lead to a Darwinian free-for-all, as vehicles are all over the road and both shoulders. Judging by the chaos, the local truck and bus drivers probably would have ignored a dividing line anyway. They were without a doubt the most aggressive drivers I'd seen during travels to more than fifty countries. The lorry drivers in particular made their Indian brethren look list-less and nonconfrontational in comparison. The driver of our van came within inches of the motor scooters in front of us before blasting them with his cacophonous horn.

Immune to it, Zaki continued where we'd left off the night before.

"On one of my last visits to the *char* we are visiting today, I asked about the situation of the girls. How was it possible that not a single girl from any of these thirteen island communities had ever finished secondary school?

"Then a village elder pointed to two girls who looked to be about eleven or twelve. 'Those two over there,' he said, 'are part of the reason. Last year they were in grade five. They are no longer in school because they are now married. Their husbands are ten years older and wanted to marry young brides.'

"I was aware that we now had a circle of local people surrounding us," Zaki continued. "They were obviously eager for a distraction, as not much really happens out on these islands. But I did not let their presence deter me. I asked him: 'Were you present at the two weddings?' He gave a wide smile, most probably remembering the tasty treats served, and nodded.

"I continued my questioning: 'Why did you not try to stop it, when we know the legal age of marriage for a girl in Bangladesh is eighteen?'

"The old man replied: 'Well, if her father is saying that she is eighteen, then who can alter that?'

"I realized then that we had a task ahead of us. We had to end the day that girls become the victims of this cruel life experience called early marriage. Until we do so, we will not be able to improve the situation of girls' education.

"When I tried to ask the two girls about their reasons for dropping out, they were silent. I persisted and asked whether anything could have been done to help them continue their education. They remained mum. To break the silence, I asked a leading question: 'If we were to provide you with study materials and pay for the school fees, could that help continue your education?'

"One of them very quickly shook her head. She looked very sad as she told me: 'We do need those materials, but that would not be enough to solve the problem. This is the way it happens here. Nobody can change that.'"

As our bus zoomed past several more terrified moped drivers, Zaki told our group that he hadn't wanted to give up hope. He knew that they'd have to change the community's mind-set but that this would be only the start.

"All was not lost. We talked to other girls about why they were not in school. They said that their *char* had only a primary school, but no secondary school. They could walk to that secondary school during the dry season, but once the monsoons hit, the river was impossible to cross. And this was not a one-week or two-week problem. It could last up to three months."

"Once a student misses that much schooling, they are all but guaranteed to fail," one of our Bangladesh staff members interjected.

Zaki nodded vigorously. "Exactly! There is a reason those girls got married right after fifth grade. The local belief is that once a girl finishes school, it's time for her to get married. But what does 'finish' mean? Should a girl finish school after grade five, at age eleven, or after grade twelve, when she's nineteen?

"As I left that island, I was thinking that if only we could find a way to extend schooling to grade twelve, it would have a big effect: an end to child marriage, fewer children born in resource-scarce areas, more options for the girl to find work that is better paid, and of course the opportunity to raise a family that is better educated and healthier.

"I was getting onto the boat we'd hired for the day and was asked by a woman from the island whether she could join me for the forty-five-minute ride to the west bank of the river. Since she was from this area, I thought it would be a great opportunity to have a focus group and get a lot of information from her during the trip."

"So her free ride would not really be free?" I laughed. One of Zaki's several graduate degrees was an MBA, so this idea of an open-air focus group, under the scorching Bangladeshi sun, should not have come as a complete surprise.

"That's true," he admitted with a smile. "My friend Showkat, who runs a local NGO that works on these islands, was with me. Immediately both of us started asking this woman questions. We learned that she had finished secondary school. 'How?' I asked. 'You are the first one I am meeting from this area who completed school.' She told me that she had actually grown up in a city on the mainland but had married a man from this *char*. Now they had two children of their own.

"When I asked how far she visualized her children being educated, she was very clear in her response: 'Well, they have to at least study up to the level that I've studied up to, and then go higher. But they do have to face many challenges. Like this river. Without your support today, I would not be able to cross these waters. This river is our biggest challenge.'"

At this point of the story, a huge smile of relief crossed Zaki's face. It was as if he were at the magical moment when he could stop talking about the problem and focus on the solution.

"I threw out a thought: 'I wish there was a boat service available for these children.' Showkat didn't allow my words to fall on the surface before he jumped up, rocking the boat with his excitement. 'Why can't that happen? We already have a boat service to carry sick islanders to the nearest hospital in the mainland. They send emergency messages through cell phones. We call this service "river ambulance." Why can't you do the same and have a school boat?'"

Zaki was now talking a mile a minute. "My mind was racing and I yelled with enthusiasm: 'We can even call it Boat to Read!'

"Showkat was already imagining this solution. 'The boat should be filled with books. This way,' he enthused, 'children will be able to use the long travel time to read. We can help girls go to school, while also encouraging the habit of reading.'

"So we did it. As you say—GSD—Get Stuff Done! And just think of this, John. In thirty minutes, we will be there, and you will be the first foreigner ever to ride on the Boat to Read!"

....

From the west bank of the Jamuna, it was impossible to see across to the east side. The monsoons that caused the record floods that put Pakistan into the news headlines in the summer of 2010 had had their own negative impact on Bangladesh. The river was as wide and fast as it had ever been. Zaki told me that during the dry season, the place where we were standing would be about two miles from the riverbank.

"During this time the students can wade across a few small streams. By walking just one or two miles they will be at school. But during the monsoons, the only young learners who can get off the *chars* are those whose parents can afford to buy a motorized boat or pay the infrequent water taxis. But of course, if you have money, you would not be living on a river island in the first place, would you?"

I thought of the headmaster in Nepal. "We are too poor to afford education. But until we have education . . ."

Just then, in the near distance, we saw a beautiful sight: Three boats were approaching, all filled with students sporting green school uniforms. As they pulled up to the bank, we saw that they were all wearing handmade hats bearing six of my favorite words, the official Room to Read motto: "World Change Starts with Educated Children."

Beaming with pride, they welcomed us on board. As we pulled out into the strong currents, the Jamuna no longer seemed so frightening. The boat felt secure, and we were among friends. Through an interpreter, a fourteen-year-old girl told me that she had never had a positive impression of the outside world that existed beyond the *chars*.

"I always thought none of the city people ever cared a bit about any of us sandbar people. I wondered why they could not see our plight and do something about it. I lived in fear of being forced into marriage with a much older man. And now . . . now anything is possible for me. Everyone on our island is realizing that you believe we can be successful."

All three boats were making parallel progress upriver. The girls on each boat waved back and forth among themselves and to the foreign guests. The Boat to Read flag on each stern flapped proudly in the breeze. I observed this scene, and then suddenly it hit me.

Baby Fish Goes to School! This is it, in real life. The children's story written and illustrated by two Sri Lankan teenage girls was coming to life here on this overflowing river in the middle of rural Bangladesh. These two hundred girls were like Baby Fish. They wanted to go to school. But their school was on land. It was inaccessible. Zaki and his team were like the animals, including the clever rabbit. Their "fishbowls" were these sim-ple open-air wooden boats.

A problem had been overcome with a creative solution that was also simple and low cost.

I allowed my thoughts to drift back to the Coffee Roastery and the day I'd made a vow. Just two years ago I had been so frustrated by Mr. X's stiffing us and then an even bigger flameout as a different investor re-neged on her family's five-million-dollar pledge. Stuck in the maw of the biggest financial meltdown since the Great Depression, I'd made a vow that day not to cut a single dollar from any of our in-country budgets. The news of the cowardly Taliban acid attacks on the girls who had "dared" to go to school had persuaded me not to delay the launch of the Girls' Education program in Bangladesh. All these forces had come to-gether to inspire a pledge that we would be a force for good in a world desperately in need of it.

Boats? Check. Girls? Check. Reading? Check. We had snatched victory from the jaws of defeat. Not through any one silver bullet. Just tenacity, a GSD attitude, and a refusal to let any extraneous factor stop our optimism and GSD spirit. Our version of the future would, we hoped and prayed, inevitably win.

CHAPTER TWENTY-THREE

"If You Cannot Read, School Can Be a Torture"

Am I dreaming? Ismat Ara Shyama asked herself. The thirteen-year-old girl, enrolled in grade seven at Kishali School, could not believe what she was seeing in the school yard; nor could the other two hundred students. They were shouting and cheering the greatest surprise in their young lives.

This was indeed perhaps the most exciting day in the history of the small village of Mohammadpur. The school was hosting a visit by Junaid Siddique, Mahmudullah Riyad, and Shahriar Nafees. You may never have heard of these three men, but they are rock stars in Bangladesh or, more accurately, cricket stars in a cricket-mad nation. The "Bangladesh Tigers" were in the midst of participating in the International Cricket Council's World Cup tournament. The eyes of the nation were on its heroes, hoping that they'd advance to the finals by beating historic rivals like India, Pakistan, and Sri Lanka.

At the sound of a whistle, five dozen students gathered around Room to Read Bangladesh country director Zaki Hasan. He announced that in just one minute, the first round of the Read and Run game would commence. Best of all, the cricket stars would be joining the students in the fun.

One of my favorite parts of the day is when our in-country teams send me "stories from the field," highlighting how our organization's work is having a real impact on children and communities. Ever since my Boat to Read trip, the Bangladesh team had continued to feed me a steady stream of inspiring anecdotes and photographs. The traffic could also be two way. When I had told Zaki that Room to Read was going to be the official education partner of the Cricket World Cup, he had reacted with elation. His team had immediately begun brainstorming on how the national cricket team could help promote a culture of reading at our libraries. "If children look up to these stars," Zaki had said, "they will listen if the cricket players tell them to read always."

Like Boat to Read, the Read and Run activity was an innovation invented by our Bangladesh team. The game combined the energy children had for playing in the outdoors with the joy of reading.

Each student participating toed the starting line. Their eyes drifted over to one of the special guests, who soon counted down: "Three, two, one—GO!"

Within a nanosecond students were running across the rocky patch of earth that served as the school's playground. After fifty meters, they each stopped at a check-in point, where one of the school's teachers handed them a book. The activity tested not only their physical stamina but also their mental endurance. After the students indicated to the teacher that they had read the two pages to which the book had been opened, they were asked a comprehension question. If they got it right, they could fly off to the next reading post. If not, they'd have to read the pages again and make a second attempt at the answer.

As they ran between the reading posts, the students' faces were lit up with the pure adrenaline that every runner knows well. When they arrived, their faces bore looks of intense concentration. After nailing the question at the fourth reading post, they screamed and yelled as they ran toward the finish line. The only ones yelling louder were their fellow students cheering them on from the sidelines.

The top two winners from each heat would go to the finals. The top ten finishers in the finals would each receive a special prize of . . . you guessed it . . . books for their own personal libraries.

As the preliminary heats continued, Zaki explained to the Tiger trio the idea behind the game: "Reading should be seen as something fun. In too many places, it's badly presented by the teachers or parents as something that's a chore, something that the kids are *required* to do. Sometimes I think we need to teach them to be better at marketing." He chuckled.

"Our approach is very different. We show the children that reading can be such a great joy, that it can be every bit as much fun as running in a footrace with your friends. And of course the prizes of books are important. We don't want to give the winners candy or soda. Instead, we want to emphasize that books are so important that they should be valued by all students. And to those who don't win, we say to them that this is okay, because their school has a library with thousands of books, so in that sense every student is a winner. No one need go home today without books."

....

The Read and Run game was one small part of a much larger transition as we approached our ten-year anniversary in 2010. We'd been hearing a lot of input from our in-country teams that they wanted Room to Read's programs to continue to evolve, with a heavier emphasis on literacy, reading, and writing skills. In many of our libraries not every child could take advantage of the opportunity we were providing. Kall Kann, our country director for Cambodia, pointed to a World Bank study showing that 43 percent of grade-three students in his country could not read at an age-appropriate level. For nearly half the children in the country, a library would therefore not be relevant unless steps were taken to elevate the children to a baseline level of literacy.

Pushkar Shrestha, head of Room to Read Nepal—the successor to Dinesh Shrestha, who was promoted into an Asia-wide regional role (Shrestha is a very common name in Nepal)—reported similar issues in his country: "Most of the curriculum in Nepalese schools makes the assumption that parents are literate. But more than half of the population here is illiterate. And once you start going to more rural areas and villages, the literacy rate goes down even further. Parents cannot help their children in the early grades, because they don't know how to read themselves. We need to make sure that the nation's roots—the primary schools—are strong. Only when primary-school children are strong in reading can they move forward."

Staff members at our global headquarters in San Francisco were making similar arguments. Stacey Warner, who had become our first global program director of literacy, suggested that we needed to step back and say to ourselves: "This is great; we've got all the books, we've got the portals, the libraries. But in a lot of our countries we are hearing that many children can't actually read."

As Erin and I heard this input, it reminded us in many ways of the early days of Room to Read and that first evaluation, in which 52 percent of our young customers were telling us they'd use the library more often if there were more books in their mother tongue. The data we'd collected had challenged us to evolve. Now we were one of the biggest children's publishers in the developing world, and in 2011 we would be awarded the Confucius Prize for Literacy by UNESCO (the United Nations Education, Scientific and Cultural Organization) for our local language–publishing program. It was further proof that we should take calculated risks and invest in the continued evolution of the organization, even if the obstacles sometimes seemed formidable.

At Room to Read we've continued to innovate, making numerous program modifications over the years. One of the biggest ones was investing in training teachers and librarians. We recognized that a library could only be a true temple of reading if the adults in charge were making it a welcoming environment for the school's students. They'd need to be skilled in organizing the library in a coherent way so that young readers could find age-appropriate books that interested them. We taught them to set up checkout systems, so that students would take books home with them. This allowed for learning to take place outside the school day, and by 2011 our evaluation reports showed that 98 percent of our libraries had functioning checkout systems in place.

We also brainstormed with teachers on how to create activities that encourage the "habit of reading," like the Read and Run games in Bangladesh.

In the best Room to Read tradition, the home-office team responded to what we heard from the field.

One of the first things Erin did when she became CEO in 2008 was to initiate a strategic planning process. As an organization, we stepped back and had a series of detailed conversations over nine months: What would the next logical evolution be for Room to Read?

The strategic planning process brought in outside experts Erin referred to as "critical friends." That adjective was quite telling and very important. We were not seeking their praise. We instead craved their constructive criticism. We wanted to know where we were weak and where we could be doing better.

Our team drew up its wish list of the superstars in international education and development: education professors from Harvard and Stanford, senior-level staff from foundations like Gates and Hewlett, experts from world-class NGOs like Grameen Bank, and girls' education experts from the Population Council and the Academy for Educational Development.

Erin and the management team were dogged and persistent in recruiting this group, even though we were asking them to work pro bono. And much to our delight, eighteen of the twenty on our wish list signed on! They would become part of a hallowed tradition at Room to Read as we exhorted ourselves: *Let's not be good. Let's be great!*

The conversations and arguments that would take place over the coming nine months were some of the most insightful, vociferous, and passionate we'd ever had. As in the discussions and debates around the Africa expansion, we were about to embark on a similarly raucous exercise.

....

Our organization was founded by three generalists; Dinesh, Erin, and I did not have academic or education backgrounds. As the organization grew, we hired more and more experts in key strategic areas, such as girls' education, librarian training, language acquisition, and mother-tongue publishing. There were times when it could be intimidating for me to be in a meeting, as I'd feel the conversation was over my head. But I knew from experience that without delegation there is no scaling, and that sometimes the best thing a founder can do is to get out of the way. But it was not easy, especially since a stern questioning or a criticism of "the ways of the past" could brush uncomfortably close to the personal.

I'd remind myself that there was no sense in hiring really smart people, or recruiting them as advisers, and then refusing to listen. So many NGOs have stayed small because the founding team never made the leap to having empowered staff willing to speak their minds. Egowise, it's a lot more fun if everyone is praising and genuflecting in your direction. But that works no better in the charity world than it does for North Korea's economy.

Some of the people I most respected were also blunt. Sunisha Ahuja, the founder of Room to Read India, opined: "We can't just build schools and fill libraries with books: We also have to examine the skills of the children reading those books and the lives they lead. To become independent readers, students must move from letter recognition to word and sentence formation to actual reading and writing on their own."

Unless we helped them to take this journey, she argued, we'd not have as deep an impact as she wanted to have in India. And since her own country contains 37 percent of all the illiterate people in the world, we needed to get India right.

A longtime advisory board member praised the organization for "already being on a journey to measuring outcomes, not just outputs." It was no longer enough, he argued, to judge ourselves by how many schools we'd built or how many libraries we'd established or books we'd published. We had to measure the outcomes: Were more children becoming literate? Did students increase the number of books they were reading? Were they more likely to develop the critically important "habit of reading" at a young age as a result of Room to Read's intervention?

The discussions also unveiled many of the challenges we'd face. We'd be required to develop the skill set of teaching teachers how to teach reading, and not just in one language but in a dozen. This would also require our team to deepen its level of cooperation and engagement with governments, as teacher training was almost always the domain of the ministries of education. Finally, we'd have to raise even more money and begin to transition our model from the direct fund-a-project approach (e.g., sponsoring a school or a library).

Something as esoteric-sounding as "literacy" might not be as sexy as "a school dedicated to your parents." But I also realized that many of our long-term investors trusted us; if we asked them to redirect their funding to this new area, we'd at least get a fair hearing.

I also thought about Muneer's rocket-ship analogy. If children could not read from a young age, the trajectory was obviously off. We needed a course correction.

This thought, plus two memorable quotes from other people I trusted, served as great closing arguments and persuaded me to salute the literacy flag. One was from Kall, our Cambodia country director. "When you are poor in reading at this stage [third grade], imagine the implications. If you cannot read, school can be a torture. And if you can't catch up with your classmates, you are filled with shame: That's one of the main reasons kids drop out."

I thought of my own third-grade self, with my teacher, Miss Burdett, looking out for me. She'd constantly encourage to me to read, help me with the words I found difficult, and then test my ability to turn these words into coherent thoughts by asking questions that tested my comprehension. We could truly change post–Khmer Rouge Cambodia if a similar scene became the "new normal" for the nation's children.

The second quote came after a daylong convening of our group of critical friends. We'd been at it for eleven hours over the course of two days, and most of our brains were scrambled by this point. In an attempt to end the day on a note of clarity, Erin and I had asked the group to boil down those eleven hours of discussion and debate and close the day with each expert offering us one coherent and, ideally, concise (not always a strong suit for academic types!) piece of advice. Halfway around the table, one of them gave us a gem. It was like a Zen koan, offering a fundamental truth disguised in a deceptively simple statement: "You know, John and Erin, there's a reason you didn't call this organization 'Room with Books.'"

....

Phuong Giang is the librarian at Ngu Hiep #1 Primary School in the Tien Giang province of southern Vietnam. She works in the library in addition to teaching classes at the school but receives no additional compensation for taking on this additional responsibility. She does it, she told me, out of her love for reading and for her students.

"The school where I work is in a remote area with so many difficulties in transportation. There is not any bookstore or library, neither in the school nor on this small islet. The only way students can access book resources is through the school library. I love reading and treasure every book I have. When I was young, my family was very poor, but I always saved money up to buy secondhand books.

"Before I came to work, my school was in the same situation as the schools in Nepal I read about in your book [in 2011 *Leaving Microsoft to Change the World* came out in Vietnamese—the twenty-second language in which it was published]; that is, without a real library. Ours was a room about half the size of the classroom, containing only two old bookshelves full of termites. Books got moldy because of dampness. The situation got worse, since no teacher volunteered to take the responsibility of taking care of the library.

"Finally I volunteered. I realized that the library is the spirit of the school, [the] cradle of knowledge. How could we improve the teaching quality without books and a functioning library?"

She spoke rapidly and with passion. I was listening intently, as our work in literacy and habit of reading depends so markedly on teachers like Phuong.

"Once a student brought me a book and asked: 'Teacher, what does the phrase "not for sale" mean?' He said this while pointing to the stamp that your team puts on the inside front cover of your Vietnamese-language books. I held gently on his shoulder and explained: '"Not for sale" means the book cannot be sold. It means books provided by Room to Read are given to poor communities like ours.' He nodded as he began to understand. Then he asked, 'Will Room to Read give us books forever?'"

She expressed her own appreciation for our Vietnam team's efforts to help her school. "I believe the Room to Read organization will develop even more strongly in the future. It's a pride and honor for anybody who works with your organization. I promise that I will always work hard to lead every generation of students to the colorful world of knowledge that Room to Read has brought to the library at my school."

Our country director for Vietnam, Mr. Phong Le, asked why she is willing to work so hard to make sure that her students gain literacy and the habit of reading.

"I will educate students that they should always have a kind heart, a deep love of their fellow humans. The children here and in many places have been given a bad living condition on this earth. But there is nothing but happiness in the innocent eyes of children holding a colorful new book. Books are a precious and meaningful gift to a child's whole life and to the next generation. If there are no books in a childhood, life will become more uncertain later on. It is your team at Room to Read and you, Uncle John, who light up the fire: the fire of heart, of compassion, of knowledge and ethics."

I reminded her that our team is only partially responsible—that we can establish all the libraries in the world, but that they only prove their worth by being utilized by the children. She is even more critical than we are, I reminded her.

She was not even close to being finished. Next she shared her goal: "To open a new horizon full of sunlight and spacious roads ahead of millions of children." She would encourage them to "walk and move forward strongly. Your futures are in front of you."

While reading my book, she said, she'd decided that "Uncle John" was dedicated to "action and action" and that this had led to Room to Read's success today. This librarian understood the GSD concept—even if she used different words to describe it!

....

In Zambia, our team was all about "action and action" in implementing our first literacy programs. I had the pleasure of seeing one of the hundreds of teachers with whom we were working during a visit to Zambia in the summer of 2011. Grace, a young woman three years out of college, was teaching words to her second-grade class. As she held up cards in both the local Bemba language and English, her forty students enthusiastically yelled, "Banana! Sunday! Cow! Flag! School!" Each word was yelled at high volume, with the kinetic energy one feels in a well-run classroom.

The students later showed us an activity that reminded me of the Read and Run game in Bangladesh. This version was more like "Run and Spell." Teams lined up, and upon hearing "Go!" the first runner in each team would sprint to a "spelling station" staffed by either teachers or older student volunteers. After a word was read from a card, the students would have to spell it aloud. If they succeeded, they ran to the next spelling station.

If not, they got one more attempt, all the while, no doubt, watching their competitors dash ahead. If they missed again, one of their teammates raced to replace them. Some of the words would have challenged me: "occasion," "anathema," "perseverance" (as I typed that last word, spell-check underlined it in red).

I was impressed, and even more so when Grace told me that this new program had been going for only six weeks. The students seemed to be learning and having fun at the same time. Grace said that she preferred active learning like this over the "old way of so-called learning, where I stand in the front of the room, say something, and the students passively repeat it. That is not learning. That is just memorization. Here we spend time with the children sitting on the floor in small circles. We give the first graders words with missing letters, while the second graders get short sentences with missing words. They have to play detective and identify what's missing. They can look so perplexed for a while. But the instant they get it, their faces just light up."

The most interesting change she's seen takes place outside the classroom. "In the morning, before school starts at seven A.M., I see children standing alongside the road, watching trucks drive by. I thought it was the usual child's fascination with big objects. Then I noticed that they were pointing, talking, and seemed to be debating something. When I walked over, I was shocked but also elated, because the students were decoding words written on the side of trucks.

"'That one is delivering beef,' a first grader told me. When another truck drove by, a second-grade student said, 'That one is a dairy truck, full of milk and ice cream.' Oh, was I ever excited to see children do something that is too rare—not only learning in the classroom but also applying that knowledge in real life."

CHAPTER TWENTY-FOUR

"Three Completely Pregnant Cows"

As the worldwide teams set our sights higher by adding literacy to our program focus, many of our students were also aiming higher and raising their own personal bars. Without knowing they were doing so, they were sending us signals that they were often thinking even bigger than we were.

The original goal of our Girls' Education program had been to help girls to complete secondary school. We had later added a second ambition: that they'd also have "the skills necessary to negotiate key life decisions." Year after year, our girls made us proud, with pass rates to the next grade averaging over 96 percent. This meant that hundreds (and soon thousands) of them were getting closer to secondary-school graduation. Many confided to their social mobilizers that while they were proud to be the first woman in their families to finish secondary school, they were not content to stop there. They'd learned during their life-skills classes that university and tertiary education were two of their postsecondary options.

Room to Read could not help them financially, as we were keeping our focus on tripling the number of girls in secondary school; but there were other options, such as local scholarships or working part time to help to cover their tuition costs.

Our field staff was inventing very creative ways to encourage the girls. Zaki and his team in Bangladesh, as one example, hosted a field trip in which more than two hundred girls from the *chars* (river islands) came into the capital city and were given a tour of the University of Dhaka. On the front steps of the university, they received a pep talk from Zaki. "One day, if you want it, you can be here, going to university. Think of that—to be a girl from the *chars* who becomes a university scholar. You can take good care of your family once you start earning money, and also help our nation to develop." When I heard about this, I thought about the acid-throwing cowards on the motorbikes. We were defeating them.

And then the encouragement being given to the girls was amplified as the university president joined the group. He also encouraged the girls to aim high. "Just because your parents did not go to school, this does not mean anything today. What matters most is what you want to do and whether you are willing to work hard to see your dreams come true."

After the tour, each girl was given a university application. You may be too young to apply today, Zaki told them, but that does not mean you can't start thinking about it. "One day you could be filling this out for real. And over the next hour, you will see that it's not a difficult process. I want you to go home today with that completed application in your backpack and visualize the day you will make this journey again. But next time, you could be doing it as an admitted student to university!"

....

Sreymom Matt is nineteen years old. She attends Cambodia's Royal University of Agriculture. A graduate of Room to Read's Girls' Education program, she now majors in agricultural economics and rural development. Sreymom grew up on a small plot of land. Like many of today's adults in Cambodia, her parents had minimal education, due to the problems of the postwar era. As a young child, she had a love of animals. In addition, she had a dream of how those animals could be a conduit through which her family could have a better life.

"I have always tried my best to study. But I live in a poor family, so I always wondered if they'd be able to afford to send me to school. If I want to rise above the life in my village and have better opportunities, then I will need to study harder and do more than the average person."

Life was being lived at the margin, and nothing was guaranteed. In 2003 she persuaded her parents to buy a baby cow, which was less expensive than an adult. When the cow was older, the milk could be sold, she enthused. Then, thinking bigger, she proposed that they team up with another family that owned a "boy cow." The families could share evenly in the calves that would be born over the years.

Sreymom even sacrificed her recess period to go behind the school and cut grass for her cow. "While the other children played, I harvested all the grasses that grew against the side of the school building and in the back field."

Our team's social mobilizers, who are responsible for keeping in close contact with our girls and encouraging them to succeed, saw a spark in Sreymom and wanted to remove the uncertainty from her life. She was also a perfect candidate for our life-skills program, which works with girls to be ready for "what comes next" once they complete secondary school. Her natural precocity, work ethic, and self-confidence touched everyone who met her.

"I have always tried my best. I realized when I was young I had to work hard to have an easier life when I get older. I worked hard and studied four to five hours a day. I made a schedule to manage my studies and my work. I even added some time to listen to music. I didn't sleep much. When I got to grade ten, the workload increased."

And then in the summer of 2010, an American couple from Michigan who had always been generous investors in Room to Read met a group of our students. They were so impressed that they make a blanket offer to the group of assembled girls. "Any of you who want to attend university, raise your hands. We will sponsor your tuition, room, and board." With a smile as luminous as the full moon during the Tet lunar holiday, Sreymom thrust her arm proudly in the air.

She is now in her second year of university and writes beautiful letters to her benefactors, describing her dream of helping her nation escape the ranks of least-developed status. "When I graduate with my Bachelor's Degree, I want to return to the countryside. I want to inform them about agriculture and increase yields. This helps the whole community to become more successful. By the time I graduate I will be able to teach them how to earn money to support their families and reduce domestic violence and improve life skills. I also want to help people find customers. I think you call this *marketing*. This will improve household income and provide people with new knowledge every day."

She once described her original plans: "If I study at university, I will sell my cows to support my study." But her benefactors had a different idea: Why couldn't the family keep the cows and continue to sell the milk, so that Sreymom's siblings could also go to school? Then the cows could eventually be sold if those siblings wanted to go to university or if Sreymom pursued graduate school.

In late 2011 she reported back to her benefactors with some good news: "With smiling face, I can tell you that I now have three cows. And they are all completely pregnant."

She was not only happy for herself but also eager to teach other families that they could follow her example. "They [the cows] are an achievement which makes possible my further study. If I can get money from cows, then other families can learn from me, and do the same. I will develop my country and I will study for a Master's degree at the same time."

She closed the letter with an invitation: "When I have a good job, I will call you. You can come back to Cambodia and eat something with me."

....

Just a few hundred miles northeast of Sreymom lives a man who also found a unique path to university and whose life was changed greatly as a result.

Nguyen Thai Vu is the young man I met in Hue, Vietnam, who asked for my help with computer lessons. We've stayed in touch via e-mail ever since the day we met in 1997. During our short time together, as I tried to give him computer lessons, it was obvious that he immediately grasped the key points of Excel. He even went so far as to suggest a few keystroke shortcuts that I was not aware of, even after seven years at Microsoft. I suggested that we buy him a few books so that he could study during his eleven-hour shifts at the hotel desk.

"No, you cannot do that. If you buy me things, you are not my friend," he said with great pride.

I appealed to him, saying that a student with his brainpower deserved books and that I'd also buy him practice time at a local computer school. Again he refused. I had little choice but to resort to an elaborate and ultimately successful subterfuge.

Sitting alone that night at a small family-run café on the banks of Hue's placid Perfume River, I made up a story that would ultimately transform his world. Knowing that Vu was too proud to accept a direct handout of cash from me, his new "coffee-drinking friend," I hit upon an alternative, a way for him to save face. Ripping a page out of my journal, I freehand sketched the best forgery of my life. The "certificate" announced that Vu was the recipient of the first-ever "Bill Gates Scholarship for Promising Vietnamese Students." The benefits of this award included money for books and for taking classes at the local academy.

Tucking a twenty-dollar bill and the certificate in an envelope, I wrote, "Congratulations, Nguyen Thai Vu," across the front. Then I asked the kind, avuncular proprietor for an ice-cold 333 Vietnamese beer. Kicking back with a toast to my plan, I rationalized that it was pretty much Bill Gates's leadership of the company that had made my stock options worth so much. So it was not a complete lie that Bill had made the scholarship possible.

Rushing back to the hotel, I wondered what Vu's reaction would be. Would he believe me? Would he accept the scholarship? Or would he react with stubborn pride and refuse the offer?

....

As I packed my bags, there was a soft knock on my hotel-room door. Vu was in tears.

"If you think I am smart, then I must be smart. And I must study; then I will report back to you. I will learn to use e-mail, and Mr. John, you will always hear from me on my results—on Excel, on Windows, on Word, and on Access. I promise you that my reports will make you proud of your friend Vu."

With those words, we cemented what would evolve into a lifelong friendship. Within three months, Vu proudly e-mailed to announce that he'd scored 97 on his Microsoft Windows exam and 98 on Excel. "But only 92 on Word; I promise to study Word with much more diligence over the next month."

I would wire him small amounts of money, with encouragement to take more advanced classes and to buy more books. "Vu, you are working eleven hours a day, six days a week. The hotel only has eight rooms, so there are a lot of hours that you can be learning. Even not being in front of a computer doesn't need to slow you down. Buy books, and read, read, read!"

From that point forward, Vu going slowly was the least of my worries. He learned programming languages like Visual Basic and C++. He studied servers and server operating systems. And then one day he announced to me with delight that he'd been accepted to university.

"Imagine that, my good friend John. My parents did not go past fifth grade, and I will be in university." With what must have been great nervousness, he pointed out that this would be possible only if I could help him out.

"My parents have been saving money for years. They are poor farmers, but every month they have been putting aside 20,000 dong (about two U.S. dollars). They can afford to pay half the tuition. Can you help with the other half, plus money for my textbooks?"

Of course I decided to run, not walk, to the nearest Western Union outlet, chortling to myself as I realized that he had asked me for the funding, rather than asking me to ask Bill Gates. Along with my amusement, I thought of a valuable lesson: You don't need to have Gates-like resources to fundamentally change lives. The five hundred dollars I was about to wire to Vietnam would allow a bright young man to be the first in his family to attend university. If we wait until we have big fortunes to initiate change, we may be waiting for Godot. Why not just start now?

I was destined to make that trip to the local wire house on several more occasions. After graduating from college, Vu was accepted to graduate school.

"I will have my Master's in Computer Science," he reported in 2004. Within a year, he had done it and began studying for a second master's, this time in "the English of Infomatics." His parents again contributed, as did I. By 2005, the bright young student I'd met eight years earlier had managed to earn his second master's degree. My protégé now had one more master's than I did!

Vu now works for the Vietnamese National Railway. He leads a team of people in the IT department whose work literally helps the trains run on time. He is married to Yen, a beautiful young woman he met at university. Yen is a nurse at the local hospital. Vu sends me periodic updates filled with pride: "Yen has been selected to go to Japan for two weeks, to learn advanced techniques for helping patients to recover from surgery."

Their two children go to school every day and have the same love of reading and learning that instigated my friendship with Vu. Six-year-old Bang—yes, that's the name of the energetic little boy—attends second grade. The daughter, Thao, is in fourth grade. She wins numerous academic awards in mathematics, Vietnamese language, and English. Each and every award certificate is scanned into an Acrobat file by her proud father and e-mailed to Uncle John.

In early 2011 Thao was chosen as the top girl in her class. "She always reads, and always studies," Vu reports. "Yen and I tell her that she can be anything she wants to be, including a doctor. She loves books. Every night she also practices a little bit of English. She tells us that when Uncle John comes to visit, she wants to be able to say hello and talk about all kinds of interesting subjects. She wants to know what your life is like in America, and whether you will play badminton with her when you visit."

Like my father, both Vu and Sreymom are the first in their families to go to university. It has cost a very small amount of money. Yet it will change their lives forever, and the future trajectory of their own children. As I tell their stories, people say to me: "Do you know what's coming? You have millions of children learning to read in Room to Read's libraries. If even a small percentage of them follow a path similar to Sreymom's and Vu's, it's going to be game changing—a youth-quake."

I have remained confident that this is just the beginning. So much more is possible, especially if we find more and better ways to make these students' stories come alive via technology. That has been one of my dreams. Then one day it became a reality when I sent a tweet that changed a life.

....

"John," she yelled as she jumped out from behind her small desk, "I have been waiting for two years to say hello again! Why haven't you come back to visit me?"

In the summer of 2010 I returned to Zambia and had the pleasure of spending an afternoon with a cohort of fifteen girls in their life-skills camp. I did not immediately recognize the girl offering me the enthusiastic greeting. And then it hit me.

"Mulenga!" I shouted as I ran to offer her a bear hug. "I did not recognize you. You have grown so much in the last three years."

As she returned the hug, I thought of the contrast with the young librarian's assistant I'd first met at Mr. Tembo's school in 2008. She had been so shy and quiet, had looked so young and tentative. What a difference two years could make. She was now fifteen years old, "but I will turn sixteen in November." She stood up straight, smiled, and treated me as a peer. It was obvious the classes our social mobilizers taught on self-confidence and oral communication skills were working.

She was still reading, she told me, but now she had a new desire. She also wanted to learn about computers and the Internet. During a Room to Read–sponsored field trip to the capital city of Lusaka, she'd caught her first glimpse of the Internet and was hooked. "I want to learn typing," she said, moving her hands to mimic the motion. "I want to learn more about the Internet and connect with the world."

I asked her why.

"In life, you have to learn about communicating by ways other than writing letters or phone calls. The Internet is a faster way for me to send messages. And it's free of charge."

As we talked, I continued to be in awe of how much she had changed in the previous thirty-six months. She was talking a mile a minute, in perfect English, all the time with a huge smile on her face. *I need to share this young woman's story with the world,* I thought. And so I asked her to spend half an hour with me as soon as the life-skills camp was over.

....

"Okay, are you ready, Mulenga? Three, two, one, action!"

We were standing outside under the shade of an acacia tree. I had a Flip video camera in hand. I was the director, the producer, and the interviewer. She was the show's only star.

"Where would you like to be in five years' time?"

"I might want to work in a bank. But I also might want to work at Room to Read."

"Really? That is great, because Room to Read is run by strong women. We also have strong men. We let them work for us, too."

She laughed.

"I don't want to turn this video into a job interview, but maybe you could tell me why you'd want to work for Room to Read."

"I like working with kids. And here I could help in changing the lives of all the ladies in the world. They have the right to speak and stand for themselves."

"Would you want to go to university first?"

"Yes, of course."

"You will have to pass your School Leaving Certificate exam. How soon is that?"

"In two years."

"Are you pretty confident you will pass the exam?"

"Definitely! I want not only to pass; I want to finish in the first division. That way I can go to a very good university."

"Having known you for a few years, I am very confident that you are going to achieve those goals."

Her face broke into a smile as wide as the Zambezi River. "Thank you!"

"And I will expect an e-mail from you, saying, 'John, I have done it. I am first division.'"

"All right! Yes!!!" she said, waving her arms above her head.

"Okay, remember, john@roomtoread.org. I will expect to get good news from you in two years."

She closed the video with her wide smile and two thumbs up. Here, clearly, was a girl whose trajectory was worth watching.

．．．．．．．．．．．．

A day later our team was in the rented van, yelling to me. "Come on, hurry up, we are going to miss our flight."

We were in a small village in South Africa, an hour's drive from the small airport in Nelspruit. I threw my bruised suitcase into the back of the van and apologized as I climbed in. "I managed to find a wireless Internet connection. It was slow, but I released Mulenga's story to the world! Her interview's on YouTube, and we've tweeted it via @johnwoodRTR and @Roomtoread. Over six hundred thousand people are now being encouraged to hear her story in her own words. You gotta love technology!"

Little did I realize how much more I would soon love it.

An hour later, as we pulled up at the airport, my BlackBerry buzzed as it downloaded thirty new messages. Scrolling through, the first one that caught my attention was titled "Mulenga-Zambia."

> *Dear John,*
>
> *I am writing to you from Dublin, where I live. I just watched your video interview with Mulenga in Zambia. It was really inspirational. Mulenga will be a great asset to Zambia now and in the future.*
>
> *Can you let me know how much it will cost to send Mulenga to university in two years time? I would like to personally fund her tuition.*
>
> > *Thanks,*
> >
> > > *Adrienne*

I let out a yelp as I shared the news with our team. How cool was this? Just twenty-four hours ago I'd shot an interview on a seventy-nine-dollar Flip camera with Mulenga, using my very limited journalism skills. With a free Internet connection from rural South Africa, I'd shared it with the world. And in the last hour, a complete stranger in Dublin had seen the post, viewed the video, and now offered a scholarship.

Things were falling into place. Our students were growing up and harboring huge ambitions, in a manner and with a speed I could have never dreamed possible. In 2011 we did a survey of the girls who had finished our program and were thrilled to learn that over 60 percent were enrolled in tertiary or university education. In yet another way, the rocket ship was on course.

CHAPTER TWENTY-FIVE

Mr. Poet and Miss Library

The young boy is dressed in khaki pants, a crisp white shirt, and a white V-neck sweater vest. The blue and red piping along the lines of the *V* make the thirteen-year-old look like a tennis player. Perhaps he is on the team at his rural South African school?

He notices the smiles of the members of the Room to Read delegation. It's rare for the school to have white visitors, and it's a little bit awkward to realize that while nearly every student is black, each of the overseas investors in Room to Read is white. But as often happens, all of the smiles and the positive energy abate any potential tension. We are all, after all, unified in our love of education and desire to support these students.

The young man approaches to shake hands, and as he comes closer we notice stitching on the left side of the sweater vest: Is it the name of his school or sports team?

Not even close. On his sweater are proudly embroidered two words: MR. POET.

He explains that the school "takes very seriously the power of words." Every year a poet laureate of the school is selected. Among this person's duties are to write the words that will be read at public meetings and assemblies to lend weight and meaning to each gathering. Beaming, he tells our team that today he has written a special poem in honor of our team's visit. He will read it in just a few minutes, at the opening convocation of the ceremony the students have planned to thank the Room to Read team for the investments we've made in their school.

As he stands in front of the group of hundreds of students, teachers, and visitors, he looks confident and eager. No stage fright will mar his performance. His feet are pressed together, and he stands taller than his thirteen years. He is clearly a boy on the cusp of manhood at that tender transitional age. The smile on his face slowly fades, and his countenance becomes quite serious. He clears his throat, glances one final time at the paper in his hands, and then fills the room with his strong and resonant voice.

"I want to welcome our guests and thank them for helping us to have this wonderful room full of books. To express our eternal gratitude, I have written this poem that I will read to you now. The poem is titled 'Miss Library.'

> *"Miss Library, you are the quiet lady full of respect and dignity.*
> *You attend to people who take time to seek information.*
> *Your shelves are full of books filled with knowledge and inspiration.*
> *Through you I shared in the ideas of important people like William*
>   *Shakespeare and Desmond Tutu.*
> *The dinosaurs became extinct before our time, but you kept record and make*
>   *them come alive for us.*
> *Anytime I visit you seeking knowledge, I depart more powerful.*
> *Knowledge is power.*
> *When I seek a good story, you leave me inspired.*
> *Oh Miss Library, you are one of a kind.*
> *You are the mother of all nations.*
> *You feed the nations with knowledge and wisdom.*
> *Feed us."*

....

I think of Mr. Poet often, just as I also hearken back to the day of the ten thousandth library opening. Both feature prominently in my presentations, speeches, and slide shows. Kavresthali School and the ten thousand figure are used to show the scale that Room to Read has hit, and also to inspire the audience to help us to reach even higher: *Six million children like Mr. Poet now have access to our schools and libraries. While we're proud of that fact, we're also aware that hundreds of millions of children have never heard of Room to Read and don't have books or reading as part of their young lives. Until they do, the job is not done. So we need your help in continuing this quest.*

Mr. Poet helps to take those abstract figures and bring them down to earth. His story and the power of his words are testimony. He illuminates the importance of the issue and helps the audience envision what just one library means to a young student.

It's also interesting to compare his childhood with that of Chris Mothupi. Both are handsome young men with magnetic smiles and charming personalities. Both clearly love books and are influenced by the power of the written word. Both talk about books with awe and reverence. There is not just an interest in reading; there is a profound and deep love for it.

For Mr. Poet, there need not be a reliance on discards found in dustbins. There is still no doubt that life as a young black South African man is not easy. But for the youth of democratic, postapartheid South Africa, there are better opportunities, ones their parents and grandparents could have only dreamed of. Chris and Mr. Poet together form a rough portrait of both "before" and "after" the birth of the free South Africa that came into being with the 1994 elections.

I recall Nelson Mandela's advice that those who wanted to help South Africa should focus on helping the new nation's children to gain an education. I hope that we have done this hero proud.

....

As I've tried to evolve as a leader, I've worked closely with a brilliant executive coach. Jeff Balin, who lives in Vancouver, volunteered to work with me, mostly by phone, on a pro bono basis. A fellow Kellogg alumnus, Jeff has taught at a Tibetan orphanage and worked on Starbucks's global-management team, and in his spare time he became a Buddhist scholar.

I once asked Jeff what he had learned in his studies: Was there anything he could share with me about the secret to a happy and fulfilled life?

Usually thoughtful and deliberative, this time he indicated there would be an immediate answer. "Figure out what you want to say on your deathbed. Then work backwards from there."

....

Before attending the ten thousandth library opening, I wanted to reconnect with the past by paying a visit to the place where it all started: Bahundanda. The entire village—at least one thousand people—turned out to greet our team of Room to Read employees and investors. Walking back up that steep hill, we were jockeying for position with a dozen donkeys, all laden with building supplies. The school was well run, and its enrollment had continued to increase. To celebrate our ten-year anniversary, we'd agreed to help the school build a new eight-room building. Scott Mead, a member of our UK advisory board, had agreed to fund it in honor of his mother. The school would soon have room for at least two hundred more students. All of whom would, of course, be using the original Room to Read library.

I had my own personal donation to make to the Bahundanda library's shelves. Two nights earlier, in a torch-lit courtyard of a Kathmandu hotel, with our entire Nepal team present, we'd been celebrating the ten-thousandth-library milestone. To surprise me, Dinesh and his team had added a more minor event to the party, and we'd launched my first children's book, *Zak the Yak with Books on His Back*.

The idea for the book had been incubating for years, since the first days back in 2003 when Dinesh, Erin, and I had discussed the need for local-language children's books in Nepal and beyond. But the ultimate implementation was different. A number of our investors had said that they'd had trouble explaining our programs to their young children, who could not conceive of a world without books. So Zak became my doppelgänger, bringing books to children who had previously lacked them, in places like Bahundanda. I teamed up with Abin Shrestha, a brilliant young Nepalese artist whose early work illustrating three of our local-language children's books had caught my eye. Abin had brought Zak to life in an inspiring way. He was indeed big and lumbering, but he had a huge heart and a desire to do his best to help the students of Nepal. He was joined by two young helpers, Arul and Manju. Together, they set out on an epic journey, across rivers and through blizzards, in order to get to the big city of Kathmandu to collect donated books. The trio arrived back at the school in Bahundanda to a hero's welcome. As flower petals rained down upon them in celebration, books were distributed to happy young children. They chanted: "Three big cheers for Zak, and for Manju and Arul. This is the best day in the history of our school."

I was excited that the original library in Bahundanda would now have children's books that featured this picturesque mountain village. The library was featured in the book, and ten copies of the new book would now be in our original library.

The headmaster interrupted my musings to walk me into the library room. I was impressed that it was packed with both books and students. He handed me off to my hosts and tour guides—the top girl and the top boy for grade ten. They told me how much they loved their school, but also their dreams to be able to go to "the big city" to pursue a university degree. They spoke in perfect English. The top boy wanted to be a civil engineer—the same job as my father, Woody. The top girl wanted to be a doctor. Commenting on their ambitions, I asked if they were good at algebra, at chemistry, at physics. Yes, yes, and yes, they replied. "We study those subjects at school, and there are additional reading materials in the library."

As I talked to them about their lofty goals, it struck me that the entire arc of their years of education coincided perfectly with Room to Read's life cycle. They would have been a year from starting grade one when Woody and I made the book-delivery trip back in 1999. I was finally meeting students who'd had a Room to Read library full of books to read for their entire lives as students—a complete overlap with my career as a social entrepreneur. We'd literally grown up together.

The top boy invited me to visit his father's small "trekking store," just fifty meters from the school. About my age and with a face tanned by the strong Himalayan sun, the father shook my hand warmly and said that for years he'd wanted to share his own story with the "esteemed founder" of Room to Read.

"I used to be a farmer, with a very small piece of land. I could barely feed my family. It could be very sad to see my children having so little to eat. And then one day my oldest son came home and told me that there was a big celebration at the school. People were coming here, and they were opening a library for our students. For many months I thought about this. Then a year later, the group came with more books. I thought to myself that here were people we did not know who believed in us and who were investing in our tiny village. And I realized that maybe they believed in my family even more than I did. That day I made a vow to my wife that I'd improve the lot of our family."

"What did you do?" I asked.

"I have always seen trekkers coming through the village. I know they have money in their pockets to spend, because they are from the rich parts of the world. But they are not going to buy crops from a farmer. What will I do, sell them raw potatoes? So I went to my brother, who lives in the city, and asked him to loan me money. With those funds I started this shop. It was very small at first; but as I got more money, I added more inventory.

"Now," he said with a smile as white as a snowcapped Himalayan peak, and as his hands swept through the air, "I have many things I can sell to the hikers, especially since my shop is right at the top of this very steep hill."

As I looked over the store, I saw cold water, bread, chocolate bars, soft drinks, and even small cans of Red Bull.

Bahundanda had changed in other ways.

"Today," he said, "we get more visitors than ever. Trekkers come through here carrying your book, looking for this famous school they have read about. A lot of Nepali people come here, too, because the Nepalese-language version of your book is titled *Microsoft desh Bahun-danda* ("From Microsoft to Bahundanda"). We are making even more money now, and all of my children go to school."

....

Two days later, I am in Kavresthali for the opening of the ten thousandth library. The energy level of the students is high as the excitement builds for the weekly "quiz show" hosted by the school's librarian. Students are divided into teams of five. They sit on the carpeted floor around a small table: six teams, six tables, thirty students in all. Each group is given ten Nepalese- and English-language children's books.

The librarian does a quick refresh on the rules. "You may not touch or open any of the books before I ask the question. If you do, you will have to sit out the round. Please do not pick up any of the books until I have finished asking the question. Once the question is finished, your team should find the appropriate book and hunt for the answer. Once you have it, put your hand in the air. I will call on the first hand that goes up. You will have three seconds, no more, to answer the question. Once you have put your hand up, all reading must cease. In other words, you can't do what you usually do." She does a mock glare at one student smiling shyly at having been caught cheating the prior week. "And put your hand in the air so that you're the first to be called on, but then keep reading."

The students all chortle, as though they had also thought of this trick.

"Okay, are you ready?"

They are all leaning forward over the small tables. Their hands hover greedily above the books. All is silent. There is tension in the air and competitive energy.

"First question: In *Tommy Tempo and the Great Tuk-Tuk Race,* what position does Tommy finish the race in?"

Just as a man crossing the Sahara will throw himself into the first sip from an oasis, each team dives onto the books. One, two, three, four, five, six times I see the familiar sky blue color from the cover of *Tommy Tempo* fly into the air. Books are opened and their pages turned quickly, as the savviest students flip first to the back of the book where the answer to the question is most likely to be.

"Miss, miss!"

Shouts erupt, turning the library's silence into cacophony.

"Miss! I know the answer."

At least four hands, then five, then six and seven, are in the air. The first responder is called upon, and she announces that Tommy Tempo finished third. Her team exchanges smiles of victory as the librarian awards them the first point scored.

"Okay, next question. Who won the race, and what was the name of both the *tuk-tuk* and the driver?"

The chaos is repeated. The kinetic energy of kids engaged in spirited competition fills the room. Within four seconds, there are at least ten hands in the air.

This time it's a young boy in grade four who's first to the metaphorical buzzer.

"The winning *tuk-tuk* was named Tilak. The driver of the *tuk-tuk* is named Rishi."

The game continues. The third question comes from a different book but elicits a similar response from the thirty quiz-show contestants. The librarian's plan was to have twenty rounds, but it seems obvious that these kids would play until midnight.

My thoughts are interrupted by a hand on my shoulder.

"Thank you for bringing us here. You have given your father and me a gift we will never forget."

My mother's eyes are welling with tears. She tightens her grip.

"I have never seen anything that makes me so happy and so proud. Just look around this room, John, and think about what you are giving to these kids. Look at the pure joy on their little faces. And the mothers!"

Several of the mothers are lining the windows, watching the activities from the outside. Their faces are lit with radiant bliss. One can guess which eager young quiz-show participant is theirs by the direction of their proud gaze.

"Every mother wants this for her children. The kids may not yet realize the significance, but the mothers do. We really do."

My own eyes flood with tears as I think of the green bike; the library card; the weekly trips to Spalding Memorial Library; Mom making me peanut butter on toast as she realized that I was paying more attention to feeding my brain than to feeding my stomach; the long hours spent curled up on the sofa with her, reading aloud from my newfound treasures. She would read the odd-numbered pages and I the even.

These mothers here in Nepal are no different from my own. Almost every parent I have met feels a profound sense of pride and confidence in the future at seeing his or her child diligently reading. If your son or daughter is a reader, the odds are pretty strong he or she is going to be more successful in life. That belief seems to be hard coded in our DNA.

What is true in the developed world is also true across the developing world. It is independent of geography, of race, and of income level.

Could a child possibly ask for more than those simultaneous embraces: the love of his parents and the love of books?

. . . .

When I left Nepal after the opening of the ten thousandth library, I made a long-planned stop in Singapore to speak at this relatively new chapter's second annual wine gala. The chapter network had continued to grow like wildfire. It seemed like every time I checked my e-mail, a new fund-raising chapter was opening up somewhere: Austin, Brisbane, and Charlotte; Geneva, Montreal, Seoul, Singapore, and Zurich. The network soon extended to fifty-seven cities. Incredibly, more than ten thousand people were involved. They carried Room to Read business cards but were not on our payroll.

Knowing that I wanted to share photos of the ten thousandth library with our Singapore supporters, my friend James gave me a USB stick full of hundreds of high-resolution images from the opening ceremony as I dashed for the airport. "Knock 'em dead in Singapore, mate! Challenge them to help us build the next ten thousand!"

The Lion City accepted the challenge. Perhaps a bit lubricated by the incredible South African wines selected by the legendary wine writer and event host Jancis Robinson, the well-heeled crowd did not stop throwing their paddles into the air until they'd given almost two million dollars.

Standing on the stage, totally in awe, I embraced my inner math geek and did the calculations. At five thousand dollars per library, this was enough to set up an additional four hundred. And with each library reaching at least five hundred children, this meant that this one evening alone could impact two hundred thousand students—two hundred thousand! I said the number slowly, over and over again. And then it hit me.

The timing could not have been more perfect. It was a brilliant bit of fate to have the ten thousandth library opening and this megasuccessful event during the same week. The world was sending me a clear signal. Kavresthali represented the "demand" for libraries across the developing world, while Singapore was offering the "supply" of capital to help our team to say yes to those communities.

And it was not happening just in Singapore. Around the world, there were events both small (fifth graders in Hong Kong holding a readathon to benefit global literacy), medium (newer fund-raising chapters that would hold parties with a "raise the roof" theme, resulting in a new library or school block being built), and large (volunteer-driven events in London, New York, Tokyo, and Sydney that would raise up to a million dollars in a single evening). To me, every story I heard from chapters, regardless of the size of the result, was equally exciting. Each helped us to move the ball closer to the goal line, and of equal importance, every fund-raising effort was full of the passion and energy of people who had bought into our dream. I've always said that I do not want to be the leader of an organization but rather *one of many leaders* of a global movement. The Andrew Carnegie of the twenty-first century would not be a rich, old, white male. It would be a global movement, and we were building it.

It was then that I decided we weren't thinking big enough. It was clearly time to take the brakes off and to brainstorm on a bigger long-term goal.

....

Watching the faces of the children at Kavresthali as they read their new Nepali-language books, I remind myself that ten thousand is a drop in the ocean. Today we celebrate; tomorrow my mantra will be, "Congratulations. You've reached about 1 percent of the children who need you. Get your ass back to work."

I take a quiet moment to reflect on how my life has evolved. I left a lucrative job and a stable future for a new and unpredictable life. It could have all blown up. Yet with the help not just of my family but also of legions of committed coworkers and volunteers in dozens of countries, I've found my place in the wide and interconnected world in which we now live, one that combines business skills with my deepest held goals.

I've managed to do what was prophesied by a former business-school teacher named Katherine Frazier, who wrote in a letter of recommendation decades ago: "The only real constraint I can imagine on John Wood's ability to advance rapidly in the business world is his strong sense of personal integrity. John Wood is a nice man, and successful people are not always nice. However, this could only be a short run problem. John Wood will find a way to succeed on his own terms."

I'm glad I didn't let her down.

I've also not let down my parents or their faith in me. The proof is here today: ten thousand libraries serving five million children. The bigger proof lies ahead. There are future milestones: ten million children served; twenty thousand libraries; double those numbers, and then double them again. Could we reach a hundred million children in this lifetime? Everything we've done is testament to our ability to ignore those who told us it could not be done. Even today people tell me that it's crazy or hubristic to believe that we can ever live in a world in which "every child" has access to books, can learn to read, can fall in love with the power of education from a young age.

Maybe it is a crazy goal. But the fact that we'd come this far this fast is confirmation of my conviction that bold goals attract bold people. The world continues to encourage us to strive for greater heights. The UNESCO award for our Local Language Publishing program came as we finalized plans to publish more than one thousand original children's titles by the end of 2013.

Our library program was given a Presidential Citation by the American Library Association. Secretary of State Hillary Clinton publicly praised our Girls' Education program as a model for helping societies develop, and the U.S. State Department made an investment in Room to Read of more than a million dollars, an affirmation of our belief that libraries, books, schools, and long-term education support for girls can be amazingly cost-efficient tools of public diplomacy.

One of Muneer's prophecies continues to be proven true with metronomic regularity. He once told me: "Every day, thousands of people wake up and will your team to greater and greater successes. John, the world is not going to let you down. Or those kids who need us."

In 2008, the *Financial Times* chose us as its charity of the year for its annual seasonal appeal; the campaign brought in more than three million dollars. The financial magazine *Barron's* twice named me (and by extension Room to Read) one of the world's twenty-five most effective philanthropists. The list was full of people who were either billionaires (Bill and

Melinda Gates, Warren Buffett, George Soros) or famous (Bill Clinton, Jimmy Carter) or in some cases both (Richard Branson). My placements in positions eleven (2009) and nine (2010) were an anomaly—the only bootstrapped social entrepreneur to appear on both lists.

With that recognition has come the usual self-imposed pressure to be worthy of the accolades. Having grown up a small-town, middle-class kid, I can still feel insecure and nervous when it's time to step onto a larger stage with brighter lights. I also wonder whether we're doing enough to take full advantage of all the opportunities in front of us. *Don't blow it,* I think; *these opportunities may not come again.*

But I always return to my true north. In my heart of hearts, I am an action-oriented optimist. Being surrounded by so many bold people, I know we can set even bolder goals. One day, I think, every community in the world could have a library like the one in Zambia where Grace's students are decoding words on the sides of trucks or like the ones in Vietnam where children read nine books in one night. Millions of students may one day emulate Sreymom (with her completely pregnant cows) in Cambodia, Vu in Vietnam, and Mulenga in Zambia and matriculate to university. Schools like the one here in Kavresthali could become part of the "new normal" that we're helping to bring to millions of children. That number could someday be in the tens of millions or hundreds of millions.

The only way we'll ever know if that's possible is if we give it a go.

....

Woody has walked across the library to stand next to me. He jokes that the children on his quiz-show team don't need him, that he's more of a hindrance than a help. I chuckle while thinking of eight-year-olds being able to beat such a smart man at a children's game. Then I notice that his face looks serious.

"John, I have something I want to say to you."

His face is tan. He radiates happiness. His eyes are dewy. "I want you to know that I am very proud of you. If I were to die now, I would die happy as a proud father."

"But you're not going to die," I plead. "You're going to be here for library number twenty thousand, and then number one hundred thousand, aren't you? Mom, too."

"You never know. But if I am still alive, you can push me into the ceremony in my wheelchair. That will make me happy. As long as I can see the faces of these kids, I won't even care if I am old and feeble. Or I'll ride in on top of a yak. Hopefully I will still have enough brainpower left to remember to put my hands together, bow, and say *namaste*."

Wordlessly, we stand together. I try to avoid letting him see my eyes.

In front of us fifteen children throw their hands in the air as they yell, "Teacher, Teacher." They are giggling as they compete to be the first to answer the question and then applaud for the nine-year-old girl who scores a point for her team. She beams like an Olympic gold medal winner.

I put my arm around my father's shoulder and draw him closer. Together we watch the young students whose faces are alight with the thrill of mental success.

"You know, Dad, I think I have figured something out."

He leans closer to hear me over the students while offering an encouraging smile.

"I think that this is what hope looks like."

AUTHOR'S NOTE

My friend Kim once opined: "A memoir is something you do when you're older, sitting in a rocking chair. You need to have that time on your hands. That's why most memoirs are written when people's lives have slowed down. Maybe you should wait a decade or two."

Alas, I did not listen, and this book is the second in what I hope will be a trilogy. I have no doubt that this is a less than perfect retelling of the formation and growth years of Room to Read. I've always believed in full disclosure—never more important than in our modern age of radical transparency. On Room to Read's Web site you don't find just one year of audited financial statements, but five. We publish not only our audited financials, but also our annual reports and our IRS Form 990s, as well as independent evaluations of the efficacy of our work, warts and all.

In that same spirit of "opening the kimono," I offer the following.

Many of the conversations in this book are recounted from memory. Though I've always been blessed with good recall, no doubt I've made mistakes. Throughout the book, I have quoted and paraphrased as accurately as possible. For any mistakes, my apologies: I take full responsibility.

I have changed the names of a few of the schools. Why? Because many headmasters and teachers have told us that while they love welcoming foreign guests, it can be a huge distraction to have unannounced groups of visitors "just drop by to say hello and to check things out." I can't imagine dropping in to my local school in Manhattan without phoning first to schedule an appointment, but for some reason people seem to feel it's all right to do this in the developing world. We want the headmasters and teachers to stay fully focused on running great schools, libraries, and long-term education programs for girls. That being said, we've hosted hundreds of visitors, and on our Web site at www.roomtoread.org you can find out more about how to visit our projects.

I've also changed the names of a few of the characters to protect their privacy.

Full disclosure: Despite our "No Land Rover" policy, we have had to buy a few vehicles. It's nearly impossible and often dangerous to travel across hundreds of miles of potholed and crowded dirt roads in Zambia or Tanzania on a motor scooter. We've done everything possible to keep our costs low. This includes donations of two used trucks from LaFarge (our free cement supplier) in Zambia and buying used vehicles in Tanzania. As I write this our team is also in the midst of a discussion with one of the world's largest car companies to provide us with free vehicles for each Room to Read country office. That way our teams can get around rural areas without heavy up-front costs.

Zak the Yak now has his own company, The Yak Pack. The Yak Pack is inspired by the Newman's Own food company and its "all profits to charity" model. We donate 100 percent of profits to Room to Read. Because the printing cost of each book is funded by corporate partners like The Republic of Tea and Scholastic, we are able to sell "zero cost" products and give more money away to help kids. We estimate that each time we sell a book for ten dollars, half that amount will be donated to Room to Read. That is enough for the organization to print five new local-language children's books. Zak the Yak is also appearing on thousands of iPads in a fun and animated version of his adventures—we call it Zak the App. You can find out more at www.yakpack.org.

To all those who have done great things for Room to Read and who were not included in this book, please know you are there in spirit. Next time?

I hope to meet many of you on a book tour or at a Room to Read event. Thank you again for reading this book, and I hope you will share it with the book lovers in your life.

ACKNOWLEDGMENTS

I am very fortunate to be surrounded by one of the best teams on the planet. There is oftentimes in the charity world a "cult of personality," which is a shame as any one individual can do only so much and his or her team usually deserves so much more of the praise and the spotlight than they receive. It was important for me to have the voices of Room to Read's amazing, dedicated, and passionate employees heard in this story. Our six hundred-plus employees are out creating more Room to Read every day, often in very remote and challenging places. It's an honor to work with them. I salute their passion for education and their dedication to our cause.

Our organization would not be close to its current size and impact were it not for the focus, talent, tenacity, and incredibly strong work ethic of my cofounders, Erin Ganju and Dinesh Shrestha. It's unusual for three cofounders to still be working together after more than a decade, and Room to Read is stronger as a result. All three of us have worn many hats. As our roles have evolved, it's always been done with complete trust and team spirit. We've never asked, "Is this right for me?" but "Will this help take Room to Read to the next level?" I hope we're still together at the twenty-year anniversary while also continuing to turn things over to the next generation of leadership.

I firmly believe that Room to Read has one of the best boards in the NGO world, and I'm so grateful to our past and current board members for their dedication. They've always given me strong psychological support, humored me when I threw out what I considered to be "new and improved" goals, and provided constructive feedback. Hilary Valentine and Muneer Satter stepped up to serve as board cochairs during critical periods of Room to Read's growth. Today we are very fortunate to have Tim Koogle serving with me as board co-chair. Other board members who have stepped up to serious leadership positions since *Leaving Microsoft to Change the World* was published are Chris Beer, Craig Bruya, Jerry del Missier, Peter Grauer, Scott Kapnick, Kim Anstatt Morton, Fernando Reimers, John Ridding, and Yusuf Alireza. My gratitude also to former board members Herb Allen, Marc Andreessen, Marjorie Benton, Christine Boskoff, Wynne Leon, Alison Levine, Alastair Mactaggart, and Dambisa Moyo.

I've always said that I don't want to be the *leader* of an organization, but instead *one of many leaders* of a movement. We've made good on that vision by building a bright "constellation of boards," each of which provides leadership in its own unique way. Our Global Advisory Board, twenty members strong, is always ready, willing, and able to offer its sage counsel. The UK Advisory Board and UK Board of Directors have turned Europe into the second largest fund-raising geography for Room to Read. Our Asia-Pacific Development board members have set a torrid pace in making their own personal multiyear commitments, getting their companies onto the Room to Read express train, and recruiting their friends and coworkers. We've also recently launched new boards in Australia and New York, with some dynamic leadership with whom I look forward to working closely.

Our chapter members, now more than ten thousand strong, are among the most passionate and talented people I've met. I'm continually in awe of their creativity as they launch new initiatives like the Big Book Swap, Beers for Books, Namaste India Global Yoga Day, Zak the Yak Read-a-Thon Packs, Yak Pack running clubs, celebrity chef events, gala wine dinners and auctions, and the list goes on. Even more impressive than their creativity are their results, raising more than fifty million dollars. A special shout-out to the chapter leaders: keeping thousands of volunteers in fifty-seven cities organized is not an easy task. We appreciate you stepping up and taking the mantle of leadership. So many of my finest hours at Room to Read have been enjoying and celebrating our shared victories.

Over the years we've had some great coaching to help us take our game to the next level. Special thanks to Jeff Balin for being my executive coach, on a pro bono basis, for eight years running. Both Lesly Higgins and Martina Lauchengco have always been willing to step in when we've needed organizational design consulting. Many professional consulting groups and law firms have helped us out in big ways without ever issuing an invoice, as has Ketchum, our communications agency.

I clearly lucked out the day Bonnie Solow walked into a Room to Read event in Silicon Valley. I did not think I had a second book in me, but she was convinced I did. Over more cups of coffee than I can count, she worked with me to come up with a structure and narrative arc. For the last few years, she showed incredible patience and confidence in my abilities as a writer. Bonnie, thank you for being everything a good agent should be. Let's do it again—just not right away!

I've been lucky to work with the team at Viking Penguin. They have constantly inspired me to produce the best book possible. Thanks to Clare Ferraro, Wendy Wolf, and Margaret (Maggie) Riggs for making this book what it is, and to the sales and marketing teams for their great work in launching the book around the world.

Patricia Mulcahy worked closely with me as a book doctor. Together we tore the original manuscript apart, debating what to scrap, what to keep, and what could be built upon and improved. She looked at a *years-in-the-making* manuscript with fresh eyes and also spent countless hours interviewing key players at Room to Read so that we could also incorporate their voices into this story. Pat, I would work with you again in a heartbeat, as should any other author who needs help taking their work to the next level.

Writing a book while working a seven-day-a-week job is not an easy feat. I was fortunate that many friends all over the world helped me sneak away to "undisclosed locations" where I could write in peace. Without these generous offers of both hospitality and solitude, this book would have never seen the light of day. Thanks to Hilary and Don for your place at Tahoe, to Robin Richards Donohoe and Chris Donohoe for the time in Sonoma, and to Scott and Kathleen Kapnick for the chalet in Verbier, where the view of the Swiss Alps inspired me. My gratitude also to Armando and the team at Four Seasons Maldives, to Tracey and her outstanding coworkers at the Amankila in Bali, to our partners at Small Luxury Hotels, to Daniel and his attentive staff at the Four Seasons in Tokyo, and to the Banyan Tree Phuket. I feel so fortunate to have had so many places where everyone looked out for me as I put my head down to crank on this manuscript.

I travel constantly and am grateful that we're able to do so much of it thanks to donated frequent flier miles. Thank you Philippe El-Asmar, Randall Bone, Kevin Burke, David Fuente, Jerry del Missier, Joe Gold, and Muneer Satter. We've also been fortunate to have corporate donors who regularly sponsor my travel, and I'm grateful to the teams at Barclays Capital, Bol.com, Credit Suisse, Goldman Sachs, Merrill Lynch, and National Australia Bank. Not content to merely travel for free, we also try to sleep cheap, and we're especially grateful to Hilton Hotels for providing our staff with 150 free room nights a year. The Upper House Hotel in Hong Kong is my home away from home in a city I visit four or five times a year, yet I never see a bill. Thanks to Dean Winter, Martin Cubbon, and the amazing Upper House staff.

Keeping me organized as I travel the world and work crazy hours cannot be easy. Over the years, I've had four amazing assistants who always managed to keep calm and smiling regardless of whatever challenge was being thrown their way. Thank you Erin Hogan, Lisa Hotchkiss, Jerry Lee, and Iris Alvarado.

In every country where we work, English is taught as the second language. We're very grateful to have so many major publishers work with us on bulk donations of books. This allows us to make sure our libraries have shelves full of high-quality books while also keeping our costs low. Special thanks to our friends at Scholastic, Pearson, Chronicle Books, Houghton Mifflin Harcourt, McGraw-Hill, Macmillan, Penguin, and Disney Publishing Worldwide. We've also had great support for shipping these books overseas from Brother's Brother Foundation, Sabre Foundation, and The Asia Foundation. Thanks also to our largest corporate and foundation funders: Artha Capital, Atlassian Foundation, Barclays, Caterpillar Foundation, Credit Suisse, Goldman Sachs, and the ELMA Foundation. Finally, a tip of the hat to Salesforce.com for donating a huge number of software licenses to us, allowing us to closely track each and every Room to Read project in a world-class and always-accessible database; to the employees of Atlassian who volunteered their time to build Zak the Yak's Web site; and to Lenovo for saving us money by donating hundreds of new and cutting-edge computers.

Room to Read is fortunate to have so many people willing to pitch in and do "whatever it takes to help our students." Dambisa Moyo and Jancis Robinson both serve as global ambassadors for Room to Read. Working with her colleagues at the *Financial Times*, Jancis has hosted wine galas to benefit Room to Read in London, Hong Kong, New York, Shanghai, Singapore, and Sydney, collectively raising more than fifteen million dollars. Her husband and noted restaurant reviewer Nick Lander has provided invaluable advice on venues and menus for our big events. Reid Hoffman and Sheryl Sanberg have always been generous with their time and advice despite insanely overpacked schedules. President Bill Clinton and his team at the Clinton Global Initiative have always tried to shine a bright spotlight on our work, for which we are so thankful. I'm very proud to serve on CGI's advisory board and to witness how much good the CGI commitments are doing for the world. Special shout-outs also to Katie Couric, Sheryl Wu Dunn, Seth Godin, Nick Kristof, and Charlie Rose and his production team. I'll never forget working with the team at *The Oprah Winfrey Show* to announce and promote "Oprah's Book Drive" for Room to Read, which raised more than three million dollars. Thank you to Melinda Gates and the team at the Gates Foundation for providing multiyear funding so that we could implement a long-term strategic plan and build a world-class system of monitoring and evaluation. What gets measured, gets done, and thanks to the foundation we're now able to measure so much of what we do and make adjustments as necessary to make sure our education programs continue to evolve and remain best in class.

We're also thrilled to be working with the teams producing two groundbreaking films focused on the importance of girls and women as change agents for the developing world: the crew at Show of Force (what an understatement) working on the film adaptation of Sheryl Wu Dunn and Nick Kristof's award-winning book *Half the Sky*, and the 10 x 10 team who have shot so many inspiring stories of our girls in Nepal that we cannot wait to show to the rest of the world.

Thanks to everyone who has invested in Room to Read, and please, please keep doing so. Every donation, small or large, counts. Ten dollars buys ten local-language children's books, and $250 funds one girl for one year in our Girls' Education program. If you can do more than that, please do so as every day we lose is a day we can't get back. Find out more at www.roomtoread.org.

Most important are all the people who keep my personal life inspiring. Most of my friends are fellow workaholics who don't think twice when asked if they'd like to order a second bottle of wine when we get together to blow off steam. I won't write a long list as you know who you are!

Thank you to my family for always being there for me. In most speeches I mention how fortunate I was to have a grandmother, an older sister, and a mother who all read to me. Our parents made so many sacrifices for us. It's with real pleasure that I've been able to take them on big adventures to Australia, Nepal, New Zealand, Singapore, and Hong Kong. Next stop, Zambia, where we will celebrate Woody's eighty-sixth birthday.

Final thanks go to my awesome travel partner, co-conspirator, and all-around-love-of-my-life Amy Powell. We've enjoyed so many adventures in the last few years, from spicy street food in Indonesia to hiking the dunes of Namibia to running trail marathons in the Swiss Alps to benefit Girls' Education, and we hope to not slow down any time soon. Fate, and Room to Read, brought us together. I can think of no better advertisement for getting involved with the awe-inspiring people in Room to Read's chapter network than the fact that I met Amy only because she was the cofounder of our Los Angeles chapter. It is to you, Amy, that this book is dedicated, with great love and excitement for our shared future.

INDEX

Abacha, Sani, 118
Academy for Educational Development, 244
Afghanistan, women, abuse of, 225–26
Africa, 119–120. *See also* South Africa; Zambia
  corruption problem, 118
  NGO failures in, 114
  poverty, scope of, 113–14
  pros/cons of involvement in, 113–19
  schools, deficiencies of, 114–17
Ahuja, Sunisha, 23, 244
Airplane, *Literacy One*, 184–194
Allen, Herb, funding, theft of, 132–35
Allen & Company, 129
American India Foundation, 119
Asia Foundation, 119
Asian tigers, education, emphasis on, 14–15
Audit committee, 134

Baby Fish Goes to School, 103–4, 238–39
Balin, Jeff, 262–63
Ballmer, Steve, 54–55, 94
Bangladesh
  Boat to Read, 228–39
  child brides, 235
  cricket team members visit school, 240–42

  Girls' Education program, 233–39, 240–42, 251
  Hasan Zaki, country director, 228–238, 240–42
  Human Development Index status, 229
  Read to Run game, 240–42
  river islands (*char*) schools, 228–237, 251
  school boats, providing, 237–39
  university tours for girls, 251
Barron's, Wood as one of most effective philanthropists, 270–71
Baxter, Charles, 109
Boats, river island (*char*) school boats, 237–39
Bokassa, Jean-Bédel, 118
Book production
  children as authors, 102–5
  first books, 98–101
  global director of, 105–6
  impetus for, 90–93, 95–98
  and local writers/artist, 7, 99–103
  for Nepal, 98–101
  scope of by 2008, 105
  for South Africa, 142, 150
  for Sri Lanka, 103–4
  types of publications, 105–6
Branson, Richard, 194

Bruya, Craig, 134
Buffett, Warren, 86
Burj Dubai, 214–16

Calello, Paul, 85
Cambodia
    Girls' Education program in, 120–25,
        127–28, 251–52
    girls in workforce in, 122
    home life in, 124
    illiteracy problem, 242
    Khmer Rouge era, 125–27, 199, 222–
        23
    local-language books, need for, 91–92
    university students, 251–53
Campbell, Rob, 99–101
Carnegie, Andrew, 7, 89, 185, 269
Cathay Pacific airliner, donated for
    flight, 184–194
Challenge-grant model, 5, 23, 48–53
    development of, 48–49
    noncash community donations, 50–
        53, 70–71
    program funding, time frame, 44
    success, factors in, 49–50
Chameli ko Basna, 99–100
Charity, Room to Read difference from
    traditional models, 76–78
Charity Navigator rating, of Room to
    Read, 86–87
Child brides, 199–200, 235
Child labor
    Nepal, 35–36, 40
    Sri Lanka, 44–45
Clinton, Bill, 8
Clinton, Hillary, 270
Clinton Global Initiative, 8, 104
Collins, Jim, 92, 136
Community involvement
    in book production, 7, 99–103
    challenge-grant model, 48–53
    in-country teams, 63–64
    fund-raising chapters, 83–84
    noncash community donations, 50–
        53
    and starting programs, 143
Confucius, on education, 156

Confucius Prize for Literacy, 243, 270
Consultants, critical friends as, 244–45
Cost control, 78–87
    compounding approach to, 86
    frequent-flier miles donations, 83
    good versus bad overhead, 81
    local events, organizing, 84
    no Land Rover policy, 78–81
    for office space, 85–86
    savings, program building with, 86
    for travel expenses, 82–83
    vehicles, donated, 86
Cricket World Cup, Room to Read
    partnership, 240–42
Critical friends, as consultants, 244–45
Cubbon, Martin, 184–87

Decision making, and leadership, 72
Delegation
    difficulty of, 244
    necessity for scaling, 244
Dhaka. *See* Bangladesh
Dubai Cares, 206–8
    donations to, 207
    Million Book Challenge, 208–16

Economic crisis (2008), impact on
    Room to Read, 219–222, 226–27,
    239
Education
    funding, versus other causes, 12
    and global economic growth, 14–15
    illiteracy, approach to. *See* Literacy
        program
    lifetime benefits of, 11–15, 26
    schools for girls. *See* Girls' Education
        program
    university. *See* Higher education
Ehrlich, Ami, 58–59, 63
Evaluation of programs, 88–98
    audit committee, 134
    consultants in, 244–45
    early model, deficiency of, 88–89
    effect on leadership style, 94
    evaluators, types of, 90
    local-language books, need for, 90–
        93, 95

necessity of, 88–89
negative feedback, dealing with, 94–
96
outcomes, importance in, 245

Financial Times
office space donated by, 86
Room to Read charity of the year
(2008), 270
Frazier, Katherine, 269
Frequent-flier miles, as donations to
save travel costs, 83
Fund-raising. *See also* Investors
broken promises, handling of, 174–
181
chapters, expansion of, 83
as constant activity, 202
donations (2005–2006), 64
and economic crisis (2008), 219–222,
226–27, 239
growth of (2007), 183
importance of, 60–61, 64
largest commitment, 193
largest commitment, withdrawal of,
217–222
Leaving Microsoft to Change the World
driving Room to Read fund-raising
revenues, 64
from local leaders, 83–84
Million Book Challenge, 208–16
raise the roof theme, 269
team, role of, 63
Wood, activities of, 135, 174–181,
268–69
Wood, role after being CEO, 137–
140

Ganju, Erin
background information, 55, 77
as CEO, 137–38, 244
chief operating officer, role as, 137–38
on factor for success, 43
as founding partner, 22–23
on local hires, 56
and self-publishing venture, 92–93
Sri Lanka decision, 72–73
strategic planning initiative, 244

and team building, 55–66
work, energy for, 55
Genocide, Khmer Rouge/Cambodia,
125–26, 223
Giang, Phuong, 246–48
GI Bill, 14
Girls' Education program, 7
in Bangladesh, 233–39, 251
in Cambodia, 120–25, 127–28, 251–52
costs per student, 24
enhanced approach of, 165
future aspirations, building, 257–59
girls, barriers to participation, 122,
170–72, 197–98
global director of, 60, 122
graduates, university students, 251–
53
in India, 200–201
initial goal of, 250
integrated approach of, 23–24
in Laos, 21–24
life skills training, 23, 122, 250
in Nepal, 195–96
social mobilizer, role of, 21–24, 122,
198, 252
student selection, 21–22
university tours for girls, 251
in Vietnam, 163–173
in Zambia, 257–59
GSD (get shit done), 54–55, 63, 114

Hasan, Zaki, 228–238, 240–42, 251
Al Hashimy, Reem, 208
Hedgehog Concept, 136–37
Higher education
Room to Read graduates, examples
of, 251–57
university tours for girls, 251
Ho Chi Minh Trail, 18–19
Home libraries, 20
in holistic approach, 22–23
Home visits, girls' homes, Vietnam,
163–69
Honest Caddie, The, 106–8, 150–51
Hong Kong
education as priority, 15
Literacy One flight to, 184–194

Hotels, cost control measures, 82–83
Human Development Index
    Bangladesh, status of, 229
    purpose of, 229

Illiteracy
    in Cambodia, 242
    damage from, 246
    eradicating. *See* Literacy program
    in India, 244
    in Nepal, 91, 242–43
    in United Arab Emirates, 204–5
In-country teams, role of, 63–64
India
    Girls' Education program, 200–201
    illiteracy problem, 244
Investors
    airliner, donated for flight, 184–194
    books, donated by publisher, 187–88
    breaking promises, Mr. X example, 174–181
    building confidence in program, 49–50, 77–78, 246
    country visits by, 47, 159
    funding, theft of, 129, 132–35
    investment versus donation, 77
    largest commitment, 193
    largest commitment, withdrawing, 217–222
    Literacy One trip, 185–194
    noncash donations, 85–86
    program growth, demonstrating to, 57
    Teen Trek, 47, 159
    university funding from, 252–53, 259
    U.S. State Department contribution, 270

Jacobsen, Bruce, 55–56, 135

Kann, Kall, 122, 124, 126, 127, 242, 246
Ketchum, 83
Khmer Rouge, 125–27, 199, 222–23
Kinetic Books, 55
Koogle, Tim, 143, 183

Lafarge, cement/trucks donated by, 86
Language, local-language books, need for, 90–93, 95
Laos
    Girls' Education program, 21–24
    national disadvantages of, 18–21
    Room to Read library in, 20–24
Le, Phong, 247–48
Leadership
    coworker impulse, 100–101
    and decision making, 72
    and delegation, 138, 244
    and improving performance, 94–96
    transparency, importance of, 130–32
Leaving Microsoft to Change the World (Wood), 8, 10, 247
    sales as funding source, 64
Leys, Emily, 59–60, 63, 122, 147, 165, 170
Libraries
    first library, 40–42
    five thousandth, celebrating, 185–193
    home libraries, 20, 22–23
    in Laos, 20–24
    librarian training, 243
    local-language books, need for, 90–92, 95
    in Nepal, 1–9, 40–42, 261–62, 265–69
    in Sri Lanka, 52, 67–71, 74–75
    ten thousandth opening, 261–62
    in Vietnam, 155–160, 246–48
    in Zambia, 47–48, 51, 144–49
Life expectancy
    and education, 26
    in rich versus poor countries, 26
Life skills training
    core skills of, 23, 122
    educational options, teaching about, 250, 252
    in integrated approach, 23
Listwin, Don, 231
Literacy One, 184–194
    donation of, 184–86
Literacy program, 244–49
    active learning approach, 249
    analysis of need for, 243–46, 244–49
    daily living, impact on, 249
    first, in Zambia, 244–49

Local activities. *See* Community involvement

Maestrelli, Laura, 187, 188–89
Al Maktoum, Sheikh Mohammad bin Rashid, 207, 211–13
Mandela, Nelson, 59, 117, 262
Matt, Sreymom, 251–53
Microsoft, team building at, 54–55
Million Book Challenge, 208–16
    progress, measurement of, 214–16
Mr. Poet, poet laureate of South African school, 260–62
Morris, Jayson, 61, 63, 210–11, 213–14
Morrison, Toni, 104
Mothupi, Chris, 149–153, 262
    book authored by, 106–8, 150–51

Nafees, Shahriar, 240
Al Nahyan, Shikh Nahyan bin Mubarak, 205
Nepal
    books produced for, 98–101
    challenge-grant model developed in, 48–49
    child abuse cases, 197–98, 200
    first library in, 40–42, 263
    Girls' Education program, 195–96
    illiteracy problem, 91, 242–43
    local-language books, need for, 90–93
    noncash community donations, 50–51
    opening celebration in, 6, 8–9, 46–47
    ten thousandth library opening, 2–9, 261–62, 265–69
    Tihar (Nepali New Year), 45–48, 50
    trip that inspired program, 34–40
Neupane, Pasupathi, 36–38, 40–41
No Land Rover policy, 78–81

Office space, donated, 85–86
Outcome measures. *See* Evaluation of programs
Overhead, minimizing. *See* Cost control

Pascual, Willi, 105–6
Pham, Thuy, 155

Philipp, Michael, 85
Poet laureate of South African school. *See* Mr. Poet
Population Council, 244
Pot, Pol, 125–26
Presidential citation, from American Library Association, 270
Programs team, role of, 63

Al Qassimi, Dr. Hanif Hassan, 204–6

Rape, child brides, 199–200
Read and Run game, 240–42
River islands (*char*) schools, 228–237, 251
Riyad, Mahudullah, 240
Robinson, Dick, 188
Robinson, Jancis, 268
Room to Read. *See also specific countries; specific topics*
    Africa, dangers and difficulties, 109–20
    brand building, 194
    as businesslike operation, 77–78
    challenge-grant model, 5, 23, 43–44, 48–53
    Charity Navigator rating, 86–87
    charity of the year (2008), 270
    Confucius Prize for Literacy, 243, 270
    difference from "charity," 76–78
    donors. *See* Fund-raising; Investors
    early model, revision of, 88–89, 243–46
    economic crisis (2008), impact on, 219–222, 226–27, 239
    evaluation of programs, 88–98
    first library, 40–42
    Girls' Education program, 7
    goals of, 7–8, 11–16
    graduates in universities, 251–57
    growing, rationale for, 55–57, 64–65
    growth of (2005), 43, 64–65
    growth of (2007), 182–84
    GSD (get shit done), 54–55, 63
    home libraries, 20, 22–23
    librarian training, 243
    life skills camp, 23

Room to Read (*cont.*)
  Literacy One, 184–194
  literacy programs, 244–49
  locations of program, deciding on, 7,
    65, 143–44
  Million Book Challenge partnership,
    208–16
  motto of, 15
  number of libraries of, 6–7, 43, 183–
    84
  Oprah's Book Drive for, 8
  overhead, minimizing. *See* Cost con-
    trol
  Presidential Citation to, 270
  priority communities for, 73
  scale, importance of, 199, 201–2
  school construction projects, 43–44
  self-publishing of. *See* Book produc-
    tion
  social mobilizer, role of, 21–24
  teacher training, 7, 243
  team building, 55–66
  Teen Trek, 47, 159
  trip that inspired program, 34–40
Rose, Charlie, 10–11, 24
Rouse, Allison, 145
Run and Spell game, 248–49

Sakoian, Carol, 187–88, 208–9
Samanmali, Chintha, 70–71
Samanmali, Kavith, 70–71
Samanmali, Shantha, 70
Satter, Muneer, 64–65, 82–83, 130–31,
    138–39
Scholastic, books donated by, 187–88
School construction
  challenge-grant model, 43–44
  criteria for building, 44
Scott, Stephanie, 62–63, 159
Seko, Mobutu Sese, 118
Self-publishing. *See* Book production
Shrestha, Dinesh
  book production activities, 99–101
  and challenge-grant model, 48–49
  on need for local-language books,
    90–93
  work ethic of, 62

Shrestha, Pushkar, 242
Shrestha, Reema, 195–96
Siddique, Junaid, 240
Singapore, fund-raising gala, 268–69
Skoll, Jeff, 92–93, 101
Skoll Foundation, 92–93, 101
Social entrepreneurship, 60
Social mobilizers, role of, 21–24, 122,
    198, 252
South Africa
  books produced for, 142, 150
  education, necessity in, 150–53
  evacuation of team, 109–11, 113,
    119–120
  funds, theft of, 111–12, 129, 132–35
  local-language books, need for, 106–8
  opening celebration in, 149
  rebuilding program, 142, 149–150
  Room to Read library in, 150
  student poet laureate, 260–62
Sri Lanka
  books produced for, 103–4
  child labor, 44–45
  local economy, 69
  noncash community donations, 52,
    70–71
  number of schools in, 67
  opening celebration in, 71, 74–75
  postdisaster decision making, 72–73
  rebuilding, 69–70, 72–74
  Room to Read libraries in, 52, 67–71,
    74–75
  tsunami, damage from, 67, 68–69, 73
Staff, hiring. *See* Team building
Starwave, 55
Strategic planning process, 244
Surveys. *See* Evaluation of programs

Teacher training, 7
  and literacy agenda, 243, 245
Team building, 55–66
  earliest members, 58–62
  financial constraints, 56–57
  hiring criteria, 58, 60, 61, 183
  local leaders, benefit of, 56
  slow hiring, danger of, 56, 65
  teams, types of, 63

Teamwork
  book production activities, 105–6
  in-country teams, role of, 63–64
  and decision making, 72–73
  experts/critical friends, consulting
    with, 244–45
  fund-raising team, role of, 63
  programs team, role of, 63
Teen Trek, 47, 159
Tight, Chris, 208–10, 214–15
Tihar (Nepali New Year), 45–48, 50
Transparency International, 118
Travel, cost control measures, 82–83
Tsunami (Sri Lanka), damage from, 67,
  68–69

United Arab Emirates
  Dubai Cares, 206–8
  illiteracy problem, 204–5
  Million Book Challenge, 208–16
  minister of education/Wood meet-
    ing, 204–6

Valentine, Hilary, 82, 87, 231
Vehicles, donated, 86
Vietnam
  Confucianism, influence of, 156
  Girls' Education program, 163–173
  home visits in, 163–69
  local-language books, need for, 91–92
  opening celebration in, 157–59
  Room to Read library in, 155–160,
    246–48
  and Vu, Nguyen Thai, 161–62, 254–
    56
Vietnam War, 18–19, 157, 166
Vu, Nguyen Thai
  computer science degrees of, 254–55
  IT profession of, 256
  meeting in Vietnam, 161–62

Warner, Stacey, 58–59, 63, 243
Winfrey, Oprah, book drive for Room
  to Read, 8
Women. *See also* Girls' Education program

abuse as girls, 197–202
child brides, 199–200, 235
child prostitution, 201
education, barriers to, 122, 170–72,
  199–200, 225–26
students, Taliban attack on, 225–26
Wood, Carolyn
  Literacy One flight, 189–192
  at ten thousandth library opening,
    2–4, 9
Wood, John
  activities as CEO, 135–36
  biographical information, 26–29
  books/library, importance in child-
    hood, 25, 29–33
  corporate experience of, 4, 77, 137
  family background, 26–29, 39
  and fund-raising. *See* Fund-raising;
    Investors
  growing organization, inspiration
    for, 55–56
  Hedgehog Concept applied to, 136–
    37
  most effective philanthropist by *Bar-
    ron's*, 270–71
  post-CEO role of, 138–140
  trip that inspired program, 34–40
Wood, Robert "Woody"
  family background, 26–28
  and first library, 40–42
  Literacy One flight, 189–192
  profession of, 13–14
  at ten thousandth library opening,
    3–4, 9, 271–72

Zambia
  AIDS orphans, funding of, 51–52
  dormitories for students, 146
  Girls' Education program, 257–59
  literacy program in, 248–49
  noncash community donations, 52–
    53
  opening celebration in, 147–49
  Room to Read library in, 47–48, 51,
    142–49

A MESSAGE FROM THE AUTHOR:
HOW YOU CAN CHANGE THE WORLD

When I am out on the road speaking to supporters and explaining why Room to Read exists, I always stress that no child should ever be told, "Because you were born in the wrong place at the wrong time, you will be denied an education." I hope for a world in which all children can pursue their right to a quality education—and I invite you to join me in making that vision a reality.

Room to Read strives to end illiteracy by educating children, like Inkham from Laos and Mulenga from Zambia, paving a path out of poverty for them and millions of others. We give children a chance to go to school, learn in a safe environment, and develop a love of books and reading. We place great emphasis on girls because they are often left on the sidelines.

Education breeds opportunity—and the ability to earn higher wages, have healthier families, and become active members of society. Remember, little of the progress outlined in this book would be possible if thousands of people like you had not been inspired to action. Here are a few simple ways you can join our global movement and make a difference today—a difference that will last across generations through the lifelong gift of education.

Invest in Room to Read

There are nearly eight hundred million people in the world who cannot read or write—two thirds of whom are female. By investing in Room to Read, you can be part of the solution. Every gift, no matter the size, can make a difference. We also accept gifts through stock donations, bequests, corporate matching, and gifts-in-kind. We have the ability to accept donations in ten currencies.

Volunteer for a Room to Read Chapter

We rely on the passion of volunteers to raise funds and awareness about our work. We now have more than fifty volunteer chapters in cities across the globe whose support helps keep our overhead low. They're also fun groups, and they're a way to expand your business and social networks while doing good for the world.

Engage Your Company

Investments in Room to Read can be leveraged further through strategic corporate partnerships. Many companies help us by donating goods and services, through cause-related marketing campaigns and by encouraging their employees to give back.

To make a donation, find the chapter nearest you, or to find out more about any of our programs, please visit www.roomtoread.org or call our headquarters at 1-415-839-4400.

Write to us at

Room to Read
111 Sutter Street, 16th Floor
San Francisco, CA 94104, USA

Start a Personalized Fund-raising Campaign

Each year, thousands of people create their own fund-raising campaign to benefit Room to Read, enlisting family and friends to help complete their goal. You can do just about anything to raise money for our work—run a marathon, organize a wine tasting, or donate your birthday gifts—we just want you to have fun with it! Ideas, tips, and instructions can be found at our Web site.

Become a Student Ambassador

Room to Read's Students Helping Students program is our global youth movement; its members raise funds and awareness for Room to Read through activities designed for primary, secondary, and university students. No longer a student? Enlist your children, grandchildren, nieces, or nephews!

You Can Also Stay Connected with Us These Ways

Twitter: Follow us at @johnwoodRTR or @roomtoread.
Facebook: Join our fan page at www.Facebook.com/RoomtoRead.
Blog: Read our blog and sign up for our RSS feed at blog.roomtoread.org.
Newsletter: Sign up to receive our quarterly e-mail newsletter at
     www.roomtoread.org/SignUp.
You Tube: See videos of our work at www.YouTube.com/RoomtoRead.

For B to B opportunities in Africa, Asia, the Middle East, Europe, and Latin America, customers can e-mail international.sales.@us.penguingroup.com.